NARRATIVES AND ADVENTURES
OF
TRAVELLERS IN AFRICA

WAR-DANCE OF KAFFIRS.

NARRATIVES AND ADVENTURES
OF
TRAVELLERS IN AFRICA

By
Charles Williams

The Black Heritage Library Collection

BOOKS FOR LIBRARIES PRESS
FREEPORT, NEW YORK
1972

First Published 1859
Reprinted 1972

Reprinted from a copy in the
Fisk University Library Negro Collection

Library of Congress Cataloging in Publication Data

Williams, Charles.
Narratives and adventures of travellers in Africa.

(The Black heritage library collection)
Reprint of the 1859 ed.
1. Africa, Southern--Description and travel.
I. Title. II. Series.
DT731.W72 1972   916.8'04'4   72-5525
ISBN 0-8369-9152-4

PRINTED IN THE UNITED STATES OF AMERICA

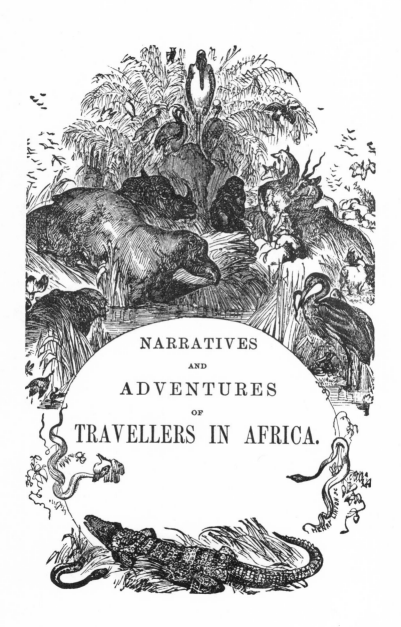

NARRATIVES
AND
ADVENTURES
OF
TRAVELLERS IN AFRICA.

Narratives and Adventures

OF

Travellers in Africa.

BY

CHARLES WILLIAMS.

Profusely Illustrated with Engravings.

PHILADELPHIA:

PORTER & COATES,

822 Chestnut Street.

CAXTON PRESS OF SHERMAN & CO.

PREFACE

An intense interest has recently been awakened, and widely extended, in regard to South Africa. Questions are, in consequence, frequently arising as to the character of its surface, its diversified tribes, its plants, and its animals; and the remarkable circumstances under which, after long concealment, they have been gradually disclosed to our view. The object of the present volume is to meet such inquiries by popular details on the highest authority, abundantly interspersed with *true* stories of chivalrous enterprise and heart-thrilling adventure. It respectfully solicits, therefore, the acceptance of all ranks, and of all ages.

CONTENTS.

CHAPTER IV.

THE EXPLORERS OF THE INTERIOR.

CHAPTER V.

ANTELOPES AND ELANDS.

CHAPTER VI.

THE DUTCH FARMER AT HOME.

CHAPTER VII.

GIRAFFES, GNUS, QUAGGAS, AND ZEBRAS, THE HYÆNA, THE CIVET.

CHAPTER VIII.

THE BUSHMEN.

CHAPTER IX.

TERMITES, OR WHITE ANTS, AND THE AARDVARK.

CHAPTER X.

SCOTCH SETTLERS ON THEIR WAY, AND SETTLING DOWN.

CHAPTER XI.

THE CAPE BUFFALO.

CHAPTER XII.

THE GREAT KARROO.

CHAPTER XIII.

INCIDENTS OF TRAVEL.

CHAPTER XIV.

HUNTING THE ELEPHANT.

CHAPTER XV.

THE CORANNAS.

CHAPTER XVI.

SERPENTS.

CHAPTER XVII:

NATIVE ARTS.

CHAPTER XVIII.

HUNTING THE RHINOCEROS.

CHAPTER XIX.

THE KAFFIRS.

CHAPTER XX.

AFRICAN INSECTS.

CHAPTER XXVIII.

ENON—REV. R. MOFFAT AND KURUMAN.

CHAPTER XXIX.

DISCOVERIES OF DR. LIVINGSTONE.

CHAPTER XXX.

BARTH'S TRAVELS AND DISCOVERIES.

CHAPTER XXXI.

MR. MOFFAT'S LAST JOURNEY.

LIST OF ILLUSTRATIONS.

Narratibes and Adbentures

OF

TRAVELLERS IN AFRICA.

CHAPTER I.

THE CAPE OF GOOD HOPE.

Pre-eminence of the Portuguese in Maritime Enterprise—The Fiction of
Prester John—Despatch of Covilham and Payva, by Don Pedro, the
Regent—Bartholomew Diaz, the Commander—The Course he pursued
—Discovery of the Great Fish River, and of the Cape of Storms,
afterwards called the Cape of Good Hope—Vasco de Gama—True
Figure of Africa—Colonisation of the Cape by the Dutch—Its Cession
to Great Britain—The Albatross—Cape Pigeons—The Fish of the
Harbour of Cape Town.

IF any are disposed to liken the Portuguese now to a
mere hull stranded on the sea-shore, it should be remembered
that there was a period when they resembled a gallant vessel,
with all its canvas spread, traversing hither and thither, the
surface of the deep.   In the fifteenth century they appeared
proudly pre-eminent among the nations, for maritime enterprise.   And thus, pursuing a brilliant career, they secured
for themselves some valuable advantages, while they conferred
benefits on others which are absolutely incalculable.

It is a curious circumstance in their history, that a mere
fiction became a mighty incentive to effort and sacrifice.
This appeared in the predominant idea of a person called
"Prester John," kept constantly before the public mind,
though no one out of the vast multitude could tell who he
was, or in what region of the globe he could be discovered.
Yet, did a ship leave the shores of Lusitania,—it was to search
for him, however long and perilous was its voyage.   Did it

1

return to port, after an adventurous and tempestuous ploughing of the ocean, the first question eagerly proposed to its
captain and its crew was, " Have you found Prester John ? "
And indescribable would have been the enkindled enthusiasm,
could any voyager have answered, "Here he is ! "   But the
ecstatic joy of such a presentation and such a reception, was
never to be realised.

It was while this meteor-like object dazzled and bewildered the eyes of the Portuguese, that Don Pedro, their
regent, sent two persons, Covilham and Payva, to attempt the
passage to India overland, and fitted out a small squadron,
consisting of two caravels of fifty tons each, and a small store-
ship, to prosecute the discoveries by sea.   This fleet was
placed under the command of a knight of the royal household,
Bartholomew Diaz, whose arrangements being completed, he
sailed at the close of August, 1486.

Having reached about two degrees beyond the southern
tropics, and a hundred and twenty leagues beyond the
furthest point visited by preceding navigators, Diaz steered
due south through the open sea, and lost sight of land.
Forced, at length, to the east by heavy gales, he approached
what he called Shepherd's Bay, from the numerous flocks
of sheep, which he descried with their keepers, near
the coast.   He was now forty leagues east of the Cape,
which he had doubled unawares.   Continuing his course
to the east, he sent ashore, from time to time, some negroes,
whom he had brought from Portugal, and who were well
dressed, in order that they might attract the attention
and respect of the natives.   He also gave them various kinds
of merchandise to exchange for the produce of the country,
and to gain all the information they could ; but the natives
with whom they met were so wild, or so terrified, that nothing
could be learned from them.

When the fleet, reduced to two vessels, reached the Bay
of Lagoa, the discontent of the crews, previously apparent,

broke out into loud murmurs; and they insisted on returning home. The stock of provisions was also exhausted; for
the small vessel containing the stores, had disappeared in the
gales. Diaz, however, succeeded in his entreaty that they
would continue their course five-and-twenty leagues further,
representing to them, how disgraceful it would be to give

PORTUGUESE SHIP OF THE FIFTEENTH CENTURY.

up the voyage without success. The direction of the coast
was now due east; and before long they arrived at the mouth
of a river, which they called *Rio do Infante*, since well known
as the Great Fish River.

On returning along the coast, to the great surprise and
joy of Diaz and his companions, they descried a promontory,

which they had long been seeking in vain. They also fell in with their store-ship, but, unhappily, only four men were remaining of its crew; the others having been massacred by the savages. To the promontory, Diaz gave the name of *Cabo Tormentoso*, or the Cape of Storms. But on his return home, the King of Portugal called it, with great satisfaction, the Cape of Good Hope ; regarding it as an omen that the Portuguese had now a fair prospect of reaching India, the great object of their maritime expeditions.

Vasco de Gama doubled it in November, 1497, on his way to the Indian Seas, and from that time the Portuguese considered the Cape as the southern extremity of Africa. But Africa does not terminate in a point : it presents to the Southern Ocean a broad line of coast running east and west. This coast is indented by numerous bays, and forms several promontories, of which the Cape of Good Hope is the most westward, and the southern extremity of a narrow peninsula.

The Dutch early saw the importance of forming a station at the Cape ; and fixed upon it as a place at which their vessels might take in water and provisions. But they did not, properly speaking, colonise it, until the middle of the seventeenth century, when they founded Cape Town, which led to further improvements, and a great extension of their territory. During the war with revolutionary France, the Cape was reduced by the British in 1797, but was ceded to Holland by the peace of Amiens. When the war recommenced it again yielded to Britain, and the permanent possession of it was confirmed by the Congress of Vienna, in 1815. Its visitors from the time of its discovery till now, have been innumerable.

Among the birds that follow the ships ploughing the ocean, the albatross is especially conspicuous. Its appearance when on the wing is very striking. It soars along with its broad pinions stretched from fifteen to eighteen feet between the tips, with an even, solemn flight, rarely seeming to stir,

THE ALBATROSS.

but as if merely floating along. Now and then a slow, flapping motion serves to raise him higher in the air, but the swift movement and busy flutter of other birds seem beneath his dignity. He sails almost close to you, like a silent spectre. Nothing of life appears in his still, motionless form but his keen, piercing eye, except that occasionally his head turns slightly, and betrays a sharp, prying expression, that somewhat shakes your belief in the lowly indifference he would fain assume. Yet, we are assured that if he be tempted to show his true qualities, there is a speedy change, for, if a piece of rusty pork be flung overboard, the disenchantment is complete, and the observer may see that long, curiously-crooked beak exercising its enormous strength in an employment in which so spectral a personage could scarcely be suspected of indulging.

The black petrel, with its keen eye, darts now and then across the stern, and the stormy petrel flutters over the ship's wake beyond the reach of gun-shot. But the Cape pigeons seem to welcome every arrival, and delight in the neighbourhood of man. As the wind dies away, and the Southern Ocean smooths her ruffled bosom, they settle upon the water, and swim gaily about, like ducks in a pond, and with quite as much familiarity. It is not uncommon for the boys on board to bait their hooks and catch them as so many fish; while the rest of the crew line the ship's side, and amuse themselves by watching the sport. When caught, placed in the hen-coops, kept there till morning, and then turned adrift, they stagger awkwardly upon the slippery deck; for they cannot take to the wing, unless they have the opportunity to start from some point of vantage, or the edge of the heaving wave. They bear captivity calmly when alone, but quarrel and fight perpetually when they are not in solitary confinement.

Their powers of flight are of no ordinary kind. When the ship is going at the rate of two hundred miles a day, the

Cape pigeon will fly round it, sheer off, or approach it, and soar aloft or descend, as if it were absolutely stationary. One that had lost a leg, and so was easily recognised, followed a vessel while progressing at this rate, for two or three days. It was computed that it traversed in its evolutions at least five times the distance run by the ship, which would give it a journey of a thousand miles each day. Cape pigeons fly, moreover, with little effort, as the strong wind bears them aloft, and aids their wings to resist the action of gravity. Their flight seems to be a series of manœuvres, and shows how instinct has taught them the practical application of the theorem, called the resolution of motion. This is most pleasingly illustrated when they fly against the wind, for they always ascend, so that a part of its force is employed in carrying them on high, and consequently, interferes not with their advance. The remaining part is easily resisted, by the oary sweep of their wings. When they fly before the wind, they usually descend, so that the exertion to keep above the water must be very small. When they would suddenly stop in rapid flight, they whirl round several times like a hawk, to exhaust the momentum of their speed.

The supply of fish which the harbour of Cape Town furnishes, is apparently inexhaustible. There is a great variety of species, several very wholesome and fine flavoured, but not worthy to be compared with those of England.

The Cape salmon, a heavy fish, in size and appearance somewhat resembling that of Britain, and the snook, a voracious marine pike, seem to be the most abundant. After an excursion of a few hours, boats return laden with these fish, which are sold very cheap, and form the principal food of the coloured population. Fish may be seen suspended on long lines, like clothes are with us, at the west end of Cape Town, that they may be dried ; and vast quantities are salted for exportation, the Mauritius being the principal market.

Fishing for snook often affords amusement. They may

be caught while the boat is in motion, by trailing a leaden
hook astern, with some white streamers of rag on it, or when
at anchor, by alternately casting the bait to a distance, and
drawing it quickly back through the water. Penguins, Cape
pigeons, and albatrosses, with some kinds of seagull surround the boat; while gannets and cormorants fly around the
fishers in great numbers.

CHAPTER II.

TABLE MOUNTAIN, the north front of which forms so prominent
an object in the view of Cape Town, extends from east to
west, for the length of two miles.   The bold face that rises
almost at right angles to meet this line, is supported, as it
were, by a number of projecting buttresses, that rise out of
the plain, and fall in with the front a little higher than mid-
way from the base ; these, and the division of the front by
two great chasms into three parts, give it the appearance of
the ruined walls of some gigantic fortress.

The table land at the summit of the mountain, is 3,582
feet above the level of the Table Bay.   The east side, which
runs off at right angles to the front, is still bolder, and has
one point higher by several feet.   The west side is rent into
deep chasms, and worn away into a number of pointed masses.
In advancing to the southward about four miles, the mountain
descends in steps or terraces ; the lowest of which communi-
cates by gorges with the chain which extends the whole length
of the peninsula.

The two wings of the front, one the Devil's Mountain and
the other the Lion's Head, make, in fact, with the Table, but
one mountain.   The depredations of time, and the force of
orrents having carried away the looser and less compact parts

TABLE MOUNTAIN.

have disunited their summits, but they are still joined at a very considerable elevation above their common base ; the height of the first is 3,315, and the latter 2,160 feet. The Devil's Mountain is broken into irregular points ; but the upper part of the Lion's Head is a solid mass of stone, rounded and fashioned like a work of art, and from some points of view, resembling very much the dome of St. Paul's, placed upon a high cone-shaped hill.

The best and readiest access to the summit of the Table Mountain is directly up the face next the town ; the ascent lying through a deep chasm to the left. The length of this ravine is about three-fourths of a mile ; the perpendicular cheeks at the foot more than a thousand feet high ; and the angle of ascent about forty-five degrees. The entrance into this chasm is grand and awful. The two sides, the one distant at the lower part about eighty yards from the other, converge within a few feet of the portal, which opens upon the summit, forming two lines of natural perspective.

On passing this portal, a plain of very considerable extent spreads out, exhibiting a dreary waste, and an insipid tameness, after quitting the bold and romantic scenery of the chasm ; and were this all, there would be but poor compensation for the fatigue of the ascent. But this is ample when the great command given by the elevation is considered ; and the eye, leaving the immediate scenery, wanders with delight round the whole circumference of the horizon. On approaching the verge of the mountain, the objects on the plain below appear dwindled away into littleness and insignificance. The flat-roofed houses of Cape Town, straight and intersecting one another at right angles, seem disposed into formal groups, like the fabrics which children are accustomed to build with cards. The shrubbery that rises in the sandy isthmus looks like dots, and the farms and their inclosures as so many lines, or the more finished parts of a plan drawn on paper.

The two most powerful winds are the north-west and

south-west. The first generally commences towards the end
of May, and blows occasionally to the end of August, and
sometimes through the month of September. The south-east
prevails for the rest of the year ; and whenever a white mist
shows itself on the mountain,—a phenomenon popularly called
" the spreading of the table-cloth,"—the wind blows in squalls
of great violence.

The poet Young has said :—

> " Fierce o'er the sands the lordly lion stalks,
> Grimly majestic in his lonely walks :
> When round he glares, all living creatures fly,
> He clears the desert with his rolling eye ;
> By the pale moon he takes his destined round,
> Lashes his sides, and furious tears the ground.
> Now shrieks and dying groans the forest fill,
> He rages, rends, his ravenous jaws distill
> With crimson foam, and when the banquet's o'er,
> He strides away and paints his steps with gore.
> In flight alone the shepherd puts his trust,
> And shudders at the talon in the dust."

The name of the Lion's Head, another portion of the mountain, is probably attributed to some fancied resemblance of a
part of the mountain to the head of that animal. At one
time it appears to have been a great haunt of lions. According to an old chronicler, a very grim one took up his residence
on this hill ; and, for a considerable time, made woeful havoc
among the cattle, and terribly annoyed the inhabitants of the
neighbourhood, some of whom he devoured. He constantly
retired with his prey to this hill ; escaped all the snares that
were laid for him ; and none, for a long time, being found
daring enough to follow him, and beat up his quarters, he
became the terror and plague of the whole settlement. At
length, Mr. Olofberg, Captain of the Fort, ventured to follow
him with a force, and had the good fortune to rid the country
of this lion.

The African differs from the Asiatic lion principally in the former being generally of a larger size, more graceful in figure, of a darker colour, with a less extensive mane. Of this quadruped two varieties are found in Africa : one which the settlers have long distinguished as the black lion, from its having a darker colour and the mane somewhat blackish ; while the other is all over of a pale colour. The black lion

THE LION'S HEAD.

is considered the more ferocious of the two, and is said to be less scrupulous than the other in attacking man, whenever it is pressed by hunger. But, happily, it appears to be more rare.

In illustration of the numbers and daring of the lions at the early period of the settlement at the Cape, an anecdote is related of a trumpeter, who, while on duty, had got drunk and fallen asleep on his post, outside the

2

fort ; in which helpless situation, being found by a prowling
lion, he was unceremoniously appropriated as lawful booty by
the latter, which, seizing him in his fangs, walked off with
his prey towards the hill in much the same manner that a
cat would carry a mouse. The extent of his danger, however,
according to the old chronicler, had apparently the effect of
sobering, as well as wakening the drunkard ; who, retaining
his presence of mind, sounded with his bugle such a thrilling
blast, that the terrified lion instantly loosed his hold ; and
the trumpeter, more frightened than hurt, lost no time in
scampering back to his *Corps de Garde*.

The Lion's Head Hill is 2,160 feet high, about 200 feet
lower than the Table Mountain ; but the ascent of the former is
far more difficult and dangerous than that of the latter. Mr.
Methuen says : " For a great portion of its height it is
necessary to climb with hands and feet, as up a wall,
over huge blocks of stone, and alongside giddy precipices.
With the assistance of several friends, I, on this occasion,
dislodged a ponderous stone of circular shape, and rolled
it down the declivity : it seemed to have for ever bidden
adieu to the *vis inertiæ*, and making the most prodigious
bounds, rushed madly forward with frightful velocity,
as if it had resolved to visit Cape Town. We stood
aghast at its progress—some silver trees grew in its course,
one of which it demolished like a sapling. On, on, it still
flew towards a herd of unsuspecting cows, which were grazing
on the mountain foot, but before reaching them it charged an
enormous indolent rock, when it happily gave one turn,
and again sunk into repose, but divided its opponent into
four fragments, which passed through the cows without touching them, and subsided in a deep gulley. This gave me some
idea of the effect which the vast masses of rock on the sides
of Table Mountain would have on Cape Town, if any convulsion of nature should set them in motion."

A day passed near the Lion's Head had been unusually

warm, but the sun went down without a cloud, while his fiery beams shed a glare on every object within their range. At ten o'clock, the stillness of the night was disturbed by a noise resembling that of distant thunder, yet so loud that it appeared as if a thousand pieces of artillery were fired behind the Lion's Mountain, over the neighbouring town. Many were aroused from their sleep, and were soon made sensible that something extraordinary had occurred, by the shaking of everything around. The earth was like a drunken man, and seemed to reel to and fro.

Immediately behind a house far distant from any other residence, were vast masses of stone on the declivity of the mountain. One of these, of huge dimensions, had before seemed to have been wrenched from the summit by some astounding force, and ready to crush the contemplative traveller. This terrific object now produced the greatest alarm, and was expected by the inmates of the house to roll upon it every moment, in which case the edifice would have been crushed as easily as a pebble beneath the wheel of a wagon. Imagination heightened the terror produced by the realities of that tremendous night. All around was solitary and frightful. If they escaped the fall of the mountain mass, the waves of the great southern ocean were dashing before them with unwonted fury, threatening to overwhelm the neighbouring rocks, and to engulf them in the surging waters. The voices of a thousand wild beasts appeared to be howling in every quarter, as if in response to Nature's throes; and there was no way of escape to the town but by a narrow road on the side of the mountain, where the scene was so terrific as to appal beholders even in a calm. Happily the night passed over the terrified inhabitants of this dwelling without any catastrophe.

Similar shocks have been experienced in other parts of the colony. Mr. Burchers, a resident, had gone a short distance from home; on his arrival, he felt very feeble, and asked for some water, but could not drink it, for it was luke-warm. The people said it was brought from the fountain just by, which was the more remarkable. He sent his own servant to the fountain, but what he brought was warm also. He went himself, and found it the same. Everybody felt languid and heavy, and even the dogs were unwell. Mr. Burchers, with his family and servants, returned home next morning.

At ten o'clock at night all were alarmed by a noise resembling a thousand wagons hurrying along the streets. The family did not know what was occurring; but all were terrified. A great light shone into the room. Supposing it had been thunder, Mr. Burchers told them not to be afraid, for the danger was over, the lightning being gone. While speaking, the same noise was repeated, and everything was shaken. "Oh!" said he, "it is an earthquake; come all out of the house into the garden," all feeling as if no life remained in them. There was then a third shock, which was inferior to the former two. The noise was not only awful because of its loudness, but, also, from its being a kind of melancholy growl or howl. The dogs and birds showed by their moans how terrified they were. This added to the terrors of the night, which was very still. There was no wind, but a great number of small fiery meteors were observed, and some little thunder-clouds, but with something new in their aspect. The effort to obtain a little sleep was utterly in vain.

CHAPTER III.

THE HOTTENTOTS.

The Hottentots, a Distinct Race of People—Their State on the Arrival of the Portuguese and the Dutch—Speculations as to their Name—Their Song of "Hottentotum Broqua"—First Case of Felony—Deterioration of the People—First Sight of a Hottentot Kraal—Structure of Huts—Singular Provision for the Safety of Children—Mode of Drinking—Remarkable Production of the Asbestos Mountains—Docility and Sagacity of the Oxen—Patience and Perseverance of their Drivers—A Hottentot chased by a Lion—The Lion's Mode of Seizing a Large Animal—A Lion carries off a Heifer and a Horse—A Tiger's Attack—Fondness of Hottentots for their Dogs—Singular Frolic of a Hottentot—Hottentot Hunting.

THE Hottentots are a distinct tribe of people, bearing no resemblance to the Kaffir, Damara, and Bechuana natives, extending from Angra, Pequena Bay on the west, to the great Fish-river on the east. They appear, as a race, to stand absolutely alone.

On the arrival of the Portuguese, they found the inhabitants rich in cattle, living comfortably, and possessed of sufficient spirit to repel aggression and resent unjust treatment. From the slight intercourse held with them, chiefly for the purpose of procuring water and refreshment for their ships, they were led to entertain very favourable notions of the character of the natives. It was said the Hottentots were remarkable for the excellence of their morals, that they kept the law of nations better than most civilised people, and that they were valiant in arms.

When the Dutch took possession of the Cape, the natives appear to have been much more numerous than they now are, and to have possessed large herds of cattle. So rapid, indeed, was the diminution occasioned by the trade carried on between

2

them and the new settlers, that it arrested the attention of
the government; and it appears from the minutes of an investigation before the governor, Van der Stell, that a single
Hottentot village had been robbed of cattle by the colonists
to the extent of 2,000 head.

The name of Hottentot has been supposed to arise in
various ways. One writer concludes, and that with some
probability, that it has been applied from the peculiar idiom
of the language of that people, which is much broken, full of
monosyllables, uttered with strong aspirations from the chest,
and a guttural articulation which it is difficult to acquire.
" It is," he says, " as if one heard nothing from them but
hot and tot." An extraordinary sound called the "click," is
emitted in pronouncing their words; it is produced by pressing the tongue against the palate.

The assertion of Arnold that the term Hottentot was a
nickname, given to the native tribes from their constantly
singing "Hottentottum Broqua," is contradicted by Kolben, a
better authority. According to him, the origin of this phrase,
and of the custom of singing it, and pronouncing it frequently
in their mirthful assemblies, was this :—The chaplain of a
Dutch ship sent a Hottentot upon an errand, and promised
if he discharged the business well, to give him a huge piece of
Dutch bread, or a certain quantity of tobacco. The Hottentot, having duly executed his trust, required of the chaplain
the fulfilment of his promise; but he, it seems, had so little
conscience that he utterly refused to give him any satisfaction.
The poor fellow telling this wrong to his countrymen, they
instantly, in derision and detestation of the chaplain, composed, after their manner, a song on him, in which the words
" Hottentottum broqua"—" Give the Hottentot his hire"
—are often repeated. This song quickly spread all over the
country, "when every one," says Kolben, was made acquainted
with the chaplain's knavery; to perpetuate the memory of
which, and to caution one another against the wiles and

circumvention of strangers, the song was sung whenever any strangers came within sight or hearing of them, as it is often at this day."

The records of the colony during the first fifty years of Dutch occupation agree in praising the virtues of the Hottentots. All the tribes, indeed, were distinguished by the appellation of "the good men." Bogaert states that, during the whole of that period, the natives had never been detected in committing an act of theft on the property of the colonists.

The first article stolen was a waistcoat with silver buttons, and could not easily be concealed among savages. Accordingly, a short time after, the waistcoat was found in the possession of a Hottentot, belonging to a kraal at a small distance from Cape Town. The discovery was no sooner made than the offender was seized by his countrymen, who took him to town, and delivered him up to the magistrates. And so great a disgrace did they consider this act to their nation, that they demanded that he should be punished, as the only means of wiping off the stain of his crime; and not satisfied with his getting a severe flogging, they banished him from their village, as unworthy to live among them.

The injuries inflicted on the Hottentots by the colonists must have had a deteriorating influence on their character, in the course of a hundred and fifty years, during which time they had been driven from the most fertile tracts of their country, and deprived of the independence to which they were passionately attached. One who knew them well has given us the following portrait :—

> " Mild, melancholy, and sedate he stands,
> Tending another's flocks upon the fields,
> His father's once, whe   ow the white man builds
> His home, and issues forth his proud commands:
> His dark eye flashes no   his listless hands
> Support the boor's huge   relock—but the shields
> And quivers of his race   a gone: he yields,
> Submissively, his freedo   and his lands.

Has he no courage? Once he nad—but lo!
The felon's chain hath worn him to the bone.
No enterprise? Alas! the brand—the blow—
Have humbled him to dust—his HOPE is gone;
He's a base-hearted hound, not worth his food;
His master cries: 'he has no *gratitude*.'"

Mr. Thompson, on awaking at dawn of day, found a
strange scene stretched out before him. He was in the midst
of a curious kraal, or cattlefold, situated on a ridge of land,
which commanded an extensive view of the windings of the
Great River. This encampment was formed partly by the
cabins of the natives, arranged in the shape of a half-moon,
and partly by a hedge of thorns, which completed the circle.
The horde consisted of about fifty souls, and were in possession
of above two hundred cattle. The huts were fronted inwards
to the kraal.

A hut, with its mats, more resembling an inverted basket
than a building, is the same which has been in use among all
the various tribes of Hottentots from time immemorial.
Such huts have their convenience for the people's mode of
life : they may be taken to pieces in an hour, and packed on
the back of a couple of oxen, together with their young
children and all their utensils, and transported with ease and
expedition to any part of the country to which they may find
it necessary or agreeable to remove, either for water or
pasture for their cattle, or for the sake of avoiding inimical
neighbours.

In some places where lions abound, the natives rear a
curious sort of house for the protection of their children ;
consisting, in fact, of a cabin, erected on the top of poles or
branches, ten or twelve feet high. The little urchins learn to
climb up these poles, and reach the cabin on the top, where
they remain in security.

The Hottentot manner of drinking water from a pool or
stream is very curious : they throw it up with the right hand
into the mouth, seldom bringing the hand nearer than a

A HOTTENTOT VILLAGE, OR KRAAL.

2*

foot's distance from the mouth, and so quickly that they are soon satisfied. The traveller has frequently tried to imitate this practice, but without success.

In the Asbestos Mountains the attention of the Hottentots, little accustomed to observation, has been directed to a remarkable production. It has the singular property of becoming, on being rubbed between the fingers, a soft cotton-like substance, resembling that which they made from their old handkerchiefs for the purpose of tinder. Hence it is called *Doeksteen,* handkerchief, or cloth-stone.

This substance is a kind of asbestos of a blue colour. It is found between the thin horizontal layers of laminated rocks. These veins of asbestos are of various thickness, and consequently their fibre, which is always transverse, is very short. But in the mountains about four and twenty miles north-eastward, some is found the fibres of which are above two inches long. This is, in fact, another species, and differs not only in the length, but in the more compact, perfectly straight and glossy fibre, and in its deeper colour.

All the rocks at the former place are formed of thin plates of clay-slate, not more than half an inch in thickness, and often scarcely the tenth of an inch. Between these plates a beautiful kind of stone is found, sometimes of a blue, and sometimes of a silky golden colour. It is a species of asbestos —allied to the substance called cat's-eye—in a less mature and flaxen state, with compact fibres of a flinty hardness, either transverse or oblique, straight or wavy. When cut and polished, this stone exhibits a very beautiful appearance. A handsome kind of jasper is also to be found here, brown striped with black ; and a green opal or pitch stone.

The oxen of the Hottentots are generally broken in for riding when they are not more than a year old. The nose is first pierced to receive the bridle ; a slit being made through the cartilage between the nostrils, large enough to admit a finger. In this hole is thrust a long stick, stripped of its bark, and having at one end a forked bunch, to prevent its passing through. To each end of it is fastened a thong of hide, of a length sufficient to reach round the neck, and form the reins ; and a sheep-skin with the wool on, placed across the back, with another folded up, and bound on with a rein long enough to pass several times round the body, constitutes the saddle. To this is sometimes added a pair of stirrups, consisting only of a thong with a loop at each end slung across the saddle. Frequently the loops are distended by a piece of wood to form an easier rest for the foot. While the animal's nose is still sore, it is mounted and put in training, and, in a week or two, is generally rendered sufficiently obedient to its rider. The facility and adroitness with which the Hottentots manage the ox, has often excited the traveller's admiration : it is made to walk, trot, gallop, at the will of its master ; and being longer-legged and rather more lightly made than the English ox, travels with greater ease and speed, walking three or four miles in an hour, trotting five, and on an emergency, galloping seven or eight.

The ox, in South Africa, seems little inferior to that most sagacious of all quadrupeds, the dog. Among the Hottentots, these animals are their domestics, and the companions of their pleasures and fatigues. While the sheep are grazing, the faithful *backeley*, as this kind of oxen is called, stands and grazes beside them. Still attentive, however, to the looks of its master, the *backeley* flies round the field, obliges the flocks of sheep that are straying, to keep within proper limits, and shows no mercy to robbers, who attempt to plunder, nor even to strangers. It is not the plunderers of the flock alone, but even the enemies of the nation that these oxen are taught to combat. Every army of Hottentots was furnished with a proper herd of these creatures, which were let loose against the foe. Thus sent forward, they overturned all before them, and often procured their masters, even before they had struck a blow, an easy victory.

A driver. on losing any of his oxen, will show much patience and perseverance in their pursuit, even under the oppressive heat of an African climate. Thus one started from the Helbeck River to return to Reed Fountain when two oxen had left the rest. At this place he arrived about sunset, and it being too late to commence the search that night, he lay down behind some sand and slept. At daybreak he examined the foot-marks of oxen all around, but could not distinguish the marks of those he wanted.

He then went to a rising ground, from whence he looked carefully in all directions, but saw nothing of them; after which he descended to the road, and searched for fresh foot-prints of cattle. Here he found the marks of three oxen, which rather perplexed him, as he only sought for two; he, however, resolved to follow their track, as they were in the direction of the wind, which African oxen generally prefer. After patiently tracing the marks for eight or nine miles, he came up to the oxen, and found that all three belonged to his employers.

By sunset that night he reached the Helbeck river, where he slept, and next morning, after eating his last piece of bread, resumed his journey. In two or three hours he reached a wagon that had been halting, and received a small supply of bread. About sunset he found water, at which he stopped for the night. Next day he was met by a man driving loose oxen, who said he was desired by the employers of the driver to take the oxen with him to his master. On asking what authority he had, and the man producing none, he drove the oxen slowly forwards, and reached his employers after an absence of three days, and walking about 100 miles. He took his usual place after his return, and there was no word, or expression of countenance, that indicated any idea on his part that he had done anything remarkable.

A Hottentot driving his master's cattle to water, perceived a lion in the pool, and being pursued, breathless and half dead with terror, he scrambled into a tree. At the same moment the lion made a spring at him, but missing his aim, fell upon the ground. In surly silence, he walked round the tree,

THE LION IN PURSUIT

casting now and then a dreadful look towards the poor Hottentot. After four-and-twenty hours, during which time he stirred not from the place, he returned to the spring to quench his thirst, and in the meantime, the Hottentot descended the tree, and scampered to his home, not more than a mile distant, as fast as his feet could carry him. So great was the perseverance of the lion, that it appeared afterwards he had returned to the tree, and from thence had hunted the Hottentot by scent, within three hundred paces of his dwelling.

The dread entertained of the monarch of the forest by both man and beast is such that every sense is at once awakened into vivid activity. At his sight, or even his smell, the greatest alarm is displayed on the part of the cattle. Though they may be in the worst possible condition, worn out with hunger and fatigue, the moment the presence of the shaggy monster is learned, they start off like race-horses; and sometimes days will elapse before they are discovered. "One night," says Mr. Moffatt, "we were quietly bivouacked at a small pool by the Oup river, where we never anticipated a visit from his majesty. We had just closed our united evening service, the book was still in my hands, and the closing notes of the song of praise had scarcely fallen from our lips, when the terrific roar of the lion was heard. Our oxen, which before were quietly chewing the cud, rushed upon us, and over our fires, leaving us prostrated in a cloud of dust and sand. Hats and hymn books, our Bibles and our guns, were all scattered in wild confusion. Providentially, no serious injury was sustained. The oxen were pursued, brought back, and secured to the wagon—for we could ill afford to lose any."

It is the habit of the lion, when he kills a large animal, to spring upon it; and, seizing its throat with his terrible fangs, to press the body down with his paws till the victim expires. The moment he seizes his prey, the lion closes his eyes, and does not open them again until life is extinct. A lion, having attacked an ox, a Hottentot herdsman ran to the spot with his gun, and fired at the lion within a few yards' distance, but from the agitation of his nerves entirely missed him. The lion, however, did not even deign to notice the report of the gun, but kept fast hold of his prey. The Hottentot reloaded, fired a second time, and missed ; reloaded again, and shot him through the head.

Sparrman relates that a lion was once seen at the Cape to take a heifer in his mouth ; and though the legs of the latter dragged along the ground, yet he seemed to carry her off with the same ease that a cat does a rat. He likewise leaped over a broad dike with her, without the least difficulty. According to the testimony of others, he can drag the heaviest ox with ease a considerable way ; and a horse, or smaller prey, he finds no difficulty in throwing upon his shoulder and carrying off to any distance he may find convenient.

A very young lion was seen to carry off a horse about a mile from the spot where he killed it. In another instance a lion having borne off a heifer of two years old, was followed on the *spoor* or track, for full five hours, by a party on horseback, and throughout the distance, the carcase of the heifer was only once or twice discovered to have touched the ground.

It is singular that the lion, which, according to many, always kills his prey immediately, if it belongs to the brute creation, is said frequently, although provoked, to content himself with merely wounding the human species ; or at least to wait some time before he gives the fatal blow to the unhappy victim he has got under him. A farmer, who had the misfortune to be a spectator of a lion's seizing two of his oxen, at the very instant he had taken them out of his wagon, stated that they immediately fell down dead upon the spot, close to each other ; though, on examining the carcases afterwards, it appeared that their backs only had been broken. In another instance, a father and his two sons, being on foot near a river on their estate, in search of a lion, the creature rushed out upon them, and threw one of them under his feet. The two others, however, had time enough to shoot the lion dead on the spot as it had lain across the youth so dearly related to them, without having done him any particular hurt.

"I myself saw," says Sparrman, "near the upper part of Duyrenhoek river, an elderly Hottentot, who, at that time (his wounds being still open), bore under one eye, and underneath his cheek-bone, the ghastly marks of the bite of a lion, which did not think it worth his while to give him any other chastisement for having, together with his master (whom I also knew), and several other Christians, hunted a lion with great intrepidity, though without success. The conversation ran everywhere in this part of the country upon one Bota, a farmer, and captain in the militia, who had lain for some time under a lion, and had received several bruises from the beast, having been, at the same time, a good deal bitten by him in one arm, as a token to remember him by; but upon the whole, had, in a manner, his life given him by this noble animal!"

Mr. Smith, of Cape Town, went with about forty others to a neighbouring hill to hunt wolves, which had committed various depredations among the sheep. While engaged in the chase, a tiger sprang from a bush, and seized one of the Hottentots by the forehead. "I could not leave the man to be killed," he said, "I therefore went with my gun to shoot the tiger. On observing me, he left the Hottentot and attacked me; my gun was useless, for, in a moment, he caught my arm in his mouth, having directed my elbow towards him to defend my face. I held his throat down with my other hand, with my knee on his belly, and called out to the Hottentots to come to my assistance. When they heard I was in danger, they ventured their lives to save mine;—they came running, and one of them shot him dead; and we brought home his skin." His teeth met to the very bone of Mr. Smith's arm, and it was a long time before he recovered.

The Hottentot who was first attacked, carried the marks of the tiger's tusks in his forehead all his days.

The Hottentots are fond of their dogs; each hut having one or two, it is said, " brave, honest, loving creatures." These animals are turned out every night to guard the cattle, a service which is discharged with great watchfulness and courage. The proverb, "love me, love my dog," is therefore strictly applicable in this case; and amply does the animal repay all the attention he receives. If it is his master's turn to go with the herds to pasture, his dog, accompanied by others, goes with him. No dogs have more skill in watching and driving the cattle than these have. While the herds are on their way to the pasture, they are incessant in their attentions to the flank and the rear, barking with due authority to keep the cattle in the proper line.

On arriving at the place where they are to graze that day, the dogs employ themselves, without bidding, partly to fetch in stragglers, and keep the cattle together, and partly in scouring the fields about the herds, which they do from time to time when required in a body, to keep off the wild beasts. When the cattle are fixed for the night, in and about the kraals, and their masters are retiring to rest, all the dogs rush out from the huts to mount guard for the night against the same enemies. Though the cattle low, and are in great disorder on the approach of wild beasts, they would often be attacked before the Hottentots could be roused and come forth to their defence, were it not for the dogs, which patrol from time to time about the herds, and on the least lowing or disorder, bark with all their might, to meet and engage the enemy. Quickly, therefore, their masters are at their heels, and often, in consequence of the watchfulness of the dogs, is the invader despatched or put to flight.

Campbell observed one of the Hottentots going to chastise a dog who had done some mischief in a vineyard, though the animal had a stick tied to his neck to prevent his entering.

The Hottentot took the dog near the spot where the offence was committed, that there the chastisement might be administered. The instant the culprit was set at liberty, the other dogs, to the number of about thirty, thought they were bound to give him a second drubbing ; for they rushed upon him from all directions. On his treating pretty roughly two or three of his first assailants, amity was restored, at which he seemed not a little pleased. A somewhat eccentric Hottentot now engaged in a curious frolic. By signs and sounds, he gathered about him all the dogs, who even seemed as if worrying him to death. In consequence of the wounds he appeared to have received, he gradually sank down, when, from the number that stood around and upon him, he became completely out of sight ; after which he arose smiling ; and the dogs went away as if their part had been done well.

The mode of Hottentot hunting has been described in terms of eulogy, from the earliest times. When the men of a kraal are out on the chase, and discover a wild beast of any considerable size, strength, and fierceness, they divide themselves into several parties, and endeavour to surround the beast, which, through their nimbleness of foot, they generally do very quickly ; though, on the sight of such danger, " the beast, of whatsoever kind," says Kolben, " always betakes himself to all his shifts and to all his heels."

When a lion, tiger, or leopard, is thus encompassed, they attack him with spears and arrows. With flaming eyes and the wildest rage, the creature flies on the Hottentots who threw them. He is nimble ; they are nimbler, and avoid him with astonishing dexterity, till they are relieved by others of the ring, who, plying him with fresh arrows and spears, bring him and all his fury on themselves.

He leaps towards one so quickly, and apparently so surely, that the looker-on shudders for the Hottentot, expecting to see him torn to pieces in an instant. But, instead of this, the Hottentot leaps out in the twinkling of an eye, and the beast spends his rage on the ground. He turns, and leaps towards another, and another, and another, but still in vain; he is avoided with the quickness of thought, and he fights only with the air. All this time the arrows and spears shower on him in the rear. He grows mad with pain; and leaping from one party to another of his foes, and tumbling from time to time on the ground, to break the arrows and spears that are fastened in him, he foams, yells, and roars most terribly. "If the beast is not quickly slain," says Kolben, "he is quickly convinced there is no dealing with so nimble an enemy; and then he makes off with all his heels, and having by this time a multitude, perhaps, a multitude of poisoned arrows and spears in his back, the Hottentots let him go freely and follow him at a little distance. The poison quickly seizes him, and he runs not far before he falls.

CHAPTER IV.

THE EXPLORERS OF THE INTERIOR.

Occupancy of only the Extreme Angle of the African Continent—Long Ignorance of the Interior—The First Explorer, Captain Henri Hop—The Swedish Naturalist, Sparrman—The French Traveller, Le Vaillant—Mr. Barrow—Messrs. Trutter and Somerville—Fatal Expedition of Dr. Cowen and Lieutenant Donovan—Dr. Lichtenstein—Dr. Burchell—Rev. John Campbell—Mr. George Thompson—Melancholy Memorial of a Wreck on the Coast of the Southern Ocean.

FOR more than a hundred years after the settlement of Cape colony, it occupied only the extreme angle of the African continent, or a part of the narrow stripe between the sea and the nearest mountains; nor does much information seem to have been obtained with regard to any of the native tribes, except the nearest Hottentots. Hence it was that Swift said, with much sarcasm and some truth :—

> " Geographers in Afric maps
> With savage pictures fill their gaps
> And o'er uninhabitable downs
> Place elephants for want of towns."

The first traveller who penetrated any considerable way into the interior was Captain Henri Hop, who was sent out on an expedition of discovery by the Dutch government, and traversed a considerable part of the country occupied by the tribe of Namaquas. He was followed by the Swedish naturalist Sparrman, and by the French traveller, Le Vaillant, whose journey extended to the territory of the Bushmen, some three or four hundred miles north of Cape Town. Mr. Barrow subsequently traversed the regions lying in this direction from the country of Kaffirs on the east to that of the Namaquas in the west, including the desert of the great Karroo, and as far north as the foot of the Sneuwberg, or Snow Mountains. The great barrier formed by this range was first passed by Messrs. Trutter and Somerville, who crossing the Gariep or Orange river, penetrated as far as Lithako, the capital of the Bechuanas.

Soon after, another party, under the charge of Dr. Cowen and Lieutenant Donovan, was sent out from Cape Town to cross the country to Mozambique, and accounts were received from them when they had advanced eleven days' journey beyond Lithako. But here the unfortunate adventurers 'appear to have been destroyed by the natives. A few years after Dr. Lichtenstein penetrated as far as Lithako, and brought back much valuable information as to the Bushmen and other tribes of Africa.

Dr. Burchell afterwards **visited** Lithako, and made important additions to our **knowledge** of the country and its people. The Rev. John Campbell, in two journeys made at the request of the London Missionary Society, visited Lithako on two occasions, and in the latter instance proceeded thence as far east as the hitherto unvisited city of Mashow, from which he directed his course northward till he reached Kureechanee; about latitude 25° south-west from this last town he found himself on the borders of a desert, which he was told extended an immense distance to the westward

Lithako was afterwards visited by Mr. George Thompson, whose accounts of many parts of the country lying between this point and the colony, as well as of some of the Kaffir tribes to the east, are exceedingly valuable.

Mr. Thompson made an excursion to the extremity of the Cape promontory—the real "Cabo Tormentoso"—in company with some naval officers. The road lay across a rugged chain of rocky hills, composed of the same materials as a great part of the mountains in this part of the Colony,—sandstone and

3

granite.   The appearance of this southern abutment of the
African continent is bold, bleak, and desolate.   In an
immense cavern at the bottom of the cliffs, washed occasion
ally by the billows of the great Southern Ocean, and apparently the resort of innumerable flocks of sea-fowl, they
found a piece of wreck, consisting of a ship's windlass, &c.,—
a melancholy memorial of some one of the many disasters
which have happened on this stormy coast since the adventurous Vasco de Gama doubled the promontory.   With the
explorers thus briefly introduced we shall have first to do,
reserving for the present the exploits of the most recent
discoveries.

The Drachenberg, or Quathlamba mountains, form a
broad range which runs nearly parallel to the south-east
coast of Africa, at a distance varying from sixty to ninety
miles from the shore.   Their height is estimated at from
8,000 to 9,000 feet above the sea.   The country gradually
rises from the ocean to the foot of the mountains ; and here
the Colony of Natal was established in the year 1845 by the
British Government.

ENVIRONS OF MOSAMBIQUE.

CHAPTER V.

ANTELOPES AND ELANDS.

Abundance of various Species of Antelopes—The Gems-buck—The Spring-buck—Its Peculiar Character and Remarkable Leaps—Immense Flocks of the Interior—Their Migrations—Their Adaption to Food and Clothing—The Pallah—The Bless-buck—The King of the Tribe, the Koodoo—A Lion springs on a Hottentot—Perilous Adventure of a Boor—A Leopard attacks Two Hunters—The Leopards and their Cubs—The Leopard compared with the Lion and the Panther—The Eland.

No country, perhaps, is more richly stocked with animals belonging to one particular tribe than Southern Africa is with antelopes. Wherever the traveller passes, he is almost sure to meet with some species or other of these animals. The antelopes are especially characterised by the symmetry of their form and the gracefulness of their motions. They are distinguished from the deer in the peculiar character of their horns, which are permanent, and are formed by the prominences of the frontal bone being covered with a sheath of horn, composed of layers of fibres, which increase during the whole life. The horns grow in various directions, usually ascending from the base, but inclining in different ways, and sometimes spirally twisted. Their ears are usually long, their eyes are mostly large, dark, and soft, and their legs are slender and elegant. Those that have spiral horns are for the most part gregarious, and frequent the open plains; the large species live in small troops in deserts or mountainous woods; while others roam over mountainous regions, finding their home amidst ravines and precipices, and the snow-clad summits of mountains, and leaping up and down to the smallest surface that will contain their collected feet, without alarm or peril. Those that frequent the plains are watchful and timid, flying with the utmost ease and swiftness, then stopping and turning to gaze.

The height of the gems-buck is about three feet and a half at the shoulders. The horns are about two feet and a half in length. The white face is crossed with two bands of black; the general colour is iron gray, and this is separated from the white body by a black band. Every part of this animal is valuable. The flesh is good, and may be salted and preserved for future use. The hide is useful, like the horns, for several purposes.

The spring-buck is generally about four feet and a half in length, and nearly two and a half high. The hair, which is usually long, sleek, and shining, is of a beautiful light cinnamon colour on the back, sides, shoulders, neck, and thighs, and of a snowy white on the other parts of the body; the cinnamon colour and the white being separated on the flanks by a band of a reddish colour. The head, face, cheeks, and chin are almost entirely white, with the exception of a brown line on each side, extending from the eye to the corner of the mouth; and of a mark of the same colour in the middle of the face. The neck is long and slender, and slightly compressed at the sides; the tail small, round, and naked, with the exception of a bunch of black hair extending along the tail, and terminating in a tuft; the legs are, in proportion to the size of the animal, remarkably long and slender; and the hoofs small, black, and of a triangular form. The horns are round, black, and surrounded by rings, from the base nearly to the point: on emerging from the head they spread backwards and outwards in a bold curve, and then turn inwards towards their inner extremities, the horn itself being slightly twisted on its own axis. The eyes are large, lively, and of a brownish colour. The ears are long, small, and cylindrical at their root, widening in the middle, and terminating in a narrow point.

There is one peculiar character which distinguishes the spring-buck from every other species of antelope. Along the

NATAL.

THE GEMS-BUCK.

top of the loins, from about the middle of the back to the tail, are two folds of the skin, from there being much more there than is necessary to cover that part of the body. The portions of this skin which are seen when the animal is at rest, are of the same cinnamon colour as the back, but the folded part is of a bright snowy whiteness. When the animal is taking the springs or jumps from which it derives its name, the folds become expanded, and form a broad circular mark of the purest white, extending round the hips.

According to Burchell, it is only occasionally that the spring-bucks take such remarkable leaps; for when grazing or moving at leisure, they walk or trot like other antelopes. When pursued, however, or when increasing their pace, they take these extraordinary bounds, rising with curved or elevated backs high in the air, often to the height of eight feet, and appearing as if about to take flight. In crossing a road or path, when moving rapidly, they will often clear it at one leap, extending even to twenty-five feet.

These animals reside in countless flocks in the interior of Africa, seldom approaching inhabited districts except in seasons of great drought, when they migrate in search of food. Their numbers are absolutely incalculable. The foremost of the mighty host are fat, and the rear ones meagre and lean, from the utter consumption of all the herbage and water that may be met with by the former before the latter can reach it; unless the cultivated fields are enclosed by thick and high hedges, all attempts to keep them out avail but little; and even when heaps of dry manure placed close together round the fields are set on fire, in hopes of keeping them off by the dense smoke that is produced, the dawn of day generally shows the land covered with spring-bucks, and every atom of verdure consumed.

Alluding to an immense multitude of these creatures, Mr. Pringle says : " I could not profess to estimate their numbers with any degree of accuracy, but they literally *whitened*, or rather speckled the face of the country as far as the eye could reach over those far-stretching plains; and a gentleman, better acquainted than myself with such scenes, who was riding with me, affirmed that we could not have fewer of these animals under our eye than twenty-five or thirty thousand." It has also been said that, to offer any estimate of the total numbers forming one migration would be impossible. Pouring down like locusts from the endless plains of the interior, lions have been seen stalking in the middle of their compressed phalanx, and flocks of sheep have not unfrequently been carried away by the living torrent. Cultivated fields, which, in the evening, appeared proud of their promising verdure are, in the course of a single night, reaped level with the ground ; and the despoiled grazier is compelled to seek pasture for his flocks elsewhere, until the rainy season supplies fresh food to the spring-bucks on their native spots, to which they instinctively return.

As spring-bucks, old and young, furnish excellent venison, vast numbers are destroyed by the Dutch farmers, not only for the sake of the flesh, but also for the skins, of which they make sacks for holding provisions and other articles, and clothing for their servants. A good marksman will kill from twenty to thirty spring-bucks every time he goes out : he lies concealed among the thickets near the springs or pools of water which the animals frequent at the close of the day to quench their thirst ; and by firing among them his enormous gun, loaded with several bullets, he often brings down four or five at one shot. No dog can attempt to approach the old spring-bucks; but the young kids are frequently caught after a hard chase.

Another antelope, the Pallah, resembles the spring-buck in form and colour, but is considerably larger in size, and has not the peculiar duplicate of skin on the back, already described. The horns, too, spread much further apart, and are more than twice the length of those of the spring-buck.

The Bless-buck is one of the largest animals of this tribe; its dimensions exceeding those of the European stag. It was once very common within the districts of the Cape Colony where in some parts it still exists, but not in such multitudes as formerly. In the country beyond the colonial borders it is tolerably abundant. The bless-buck is fleet and active; and its markings are very ornamental. The colours of the head and body are most singularly disposed ; the whole animal appears as if it had been artificially painted with different shades, laid on in separate masses.

The hartbeest has a very long head, in proportion to the size of the body ; the horns are thick, strongly annulated obliquely, and bent back ; the hair is a bay, or high-toned fawn colour, deepest on the back, with black or brown at the base of the horns, and the front of the legs ; there is also a stripe of very dark brown running from the insertion of the neck to the tail. It is sometimes four feet in height.

Another remarkable animal is the harness deer, so called from the singular marks like the straps of harness which appear on its body.

The white-footed antelope, or nyl-ghau, is one of the antelopes. It seems to combine the characters of the antelope and the ox. When brought to this country for exhibition in the zoological collections they have appeared very tame, delighting to be caressed, and licking the hands of those who feed them. But when irritated they manifest the utmost determination in attack or defence. Bingley mentions an illustration in point of one of the finest ever seen in England. A labouring man, without knowing that the animal was near him, and therefore without meaning to offend, nor suspecting that he was exposed to any danger, came to the outside of the pales of the enclosure where it was kept. But the nyl-ghau, regarding him as a foe, darted with the swiftness of lightning against the wood-work, and with such violence that he shattered it to pieces, and broke off one of his horns close to the root. This violence, it is believed, occasioned his death, for he died not long afterwards.

"Majestic in its carriage, and brilliant in its colour," says

Captain Harris, "there is one species which may with propriety be styled the king of the tribe. Other antelopes are stately, elegant, or curious — but the solitude-seeking koodoo is absolutely regal! The ground colour is a lively French gray, approaching to blue; the horns, spirally twisted, exceed three feet in length. These are thrown along the back, as the stately wearer dashes through the mazes of the forest, or clambers the mountain-side."

A Hottentot was out hunting, and perceiving an antelope feeding among some bushes, he approached in a creeping posture, and had rested his gun over an ant-hill to take a steady aim, when, observing that the creature's attention was suddenly and peculiarly excited by some object near him, he looked up and perceived with horror that a large lion was at that instant creeping forward and ready to spring on himself. Before he could change his posture, and direct his aim at this antagonist, the lion bounded forward, seized him with his talons, and crushed his left hand, as he endeavoured to ward him off with it, between his savage jaws. In this extremity, the Hottentot had the presence of mind to turn the muzzle of his gun, which he still held in his right hand, into the lion's mouth, and then drawing the trigger, shot him dead through the brain. He lost his hand, but happily escaped any further injury.

A boor, named Lucas, was riding across the open plains, near the Little Fish River, one morning, about daybreak, and, observing a lion at a distance, he endeavoured to avoid him by making a wide circuit. There were thousands of spring-bucks scattered over the extensive flats; but the lion, from the open nature of the country, had probably been unsuccessful in hunting.

Lucas soon perceived, at least, that he was not disposed to let *him* pass without further parlance, and that he was rapidly advancing to the encounter; and being without his rifle, and otherwise little inclined to any closer acquaintance, he turned off at right angles, laid the whip freely to the horse's flank, and galloped for life. But it was too late. The horse was fagged and bore a heavy man on his back,— the lion was fresh and furious with hunger, and came down upon him like a thunderbolt. In a few seconds he came up, and springing up behind Lucas, brought horse and man instantly to the ground. Happily the poor boor was unhurt, and the lion was fully occupied in worrying the horse.

Hardly knowing how it was done, he contrived to scramble out of the fray, and hurried at the top of his speed to the nearest house. Lucas, when relating his adventure, did not describe it as in any way remarkable, except as to the lion's audacity in pursuing a "Christian-man" without provocation, in open day. His greatest vexation appeared to arise from the loss of his *saddle*. He returned next day, with a party of friends, to search for it, and to avenge himself on his foe, but they found only the horse's clean picked bones. Lucas remarked that he could excuse the *schelm* (the rascal) for killing his horse, as he had let himself escape ; but then, as he said gravely, the saddle could be of no use to him, and he considered the depredator well deserved his most vehement invectives.

Two boors, returning from hunting a species of antelope, fell in with a leopard in a mountain ravine, and immediately gave chase to the creature. At first, he endeavoured to escape by clambering up a precipice, but, being hotly pressed, and slightly wounded by a musket-ball, he turned on his pursuers, with that frantic ferocity which, on such emergencies, he so frequently displays, and, springing on the man who had fired at him, tore him from his horse to the ground, biting him, at the same time, very severely on the shoulder, and tearing his face and arms with his claws. The other hunter, seeing the danger of his comrade, sprung from his horse, and attempted to shoot the leopard through the head ; but, whether owing to trepidation, the fear of wounding his friend, or the sudden motions of the animal, he unfortunately missed his aim.

The leopard, abandoning his prostrate enemy, darted, with redoubled fury, on his second antagonist; and so fierce and sudden was his onset, that before the boor could stab the leopard with his hunting-knife, the beast struck him in the eyes with his claws, and even tore the scarf over the forehead. In this frightful condition, the hunter grappled with the raging beast, and, struggling for life, they rolled together down a steep declivity. All this occurred so rapidly that the other man had scarcely time to recover from the confusion into which his feline foe had thrown him, to seize his gun, and rush forward to aid his comrade, when he beheld them in mortal conflict, rolling together down the steep bank. In a few moments he was at the bottom with them, but too late to save the life of his friend, who had so gallantly defended him. The leopard had torn open the jugular vein, and so dreadfully mangled the throat of the unfortunate man, that his death was inevitable; and his comrade had only the melancholy satisfaction of completing the destruction of the leopard, which was already much exhausted by several deep wounds in the breast, from the desperate knife of the expiring huntsman.

On one occasion, a pair of leopards, with three cubs, entered a sheep-fold at the Cape of Good Hope. The old ones killed nearly a hundred sheep, and regaled themselves with the blood. When they were satiated, they tore a carcase into three pieces, and gave a part to each of the cubs. They then took each a whole sheep, and thus laden, began to move off, but were discovered in their retreat; and the female, with the cubs, were killed, while the male effected his escape.

The leopard resembles in its habits the lion and the panther, but he is not so powerful. In one respect, however, he is superior to them; that is the extreme pliability of

4

his spine, which gives him a degree of velocity and agility surpassed by no other animal. With such astonishing rapidity does he climb trees, that few animals are safe from his ravages. Man alone seems to excite some respect; but if pressed hard in the pursuit by the hunter, he will turn upon him, and it requires both skill and prowess to guard against a leopard's attacks. Many instances have occurred of man becoming his victim, although generally he must be pressed to the onset; as when impelled by hunger.

Sometimes leopards are used in the pursuit of antelopes. On these occasions the leopard is first hoodwinked, as falcons are ; and as soon as the huntsman is near enough to the game the cap is taken off, the leader strokes his hands several times over the eyes of the animal, and turns his head towards the antelope. Scarcely does the leopard perceive it when he immediately springs forward ; but if he does not succeed in overtaking the antelope in two or three leaps, he desists and quietly lies down. His leader again takes him up in his cart and gives him some meat and water to strengthen him. The attempt is then renewed ; but, if he fails a second time, he is quite discouraged, and is unfit for the chase for some days. The antelope possesses such elasticity, that it makes leaps of from thirty to forty paces, and therefore easily escapes from the leopard, and hence it is indispensable to get as near the game as possible. But if the leopard succeed in catching the antelope, he leaps upon its back, and clings to it with his paws ; it falls down ; he thrusts his fangs in the neck of his hapless victim and sucks the blood, and then quietly follows his leader.

In size and shape, the body of the male eland resembles that of a well-conditioned Guzerat ox, not unfrequently attaining the height of nineteen hands, and weighing 2,000 pounds. The head is strictly that of the antelope, light, graceful, and bony, with a pair of magnificent straight horns, about two feet in length, spirally ringed, and pointed back-

THE ELAND.

wards. A broad and deep dewlap, fringed with brown hair, reaches to the knee. The colour varies considerably with the age, being dun in some, in others an ashy blue with a tinge of ochre ; and in many, also, sandy gray approaching to white. The flesh is esteemed by all classes in Africa, above that of any other animal ; in grain and colour it resembles beef, but is better tasted, and more delicate, possessing a pure game flavour, and the quantity of fat with which it is interlarded is surprising, greatly exceeding that of any other game quadruped. The female is smaller, and of slighter form, with less ponderous horns.

A traveller who had killed one of these animals, says :— "The stoutest of our savage attendants could with difficulty transport the head of the eland to the wagons, where one of the Hottentots had just arrived with the carcase of a sassayby that he had dragged a considerable distance, assisted by upwards of twenty savages. These men were no sooner made acquainted with the occurrences of the morning, than they set off at speed on the tracks of our horses, and were presently out of sight. About sunset, the party returned gorged to the throats, and groaning under an external load of flesh, which, having been unable to consume, they had brought about their necks."

CHAPTER VI.

THE DUTCH FARMER AT HOME.

The Boor's Horse described—Attendants of the Family—The Travelling
Tutor—Dealing in Cattle—Folding of the Herds and Flocks—Travelling
from the Interior to Cape Town—Another Farm described—Singular
Sight—Multitudes and Ravages of Locusts—A Boor surprised by a Lion
—A Death Grapple with a Lion—The Lion Victorious—A Hottentot
surprised—Diedrick, the Lion Hunter—Depredations of the Tiger—A
Tiger seizes a Hottentot—A Tiger Hunt—A Farmer attacked by a Tiger
—A Lion's Fear of Man—A Lion Increasingly Fierce from Success—
The Power of the Human Eye.

BURCHELL met with much hospitality from opulent Dutch
farmers in Cape Colony, but even among those of the lowest
class, there was ever a readiness to open the door to the
hungry and benighted stranger. In the family of a farmer
of the middle class, whose dwelling did not indicate much of
either affluence or comfort, but whose members appeared
contented and happy, he spent a short time. The following
particulars are taken from his observations.

The situation of the house was bleak and exposed, and
there was not much display of art or culture around. It
was situated on a wide flat, bounded by rocky mountains.
One large room, having a mud floor, and a single glazed
window, whose broken panes betokened the scarcity of glass,
formed the principal part of the house. At one end were
the bed-rooms, and at the other a very deep and wide fire-
place, exactly resembling that of an English farm-house.

As the boors often find it better economy to consume the
sheep in their own families, and convert the fat into soap to
be sold at their annual visit to Cape Town, than to sell the

animals at a low price, a large cauldron of boiling soap stood
over this fire. A door in the back wall of the apartment
opened into the kitchen. At the time of Burchell's visit, a
small window near the fire-place was kept constantly closed
with a wooden shutter, to exclude the cold wind, as it had
neither sash nor glass. Near the glázed window stood a
small table, and on it a little old-fashioned coffee-urn, an
article in constant use. On each side of the table were two
homely-looking chairs, for the use of the master and mistress.
A few chairs and benches, with a large dining-table, were
duly ranged round the room. A large Bible and a few books
lay on a shelf.

A black slave and a Hottentot girl assisted in the domestic duties, while the more laborious work of the farm was
performed by a man slave and a few Hottentots. The three
daughters of the farmer were under the instruction of an
itinerant tutor, who had been, for several months, an inmate
of the family. He could make himself understood in English
and French, and appeared fully able to complete the education
of such a family as was gathered around him. He was a
native of Holland, and had passed the last twenty-nine years
of his life in Cape Colony. Teachers of this class are scattered
everywhere throughout it. Their abilities, in many instances,
are too humble to allow of their getting a living in their
native land by the same occupation. They generally traverse
a great portion of the colony; for their usual stay at each
house is only from six to twelve months, and in this time they
must engage to "finish" their pupils in what the village schoolmaster called "the three *rs*—reading, 'riting, and 'rithmatic."

The head of this family employed his farm only in rearing
cattle, for the purchase of which he was visited by a *slagter's
knegt*,—a butcher's man. This person was commissioned by
his employer in Cape Town, to travel into the grazing districts, and buy up the number of sheep or oxen he might
require, paying, however, not in money, but in small notes of

hand, previously signed by his employer, and the validity of which was certified at the fiscal's office. Such notes were considered as good as cash, into which they were converted by the grazier on taking them to town, or they were sometimes negotiated in payment with his neighbours.

The inland traffic connected with Cape Town, was long carried on with much risk and difficulty, on account of its remote position at the extreme corner of the country, and of the miserable state of the roads by which it was approached. The barrenness and deficiency of pasturage in the tract of land lying around the town, exposed the boors, or Dutch farmers, trading there to serious inconvenience.

Those residing at a distance of five or six hundred miles, generally made but one journey there in the course of a year. On such occasions, the vehicles which conveyed them had much the appearance of a travelling menagerie; for, in addition to the principal members of the family, there were poultry, goats, sheep, dogs, monkeys, and other animals. A musket or two, with ammunition were taken, not only to afford means of protection, but also to procure game for subsistence by the way. The wagon bearing this motley group, drawn by a team of eight, ten, or even sixteen oxen, with the immoderately long whip of the driver, and the naked figure of a little Hottentot leading the foremost pair, presented to a stranger in the country a novel and amusing spectacle. The driving seat was considered an honourable post; but the office of leading the oxen was looked on as degrading to any but a Hottentot or a slave.

Between the capital and the cultivated districts, lie the extensive sandy plains, commonly called the Cape Downs, which were and are traversed by numberless roads and wheel-tracks in every direction. The soil is composed of loose white sand on a substratum of clay, supporting only a few stunted shrubs and rushes. A few solitary huts are scattered here and there.

From the general barrenness of the country, the travellers often stop but a single day at Cape Town. After having come the distance of perhaps twenty days' journey, they cross the barren heath already described, and frequently *outspan*, as they call it, or unyoke, at Salt River, to be ready to enter the town at daybreak the next morning. Thus they are often able to sell their produce, and to make the purchases they require during the day, and immediately set out on their return home.

Another boor rejoiced in a more extensive domain. The visitor descended from the ridge of a mountain, by a steep and stony path, tracked out by the hartbeests, elands, and other large game, and followed the rugged course of a solitary brook, or rather torrent, for the greater part of its bed was now dry, until, after a ride of about three hours, he reached the farm of Elands'-drift, in the valley of the Tarka, and the residence of Winsel Koetzer.

On riding up to the place, consisting of three or four thatched houses and a few reed-cabins, inhabited by the Hottentot servants, he was encountered by a host of some twenty or thirty dogs, which had been lying about in the shade of the huts, and now started up around him, open-mouthed, with a prodigious barking and clamour, as is generally the case at every farm-house on the approach of strangers. In daylight these growling guardians usually confine themselves to a more noisy demonstration; but at night it is often a matter of no small peril to approach a farm-house, for many of these animals are both fierce and powerful, and will not hesitate to attack a stranger, if in their eyes, he has the ill-luck to appear in any way suspicious. The noise of the dogs brought out Arend Koetzer, one of the farmer's sons, from the principal dwelling-house, a fine, frank young fellow. Seeing the visitor thus beset, he came instantly to his help against the canine rabble, whom he discomfited with great vigour, by hurling at them a few of the half-gnawed bones and

bullocks' horns which were lying in scores about the place.
An introduction now took place to the young boor's mother
and sisters—a quiet looking matron, and two bashful girls,
who appeared from one of the outhouses. "Wil Mynheer aff-zadel?" ("Will the gentleman unsaddle?") was the
first inquiry. The visitor readily agreed, intending, indeed,
though it was still early in the afternoon, to spend the night
at this farm.

On entering the house, he found that the old boor had
not yet risen from his afternoon nap, or siesta, a habit which
is generally prevalent throughout the colony. He was not
long, however, in making his appearance ; and, after shaking
hands with a sort of gruff heartiness, he took down a bottle
of brandy from a shelf, and urged his visitor to drink a
"zoopje" (dram) with him, declaring it was good "brandi-
wyn," distilled by himself from his own peaches. The spirit,
which was colourless, had something of the flavour of bad
whisky, but the visitor preferring a cup of "thee-water," it
was in the meantime prepared and poured out for him by the
respectable and active-looking dame. This "tea-water"
(properly enough so termed), was made by a decoction, rather
than an infusion, of the Chinese leaf, and which, being diluted
with a certain proportion of boiling water, without any
admixture of milk and sugar, was offered to every visitor who
might chance to arrive during the heat of the day. A small
tin box with sugar-candy is sometimes handed round with the
"tea-water," from which each person takes a little bit to keep
in his mouth, and thus to sweeten, in frugal fashion, the bitter
beverage as he swallows it. During this refreshment, the
visitor carried on a tolerably fluent conversation, in broken
Dutch, with his host and his "huis-vrouw," and he gratified
them not a little by communicating the most recent information he possessed of the state of European politics, respecting
which old Koetzer was very inquisitive.

The domicile of this family would not, probably, have

suggested any ideas of peculiar comfort to an Englishman. It was a house somewhat of the size and appearance of an old-fashioned Scotch barn. The walls were thick, and substantially built of strong adhesive clay ; a material which, being well prepared or *tempered*, in the manner of mortar for brick-making, and raised in successive layers, soon acquires, in this dry climate, a great degree of hardness, and is considered scarcely inferior in durability to brick. These walls, which were about eight or nine feet high, and tolerably smooth and straight, had been plastered over within and without with a composition of sand and cow-dung, and this being well white-washed with a sort of pipe-clay, or with wood-ashes diluted with milk, the whole had a very clean and light appearance.

The roof was neatly thatched with a species of hard rushes, which are considered much more durable and less apt to catch fire than straw. There was no ceiling under this roof ; but the rafters over-head were hung with a motley assemblage of several sorts of implements and provisions, such as hunting apparatus, *bill-tongue* (that is, dried flesh of various kinds of game), *sjamboks* (large whips of rhinocerus and hippopotamus hide), leopard and lion-skins, ostrich eggs and feathers, strings of onions, rolls of tobacco, bamboo for whip-handles, calabashes, and a variety of similar articles. A large pile of fine home-made soap graced the top of a partition wall.

The house was divided into three apartments : the one in which they were now seated (called the *voor-huis*) opened immediately from the open air, and is the apartment in which the family always sit, eat, and receive visitors. A private room or (*slaap-kamer*) is formed at either end of this hall, by partitions of the same height and construction as the outer walls running across, and having doors opening out of the sitting-room.

The floor, which, though made only of clay, appeared uncommonly smooth and hard, was formed of ant-heaps, which, being pounded into dust, and then watered and well stamped, assume a consistency of great hardness and tenacity. The floor was carefully washed over every morning with water mixed with fresh cow-dung, in order to keep it cool and free from vermin—especially fleas, which are apt to become an intolerable pest in this country.

This house was lighted by four square windows in front, one in each of the bed-rooms, and two in the *voor-kamer*, and by the door, which appeared only to be shut during the night. The door consisted merely of some reeds, rudely fastened on a wicker frame, and fixed to the door-posts by thongs of bullock's hide. The windows also were without glass, and were closed in the night, each with the untanned skin of the quagga, or wild ass.

The furniture amounted to little more than a dozen of chairs and stools, bottoms formed of thongs, and a couple of tables, one large and roughly constructed of common plank from the *geelhout* tree, the other small, and more highly finished, of ornamental wood. At the smaller table was the station of the old dame, who had before her a brass tea-urn, and the other apparatus, whence she dispensed the beverage already mentioned. Opposite her sat the *baas* (as the Hottentot attendants called their master), with the flask of brandi-wyn at his elbow, and his long clumsy Dutch tobacco-pipe in his mouth. At the further end of the apartment, a couple of wooden pails bound with bright polished hoops of brass, were suspended from crooked antelope's horns built into the wall; these pails were filled with spring-water, and had bowls of calabash affixed to them, in order that whoever was athirst might drink with facility. Sour milk, however, is the favourite beverage in this country; and when that is to be had, no one drinks water. In another corner stood a huge churn, into which the milk is poured every night and morning until it is filled, when it is churned by two Hottentot women.

In the same end of the hall, part of the carcase of a sheep was suspended from a beam; two sheep, and sometimes more being slaughtered for daily consumption ; the Hottentot herdsmen and their families, as well as the farmer's own household, being chiefly fed on mutton, at least during summer, when beef could not be salted. The carcases were hung up in this place, it appeared, chiefly to prevent waste, by being constantly under the eye of the mistress, who, in this country, instead of the ancient Saxon title of "giver of bread" (*levedy*, whence our English term of lady) might be appropriately called the "giver of mutton." Mutton, and not bread, is here the staff of life ; and they think it no more odd to have a sheep hanging in the *voor-huis*, than a farmer's wife in England would to have the large household loaf placed for ready distribution on her hall-table. At this very period, in fact, a pound of wheaten bread in this quarter of the colony was six times the value of a pound of animal food.

In regard to dress, there was nothing very peculiar to remark. That of the females, though in some respects more slovenly, resembled a good deal the costume of the lower classes in England fifty or sixty years ago. The men wore long loose trowsers of sheep or goat-skin, tanned by the servants, and made in the family ; a check shirt, a jacket of coarse frieze or cotton, according to the weather, and a broad-brimmed white hat completed the dress. Shoes and stockings appeared not to be essential to either sex, and were seldom worn, except when they went to church, or to *vrolykheids* (merrymakings). Sandals, however, of a certain kind, called "country shoes," are in common use, the fashion of which appears originally to have been borrowed from the Hottentots. They are made of raw bullock's hide, with an upper leather of dressed sheep or goat-skin, much in the same way as the old brogues of the Scottish highlanders. They do not last long, but they are light and easy in dry weather : every man can make his own sandals, and the leather costs little or nothing.

The visitor, having previously heard that the industrious dame, the Juffrouw Koetzer, sometimes manufactured leather dresses for sale, bespoke a travelling jacket of dressed spring-buck skin, the latter to be faced with leopard-fur, the price of which, altogether, was thirteen rix-dollars, or about one pound sterling. He purchased also the skin of a leopard, which one of the young Koetzers had lately shot, for about a pound of gunpowder.

Old Koetzer and his family, like the old Dutch colonists generally, were extremely inquisitive, asking a great variety of questions, some of them on very trifling matters. English-men are apt to feel annoyed at this practice, but without any sufficient cause. Though it betokens a lack of refinement, it is not at all allied to rudeness or impertinence ; it is simply the result of untutored curiosity in the manners of people living in a wild and thinly inhabited country, to whom the sight of a stranger is a rare event, and by whom *news* of any description is welcomed with avidity. Instead, therefore, of haughtily or sullenly repelling their advances to mutual con-fidence, the visitor answered all their questions with good humour, including those that respected his own age, the num-ber, names, and ages of his family and relations, the object and extent of his present journey, and such like. In return, he plied them with similar interrogations, to all of which they not only replied with the utmost openness, but seemed highly delighted with his frankness. In this manner he soon learned that his host had eight or ten brothers, all stout frontier graziers like himself, and all with numerous families. His own family consisted of six sons and as many daughters, several of whom were married and settled in the neighbour-hood. Two of his sons, with their wives and families, were now living at this place in cottages adjoining to the house. The old dame stated that she was herself by birth a Jourdan, and was descended from one of the French Huguenot families who settled in the colony after the revocation of the Edict of

4

Nantz. Her father, she said, could speak French; but she herself knew no language but Dutch. Her manner and address, however, retained something of French urbanity and politeness, which the Belgian bluntness of her husband rendered the more obvious.

Having exhausted the usual topics of country chat, the visitor suggested a walk round the premises, and sallied forth, accompanied by the boor and his son Arend. They first went to the orchard, which was of considerable extent, and contained a variety of fruit trees, all in a thriving state. The peach-trees, which were now in blossom, were the most numerous; but there were also abundance of apricot, almond, walnut, apple, pear, and plum trees, and whole hedges of figs and pomegranates. The outward fence, when there was any, consisted of a hedge of quinces. There was also a fine grove of lemon and a few orange trees. The latter required to be sheltered during the winter, until they had attained considerable size, the frost being apt to blight them in this upland valley. All the other fruits were raised with ease : peach-trees would bear fruit the third year after the seeds had been put in the ground. From the want of care and skill, however, in grafting, few of the fruits in this part of the colony were of superior sorts, or of delicate flavour. The peaches especially, were but indifferent; but as they were chiefly grown for making brandiwyn, or to be used in a dry state, excellence of flavour was but little regarded. Two mulberry trees, which were planted in front of the house, were large and flourishing, and produced an abundance of fruit. This was not the wild or white mulberry raised in Europe for feeding silk-worms; but the latter sort thrives also very well in different parts of the colony.

The garden, if it deserved the name, was very deficient in neatness, but contained a variety of useful vegetables : a large plot of beet-root, some beds of very fine cabbages, and plenty of mint, sage, and garlic, catching the eye. Onions were raised in great abundance, and of a quality equal to those of Spain. Pumpkins and melons were cultivated in considerable quantities. The sweet potato is raised here; but the common ones, though growing well, appeared not to be in much request in this part of the colony. Until the arrival of English settlers, indeed, the value of this useful root was not generally appreciated by the inhabitants, and the quality of the few they raised was very inferior. Since that period, however, the cultivation of potatoes has greatly extended itself in the eastern districts, and their quality has been so much improved by the seed brought out by the settlers, that they now are scarcely, if at all, inferior to those of England; and the prejudices with which the native population, particularly the Hottentots, regarded them, rapidly declined. Adjoining to the garden and orchard was a small, but well-kept vineyard, from which a large produce of very fine grapes is obtained, which, as well as the peaches, are chiefly distilled into brandy for home consumption.

The whole of the orchard, vineyard, and garden-ground, together with about twenty acres of corn-land adjoining, was irrigated by the waters of a small mountain-rill, collected and led down in front of the house by an artificial canal. Without irrigation little can be done in this part of the colony; and though the river Tarka passes only a short distance from the back of the orchard, the channel is here too deep to admit of its water being led out upon the banks. The limited extent, therefore, of from twenty to thirty acres was the whole that could be cultivated on this farm, comprising at least 6,000 acres, exclusive of the waste and inappropriated tracts adjoining. But this is quite sufficient for the wants of a large family; the real wealth of the farm, so far as respects marketable commodities, lies in the stocks of herds which are raised on its extensive pastures. This old Winsel himself hinted to his visitor—as, shutting up a gap in the garden hedge with a branch of thorny mimosa, they issued out towards the "kraals" or cattle-folds—the boor exclaiming in a tone of jocund gratulation, while he pointed to a distant cloud of dust moving up the valley—" Maar daar koomt myn vee !" (But there come my cattle.)

The appearance of the boor folding his herds and flocks is patriarchal and picturesque, and may well recall the words of the ancient poet:—

> " On came the comely sheep,
> From feed returning to their pens and folds,
> And those the kine in multitudes succeed ;
> One on the other rising to the eye,
> As watery clouds which in the heavens are seen,
> Driven by the south or Thracian Boreas ;
> And numberless along the sky they glide ;
> Nor cease ; so many doth the powerful blast
> Speed forward ; and so many, fleece on fleece,
> Successive rise reflecting varied light.
> So still the herds of kine successive drive
> A long extended line ; and filled the plain
> And all the pathways with the coming troop."

As the boor and his visitor were now conversing, the clouds of dust which had been observed approaching from three different quarters came nearer, and it was manifest that they were raised by two numerous flocks of sheep and one large herd of cattle. First came the wethers, which are reared for the market, and are often driven even down to Cape Town, seven hundred miles distant. These being placed in their proper fold, the flock of ewes, ewe goats, and lambs, was next driven in, and carefully penned in another ; those having young ones of tender age being kept separate. And finally, the cattle herd came rushing on pell-mell, and spontaneously assumed their station upon the summit of their guarded mound ; the milch cows only being separated, in order to be tied up to stakes within a small enclosure nearer the houses, where they were milked by the Hottentot herds-men, after their calves, which were kept at home, had been permitted to suck for a certain period. Not one of these cows, it was said, would allow herself to be milked until her calf was first put to her ; if the calf dies, of course there is an end of her milk for that season. This appears to be the effect of habit, and might be remedied by proper management. About thirty cows were milked ; but the quantity obtained from them was very small, not so much as would be got from six or eight English cows.

The boor and his wife, with all their sons. daughters, daughters-in-law, and grandchildren, who were about the place, were assiduously occupied, while the herds and flocks were folding, in examining them as they passed in, and in walking through among them afterwards, to see that all was right. The people thus employed declared that though they do not very frequently count them, yet they know at once whether any individual ox is missing, or if any accident has happened among the flocks, from beasts of prey or otherwise.

This faculty, though the result, doubtless, of peculiar habits of attention, is certainly very remarkable ; for the herd of cattle at this place amounted altogether to nearly 700 head, and the sheep and goats (which were mingled together) to upwards of 5,000. This is considered a very respectable, but by no means extraordinary, stock for a Tarka grazier.

Every individual of an African boor's family, including even the child at the breast, has an interest in the welfare of the flocks and herds. It is their custom, as soon as a child is born, to set apart for it a certain number of the young live stock, which increase as the child grows up ; and which, having a particular mark regularly affixed to them, form, when the owner arrives at adult age, a stock sufficient to be considered a respectable dowry for a prosperous farmer's daughter, or to enable a young man, though he may not possess a single dollar of cash, to begin the world respectably as a " Vee Boor."

On approaching the cattle kraals, the visitor was struck by the great height of the principal fold, which was elevated fifteen or twenty feet above the level of the adjoining plain, and his surprise was certainly not diminished when he found that the mound, on the top of which the kraal was constructed, consisted of a mass of solid dung, accumulated by the cattle of the farm being folded for a succession of years on the same spot. The sheep-folds, though not quite so elevated, and under the lee, as it were, of the bullocks' kraal, were also fixed on the top of similar accumulations. The several folds (for those of the sheep and goats consisted of three divisions) were all fenced in with branches of the thorny mimosa, which formed a sort of rampart around the margin of the mounds of dung, and were carefully placed with their prickly sides outwards, on purpose to render the enclosures more secure from the nocturnal assaults of the hyænas, tigers, and jackalls. Against all these ravenous animals, the oxen are, indeed, able to defend themselves ; but the hyænas, tigers, and leopards are very destructive to calves, sheep, and goats, when they can break in upon them, which they will sometimes do in spite of the watch-dogs kept for their protection ; the cunning jackal is not less destructive to the lambs and kids.

Some travellers approaching the residence of a farmer, had their attention attracted to a novel sight. Several people were waving white flags in some cultivated ground near the house. On drawing nearer they ascertained that this was a method adopted by the farmer and his family to expel an army of locusts, that had just alighted on their corn. They had been employed since sunrise, and it was now towards afternoon, and they described the insects as being so numerous, that it would take an hour's ride on horseback, to reach the extremity of the ground that they covered. No idea can be formed of such countless multitudes, except by those who have actually witnessed them. Their appearance when alighting, somewhat resembles a dense crimson cloud, resting on the land, and when they rise up to proceed onward, the air is literally darkened beneath. Every green herb—every blade of grass, is destroyed in their course, and in their track there remain nothing but barrenness and desolation. Still they are turned to some use. Hottentots have been observed feeding fowls with locusts out of a large sack, and it was surprising to see with what voracity they were devoured. Bushmen are particularly partial to locusts, which contribute largely to their subsistence.

A boor, of the name of De Clercq. one day riding over his farm, had alighted in a difficult pass, and was leading his horse through the long grass, when a lion suddenly rose up before him, at a few yards distance. He had in his hand only a light fowling piece, loaded with slugs ; and hoping that the lion would give way, he, according to the plan always recommended in such emergencies, stood still and confronted him ; but the lion, on the contrary, advancing and crouching to spring, he found himself under the necessity of firing ; he took a hurried aim at the forehead, but the slugs lodged in the breast, and did not prove instantly mortal. The furious animal sprang forward, and seized De Clercq on either side with his talons, but at the same time bit his arm almost in two, as he mechanically thrust it forward to save his face. In this position he held him for a few seconds, till his strength failing from loss of blood, the lion tumbled over, dragging the boor with him in a dying embrace.

De Clercq, however, escaped without any serious injury, and before long entirely recovered.

Gert, a boor of the Cradock district, was out hunting with a neighbour. Coming to a fountain, surrounded, as is common, with tall reeds and rushes, Gert handed his gun to his comrade, and alighted to search for water. But he no sooner approached the fountain, than an enormous lion started up close at his side, and seized him by his left arm.

The boor, though taken by surprise, stood stock still,

without struggling, aware that the least attempt at escape would ensure his instant destruction. The lion also remained motionless, holding fast the boor's arm in his fangs, but without biting it severely,—shutting his eyes at the same time as if he could not withstand the countenance of the victim. As they stood in this position, Gert, maintaining his presence of mind, began to beckon his comrade to advance and shoot the lion in the forehead. This might have been easily effected, as the lion still closed his eyes, and Gert's body concealed from his view any object advancing in front of him.

But the fellow proved a wretch, for, instead of complying with Gert's directions or making any attempt to save him, he cautiously retreated to the top of a neighbouring rock. As the lion continued quiet, Gert continued to beckon for aid; and lion hunters say that if he had persevered a little longer, the lion would have relaxed his hold, and left him uninjured. But Gert, indignant at his comrade's pusillanimity, and losing patience with the lion, drew his knife, which he wore sheathed at his side, and with the utmost force of his right arm, plunged it into the lion's breast.

The thrust was a deadly one, for Gert was a bold and powerful man; but it did not prove effectual in time to save his own life—for the enraged lion, held at arm's length by the utmost efforts of Gert's strength and desperation, so dreadfully lacerated the breast and arms of the unfortunate man with his talons, that his bare bones were laid open. The lion fell at last from loss of blood, and Gert fell along with him.

His rascally companion who had witnessed this fearful struggle from the rock, had now sufficient courage to advance, and bore poor Gert to the nearest house—where such aid as the neighbours could give was afforded, but utterly in vain. Gert expired the third day after this most courageous but frightful struggle, of locked jaw.

Kupt, one of the settlers, proceeding with several companions on a journey into the country, to obtain some young oxen for the Dutch East India Company, met with the following adventures. On the arrival of the wagons, which were obliged to take a circuitous route, they pitched their tent a musket-shot from the kraal, and after making the usual arrangements, went to rest. They were, however, soon disturbed ; for about midnight, the cattle and horses, which were standing between the wagons, began to start and run, and one of the drivers to shout, on which every one, with his gun in his hand, ran out of the tent.

About thirty paces off there stood a lion, which, on seeing them, walked very deliberately about thirty paces further, behind a small thorn-bush, carrying something with him, which Kupt supposed to be a young ox. The south-east wind blew strong, the sky was clear, and the moon shone very bright, so that they could see clearly ; and firing more than sixty shots at that bush, which they stoutly pierced, they could not perceive any movement. After the cattle had been quieted again, and they had looked carefully around, they missed Smit, the sentry, from before the tent. They called as loudly as possible, but in vain ; nobody answered, and it was then concluded that the lion had carried him off. Three or four men then advanced very cautiously to the bush, which stood right opposite the door of the tent, to see if they could discover anything of the man, but returned greatly alarmed, for the lion, who was there still, rose up, and began to roar; they saw too, the musket of the sentry, which was cocked, and also, his cap and shoes.

As the bush was sixty paces from the tent and only thirty from the wagon, and they were able to point at it as a target, they fired into it about a hundred shots, without perceiving anything of the lion, from which they concluded that he was killed, or had run away. This induced Stamansz to go and see if he were there or not, taking with him a firebrand. But no sooner did he approach the bush, than the lion roared

4*

terribly and leaped at him ; on which he threw the firebrand at his assailant, and the others having fired about ten shots, he retired directly to his former place behind the bush.

The firebrand had fallen into the midst of the bush, and, favoured by the strong south-east wind, it began to burn with a great flame, so that they could see very clearly into, and through it. They continued firing into it; and as the night passed away and the day began to break, every one was anxious to aim at the lion, as he could not go from thence without exposing himself entirely to their fire. Seven men, posted on the furthest wagons, watched him that they might fire, if he should come out.

At last, before it became quite light, he walked up the hill with poor Smit in his mouth, when about forty shots were fired at him, but, although some were very near, he escaped unhurt. Every time a ball approached him, he turned round towards the tent, and roared at his enemies ; and Kupt was of opinion that if he had been hit, he would have rushed on the people and the tent.

On the arrival of broad daylight, they saw by the blood, and a piece of the clothes of the man, that the lion had carried away his victim. They also found behind the bush the place where the lion had kept him, and it appeared exceedingly strange that no ball should have struck the lion, as several of them were beaten flat. As it was hoped he might have been wounded and not far off, the people asked Kupt to be allowed to go in search of Smit's corpse, in order to bury it, supposing that by the fire that had been constantly kept up, the lion would not have had time to devour much of it.

Kupt gave permission to some, on condition that they should take a good party of armed Hottentots with them, and made them promise that they would keep a good look-out, and avoid all unnecessary danger. Seven of the party, assisted by forty-three armed Hottentots, followed the track, and found the lion about half a league further on, lying behind a little bush. On the shout of the Hottentots, he sprang up, and ran away, on which they all followed in pursuit. At length, the lion turned round, and rushed, roaring terribly, amongst the crowd. The people, fatigued and out of breath with running, fired, but missed him, on which he made directly towards them. Two of the people were now attacked by the lion, when the captain, or chief man of the kraal, threw himself between them and the lion, and that so closely, that the claws of the lion were struck into his sheep-skin garment. Instantly the lion hunter doffed his mantle, and stabbed the lion with his spear ; and the other Hottentots striking into the lion their spears, Kupt says "he looked like a porcupine." Still he did not leave off roaring and leaping ; but bit off some of the spears, until Stamansz fired a ball into his eye, which made him turn over, and the others shot him dead. This was a very large lion, and had but a short time before devoured a Hottentot whom he had carried off from the kraal.

On another occasion, the grass was exceedingly tall, and the country abounded in spring-bucks. A Hottentot thought he perceived one amidst the grass, and crept closely up to it in order to make sure of his shot, when, on rising to discharge his piece, he found himself close on a large male lion, which instantly set up a loud roar. His own tale, however, was not a little amusing. "I saw," said he, "a spring-buck, which I made sure of having in the pot to-night; but when I got close to it, I found it to be *the Governor*. I was just going to fire, when he asked me in a loud tone, 'What are you going to do ?' 'Oh,' said I, 'I beg your pardon, I did not know it was your honour, or I should not have presumed to draw so near you ; I hope your honour will not consider it an insult, and I shall instantly retire.' So I scampered away a great deal quicker than I went to him."

Diederik Muller and his brother Christian were accustomed

to hunt in company, and between them killed a large number of lions. They did not achieve this, however, without many hair-breadth escapes, and have more than once saved each other's lives. On one occasion, a lion sprang suddenly on Diederik, from behind a stone,—bore man and horse to the ground, and was proceeding to finish his career, when Christian galloped up and shot the savage brute through the heart. In this encounter Diederik was so roughly handled that he lost his hearing in one ear—the lion having dug his talons deeply into it.

When the nightly depredations of a tiger have roused the farmers, the following is the course pursued :—The animal is tracked to its lair in the thick underwood, and, when found, attacked by large dogs. If possible, it flies ; but, when unable to escape, makes a desperate defence, raising itself above the assailants by leaping on a bush, and from thence striking them down with its paws as they rush in, and from its great strength and activity, frequently destroying them. But the tiger seems to know its master foe, and should a man approach within the range of its tremendous spring, it at once leaves the dogs, and darts upon him, and the struggle is then for life.

A slave, going out early one morning, to look after cattle, heard his dogs baying at a distance in the jungle, and, on coming up to ascertain the cause, was met by a tiger's spring. The tiger clung, and, seizing him by the nape of his neck, tore the skin off, until the scalp hung over his eyes ; but, even in this state of torture, the slave drew his wood-knife from his belt, and stabbed him to the heart. In general, the man stands at a distance, waiting his opportunity till he can fire without injuring the dogs.

Mr. Shaw, the missionary, says : "News was brought one evening, that a horse had been laid hold of by a tiger, and partly devoured. The chief gave orders that the hunters should be on the spot at sunrise the next morning. I

engaged to accompany them, and took my dog and gun, the
Namaquas had their clubs, and all the dogs which they
were able to procure. A little terrier having obtained the
scent, ran forward till it came to the cavern where the tiger
had taken up his abode. It stood at the entrance and barked,
not knowing the kind of game it had been pursuing. The
tiger rose, and fixing its eyes on the terrier, it scampered
away at its utmost speed. The tiger now stood on the surface of a large sloping rock, and, on seeing the other dogs, he
looked angrily at them, and began to grumble, as though he
would challenge them to an attack. My own dog and two
others instantly accepted the challenge, and a furious contest
ensued. It was impossible for me to make use of my gun ;
but at this crisis, a native, on seeing that the dogs were faithful to each other, ran and seized the tiger's tail, which he held
with all his might. The tiger roared, the dogs became more
furious, the men with their clubs approached, and beat him
on the head ; and thus assailed, he soon groaned his last.'

A resident in the colony, named Bournan, was suddenly
attacked by a tiger, who stuck its claws into his head, aim-
ing at his throat, that he might suck out the blood of the
victim. Bournan, an athletic and powerful man, wrestling
earnestly with his foe, succeeded in throwing the tiger on the
ground, where, for a time, he held it down. He soon found,
however, that the animal was too strong for him, but when
about to give himself up as lost, recollected that he had a knife
in his pocket. Instantly taking it out, he pressed with all his
might the tiger to the ground, and succeeded in cutting its
throat. Bournan was covered with wounds from which the
blood during the fearful struggle copiously flowed; but though
his life was preserved, it was long before his previous strength
was restored.

The testimony of old Teysho to one of our travellers,
entirely corresponded with what he had heard on the same
subject from the boors and Hottentots. The lion, he said, very

seldom attacks man if unprovoked; but he will frequently approach within a few paces and survey him steadily; and sometimes he will attempt to get behind him as if he could not stand his look, but was yet desirous of springing upon him unawares. If a person in such circumstances attempts either to fight or fly he incurs the most imminent peril; but if he has sufficient presence of mind coolly to confront him, the animal will, in almost every instance, retire. But, it was added, when a lion has once conquered man, he becomes tenfold more fierce and villainous than he was before, and will even come into the kraals in search of him, in preference to other prey.

The power of the human eye is felt by other animals. A British officer in India, having chanced to ramble into a jungle adjoining the encampment, suddenly encountered a royal tiger. The rencounter appeared equally unexpected on both sides, and both parties made a dead halt—earnestly gazing on each other. The officer had no fire-arms, and was aware that a sword would be no effective defence in a struggle for life with such an antagonist. But he had heard that even the Bengal tiger might be sometimes checked by looking him firmly in the face. He did so. In a few minutes the tiger, which appeared preparing to make his fatal spring, grew disturbed—slunk aside—and attempted to creep round upon him behind. The officer turned constantly on the tiger,— which still continued to shrink from his glance;—but darting into the thicket and again issuing forth at a different quarter, it persevered for about an hour in this attempt to catch him by surprise; till at last it fairly yielded the contest, and left the officer to pursue his walk. The direction he now took, it may easily be believed, was straight to the tents, at *double-quick time.*

ANIMALS OF SOUTH AFRICA

CHAPTER VII.

LE VAILLANT was struck by a distinction he observed on one
of the huts, which he found to be entirely covered with the
skin of the giraffe. "I had never seen," he says, "this
quadruped, the tallest of all those upon the earth. I knew
it only from false descriptions and designs, and thus I could
scarcely recognise its robe. And yet this *was* the skin of the
giraffe. I was in the country that this creature inhabits.
I might, probably, see some living ones. I looked forward
to the moment when I should be thus recompensed, at least
in part, for all the sufferings and annoyances of my
expedition.

"One of the Namaquas, who were my guides, came in
great haste to give me information, which he thought would
be agreeable to me. He had seen the strong feeling of
pleasure which I had evinced at the sight of the skin of the
giraffe ; and he had run to say that he had just found in the
neighbourhood, one of these animals under a mimosa, the
leaves of which he was browsing upon. In an instant, full
of joy, I leaped upon my horse ; I made Bernfry, one of my

men, mount another, and, followed by my dogs, I flew to the mimosa.

" The giraffe was no longer there. We saw her cross the plain towards the west; and we hastened to overtake her. She was proceeding at a smart trot; but did not appear to be at all hurried. We galloped after her, and occasionally fired our muskets; but she insensibly gained so much upon us, that, after having pursued her for three hours, we were forced to stop, because our horses were out of breath, and we entirely lost sight of her.

" The pursuit of her had led us so far away from each other and the camp, and the giraffe having made many turns and doubles, I was unable to direct my course towards home. It was noon already. I began to feel hunger and thirst; and I found myself alone in a sterile and arid spot, exposed to a burning sun, without the least shelter from the heat, and destitute of food." The distress of Le Vaillant, in this instance, was only temporary; he shot some birds, like partridges, which he cooked and ate to his great refreshment; and in the evening he had the high pleasure of joining his companions.

" The next morning," he says, " my whole caravan joined me again. I saw five other giraffes, to which I gave chase; but they employed so many stratagems to escape that, after having pursued them the whole day, we entirely lost them as night came on. I was in despair at this ill success.

" The next day was the happiest of my life. By sunrise I was in quest of game, in hope of obtaining some provisions for my men. After several hours fatigue we descried, at the turn of a hill, seven giraffes, which my pack instantly pursued. Six of them went off together; but the seventh, cut off by my dogs, took another way. Bernfry was walking by the side of his horse; but, in the twinkling of an eye, he was in the saddle, and pursued the six. For myself, I followed the single one at full speed; but, in spite of the efforts of my horse, she got so much ahead of me that, in turning a little hill, I lost sight of her altogether, and gave up the pursuit.

"My dogs, however, were not so easily exhausted. They were soon so close upon her, that she was obliged to stop, to defend herself. From the place where I was, I heard them give tongue with all their might; and, as their voices appeared all to come from the same spot I conjectured that they had got the animal into a corner; and I again pushed for ward. I had scarcely got round the hill than I perceived her surrounded by the dogs, and endeavouring to drive them away by heavy kicks. In a moment I was on my feet; and a shot from my carbine brought her to the earth. Enchanted with my victory, I called my people about me, that they might assist in skinning and cutting up the animal. While I was looking for them, I saw Klaas Baster, who kept making signals, which I could not comprehend. At length I went the way he pointed; and, to my surprise, saw a giraffe standing under a large ebony tree, assailed by my dogs. It was the animal I had shot, who had staggered to this place; and it fell dead the moment I was about to take the second shot.

"Who could have believed that a conquest like this would have excited me to a transport almost approaching to madness! Pains, fatigues, cruel privation, uncertainty as to the future, disgust sometimes as to the past—all these recollections and feelings fled at the sight of this new prey. I could not satisfy my desire to contemplate it. I measured its enormous height. I looked from the animal to the instrument which had destroyed it. I called and recalled my people about me. Although we had combated together the largest and most dangerous animals, it was I alone who had killed the giraffe. I was now able to add to the riches of natural history. I was now able to destroy the romance which attached to this animal, and to establish a truth. My people congratulated me on my triumph. Bernfry alone was absent ; but he came at last, walking at a slow pace, and holding his horse by the bridle. He had fallen from his seat, and had injured his shoulder. I heard not what he said to me. I saw not that he wanted assistance; I spoke to him only of my victory. He showed me his shoulder ; I showed him my giraffe. I was intoxicated, and I should not have thought even of my own wounds."

Mr. Pringle has thus graphically described the lion's attack on the giraffe :—

> "Wouldst thou view the lion's den ?
> Search afar from haunts of men—
> Where the reed-encircled rill
> Oozes from the rocky hill,
> By its verdure far descried
> 'Mid the desert brown and wide.
>
> Close beside the sedgy brim
> Couchant lurks the lion grim ;
> Watching till the close of day
> Brings the death-devoted prey.
> Heedless, at the ambush'd brink,
> The tall giraffe stoops to drink :
> Upon him straight the savage springs
> With cruel joy !—The desert rings
> With clanging sound of desperate strife—
> The prey is strong, and strives for life.
> Now plunging tries, with frantic bound,
> To shake the tyrant to the ground—
> He shrieks—he rushes through the waste
> With glaring eyes and headlong haste.
> In vain !—the spoiler on his prize
> Rides proudly—tearing as he flies.
>
> For life the victim's utmost speed
> Is muster'd in this hour of need :
> For life—for life—his giant might
> He strains, and pours his soul in flight ;
> And, mad with terror, thirst, and pain,
> Spurns with wild hoof the thundering plain.

" 'Tis vain ; the thirsty sands are drinking
His streaming blood—his strength is sinking;
The victor's fangs are in his veins—
His flanks are streaked with sanguine stains;
His panting breast in foam and gore
Is bathed—he reels—his race is o'er !
He falls—and, with convulsive throe,
Resigns his throat to the raging foe:
—And lo ! ere quivering life has fled,
The vultures wheeling overhead,
Swoop down, to watch, in gaunt array,
Till the gorged monarch quits his prey ! "

The Gnu is about the size of a full-grown ass. The neck
and tail precisely resemble those of a small horse, and its
pace, which is a species of light gallop, is so perfectly similar,
that a herd of gnus, when seen at a distance scampering
over the plains of South Africa, might be easily mistaken for
a troop of wild horses, but for their dark and uniform
colour.

They live in large herds on the Karroo, a great desert.
When first alarmed, they fling up their heels and caper like
a restive horse, tossing their heads and tails, and butting at
the mole-hills, or any other object that might be in their
way ; but immediately after, off they start, traversing the
desert with a speed which soon carries them beyond the reach
of danger. They do not run in a confused crowd, like sheep
or oxen, but in single file, following a leader, and exhibiting
an agreeable regularity as they bound over the plains. When
hunted they will turn upon the hunter, and pursue him,
dropping on their knees before making an attack, and then
darting forward with amazing alacrity and force.

"In common with the ox and buffalo," says Captain
Harris, "the gnu has an unconquerable aversion to scarlet—
pawing the earth and becoming perfectly furious on the sudden display of that colour. In situations where these
whimsical animals had been rendered more than usually wild

6

by the incessant persecutions of the border colonists, I frequently found it requisite, in order to allure the herd within range, to hoist a red pocket handkerchief upon the muzzle of my rifle. This exhibit on invariably produced the most violent tumult and excitement, and caused the whole troop to charge past in single file—'with mane erect and blazing eye'—following their leader, flinging out their taper heels, whisking their streaming tails, butting with their horns in so menacing a manner, and displaying emotions of such violent frenzy, that I was fain to strike my colours and have recourse to my weapons—when they instantly whirled and·pranced confidently round at a safer distance, headed by their swarthy chief—

> 'Fierce on the hunter's hostile land,
>   He rolls his eye of burnished glow:
> Spurns with black hoof and horns the sand,
>   And tosses high his mane of snow.' "

Two gentlemen were hunting gnus on the plains, and one having been wounded by a musket-ball (in which condition these animals are very furious), it gave chase to one of them, and gained fast upon him, when all at once he disappeared, by tumbling into an ant-eater's hole, which was concealed by the long grass. There he lay for some time secure from the enraged animal, which, after searching for him in vain, scampered off in another direction; nor could this gentleman's companion, who was galloping up to his assistance, conceive what had become of him, until he saw, to his great satisfaction and amusement, his head cautiously emerging from the bowels of the earth.

The quagga is a timid animal, with a figure and gait much resembling those of an ass, but stouter and handsomer than that animal as found in Europe. Though its flesh is carrion and its hide almost useless, it is often pursued merely for pastime. It is inferior ·to the horse in swiftness, but it baffles the hunter by seeking refuge in the most rugged parts of the mountain, where his steed can only follow with extreme difficulty.

The farmers are in the habit of driving a troop of quaggas to the brink of a precipice, when they rush over the declivities, and fall an easy prey to their pursuers. In one instance temerity was dearly paid for. A farmer was pursuing a herd, and being closely on some which were exhausted, he attempted, merely for the sake of saving his shot, to drive one of them over a precipice, on which the desperate animal turned suddenly round, and seizing him by the leg with its teeth, dragged him from his horse, and actually tore his foot off at the ankle. The consequences were fatal to the huntsman, for, in spite of medical aid, mortification ensued, and he died a few days afterwards.

Captain Harris, with a companion, and four savages of the Batlapi tribe, left the wagons at daybreak, and crossing the river, proceeded through a park of magnificent camelthorn trees, many of which were groaning under the huge nests of the "sociable grosbeaks," while others were decorated with green clusters of misletoe, the bright, scarlet berries of which were highly ornamental. They soon perceived large herds of quaggas and brindled gnus, which continued to increase, until the whole plain seemed alive. The clatter of their hoofs was perfectly astounding; and the captain could compare it to nothing but the din of a tremendous charge of cavalry, or the rushing of a mighty tempest. He could not estimate the accumulated numbers at less than 15,000; a great extent of country being actually chequered black and white with their congregated masses.

As the panic caused by the report of the rifles extended, clouds of dust hovered over them; and the long necks of troops of ostriches were also be seen, towering above the heads of their less gigantic neighbours, and sailing past with astonishing rapidity. Groups of purple sassabys, and brilliant red and yellow hartebeests, likewise lent their aid to complete the picture, which must have been seen to be properly under-stood.

"The savages," he says, "kept in our wake, dexterously despatching the wounded gnus by a touch in the spine, with the point of an assagai, and instantly covering up the carcases with bushes, to secure them from the voracity of the vultures. which hung about us like specks in the firmament, and descended with the velocity of lightning, as each discharge of our artillery gave notice of prey. As we proceeded, two strange figures were perceived standing under the shade of a tree ; these we instantly knew to be elands, the savages exclaiming at the same moment, with evident delight, "*Impoofo, impoofo*," and pressing our horses to the utmost speed, we found ourselves, for the first time, at the heels of the largest and most beautiful species of the antelope tribe. Notwithstanding the unwieldy shape of these animals, they had at first greatly exceeded the speed of our jaded horses, but being pushed, they soon separated ; their sleek coats turned first blue and then white with froth ; the foam fell from their mouths and nostrils, and the perspiration from their sides. Their pace gradually slackened, and with their full brilliant eyes turned imploringly towards us, at the end of a mile, each was laid low by a single ball. They were young bulls, each of them measuring upwards of seventeen hands at the shoulder.

"I was engaged in making a sketch of the one I had shot, when the savages came up, and in spite of all my remonstrances, proceeded with cold-blooded ferocity to stab the unfortunate animal, stirring up the blood and shouting with barbarous exultation as it issued from each newly inflicted wound, regardless of the eloquent and piteous appeal, expressed in the beautiful clear black eye of the mild and inoffensive eland."

Zebras were formerly abundant in different parts of the Cape Colony, but latterly their number has been greatly diminished   Troops of six or eight have been seen to stand at a distance, gazing on a wagon as it moved slowly onwards; but startled by the sound of the whip, they set off eagerly, scampering over stones and bushes, and leaving behind them a thick cloud of dust.

The hyæna is remarkable for his voracity, and also for the singular fact that he will feed with the vulture from the same carcase.   Mr. Burchell explains this circumstance by stating that the flesh of vultures themselves smells like carrion, and no other animal, however pressed with hunger, will eat it, a quality which gives them impunity which they would not otherwise enjoy, inasmuch as they have often to eat in company with hyænas, and other beasts of prey.   Hence they are in no danger of attack from any animals, while the services they perform as scavengers of the country gives them safety even from the assaults of men.   Often, when the vulture has finished, the hyæna will persevere, and not be content till he has consumed all the manageable bones that are left in the carcase.   When pressed by hunger they are very determined in their efforts to satisfy it, and will then kill dogs and asses even within the enclosures of the houses, and in some instances have carried off human beings.   It is also asserted that whenever one of these animals was wounded, its companions always tore it to pieces and devoured it.   Bruce tells us that they were a general scourge in Abyssinia, both in the city and the field ; and that many a time in the night, when the king had kept him late in the palace, on crossing the square which lay on his route home, he was apprehensive lest they should attack him, although he was surrounded by armed men, who seldom passed a night without wounding or killing some of them.   "One night," he says, "I went out of my tent, and returning immediately, I perceived two large blue eyes glaring at me in the dark.   I called my servant to bring a light ; and we found a hyæna standing near the head of the bed, with two or three large bunches of candles in his mouth, by keeping which he seemed to wish at that time for no other

5

THE HYÆNA.

prey. I was not afraid of him, and with a spike struck him
as near the heart as I could. It was not until I had done
this that he showed any signs of fierceness ; but when feeling
his wound he dropped the candles, and endeavoured to run
upon the shaft of ∴he spear to arrive at me, so that I was
obliged to draw a pistol from my girdle and shoot him, and
nearly at the same time my servant cleft his skull with a
battle-axe. In a word, the hyænas were the plague of our
lives, the terror of our night-walks, and the destruction of our
mules and asses, which are their favourite food."

The civet is somewhat more than two feet long from the
nose to the insertion of the tail, which is upwards of a foot
in length. The colour of the animal's fur is an ash gray, and
is marked with large blackish or dusky spots. The hair is of
coarse texture, and along the back stands somewhat erect
like a mane. The body is rather thick ; the forehead is broad,
the muzzle acute, and black at the tip. There are three black
stripes which proceed from the back of the ear, and terminate
at the shoulders and throat. Like all nocturnal animals, the
civet is torpid and indolent during the day, nor does it ever
display much of either intelligence or docility.

This animal is celebrated for its musky perfume, the
product of a peculiar glandulous apparatus. The name civet,
first applied to the odoriferous substance, is of Arabian origin,
but the animal has received the same appellation. The civets
are found in all the warm parts of Asia and Africa, in the
island of Madagascar, and in the East Indian islands.

The perfume of the civet is so strong, that it infects every
part of the creature, and so completely are the skin and hair
penetrated with it, that they will retain the odour long after
their removal from the body. If the animal is irritated, the
scent becomes exceedingly powerful ; and were a person shut
up in a room with a civet, the odour would be scarcely
supportable.

The peculiar substance by which it is yielded is a fatty
secretion, about the consistence of honey or butter, of a lively

white colour when fresh, but darker when it has been kept
for some time. It is produced by both sexes, and is contained

THE CIVET.

in two cavities, or pockets, placed beneath the tail ; these cavities are smooth internally, and covered with numerous small
pores, connected with the glands from which it is secreted.

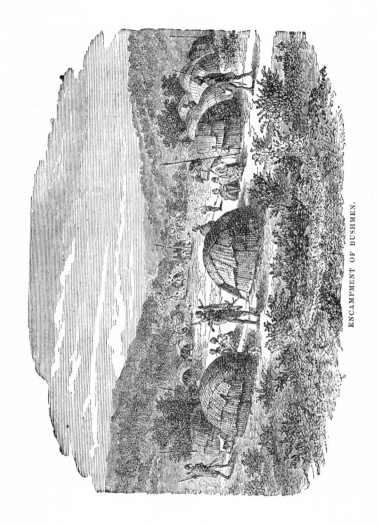

ENCAMPMENT OF BUSHMEN.

CHAPTER VIII.

THE BUSHMEN.

THE Bushmen, like the Hottentots, Corannas, and Namaquas, are rather sallow than black. They are generally smaller in stature than their neighbours of the interior, and are considered by Mr. Moffat, as well as Mr. Barrow, more to resemble the Chinese in features and colour than any other people. They have evidently arisen from a race distinct from that of their neighbours, and extended inland, inhabiting the most fertile spots, till their course was arrested by the progress of colonisation. At length they sought refuge from superior power in the wastes and barren mountain ravines, and became emphatically, " the children of the desert."

The locusts, which, as we have seen, produce such devastation wherever their countless multitudes go, are hailed with delight by the Bushmen and Corannas, with whom they form an important article of food. Thus, in a song of the wild Bushmen, are words which are interpreted as follows :—

> " I plant no herb nor pleasant fruits,
> I toil not for my cheer,
> The desert yields me juicy roots,
> And herds of bounding deer.

"Yea, even the wasting locusts' swarm,
   Which mighty nations dread,
  To me nor terror brings nor harm,
   I make of them my bread."

They are also fond of many plants and bulbs which are despised by many other people. Their huts are far inferior to those of other tribes. The holes in the ground, which sometimes answer the purpose of beds, are only a few inches deep, of a longish round form, and not more than five or six feet wide. In very cold weather they heap up twigs and earth on the windward side of the hole ; in summer they prefer the beds of rivers, and lie there beneath the shade of the mimosas, drawing down the branches to screen them from the sun.

The country of the Bushmen, as it appeared to an experienced traveller on his entrance from Cape Colony, presented an even, bare, and open surface, relieved, here and there, by a broad and far-extended undulation. This wide desert was void of all vegetation, and creation seemed nought but earth and sky. After two or three days' journey, there was a little variety in the landscape, but all was desolate, wild, and singular. A belt of mountains of from five to ten miles in breadth, crossed the country, stretching out of sight on either side, and exhibiting a vast assemblage of stocks and stones, without the slightest verdure. Occasionally the traveller arrives at some friendly nook or dell, where springs a refreshing fountain, with a few plants and reeds, but these are generally concealed, and form no part of the general landscape. Nothing deserving the name of a tree is to be seen in all the Bushman's country.

In the Bushman country the lion is considered exceedingly fierce and dangerous. An English gentleman was travelling through some portion of it, and when the wagons were outspanned, the party was attacked by several lions ; and though the Hottentots fired at the ravenous beasts, and threw forth pieces of burning wood, one of them tore away a horse which had been tied to the wagon-wheel, and afterwards

AN AGED BUSHMAN PLAYING ON THE GORRAH.

a second. These he carried off with the greatest apparent ease, and placed before his companions, who were at a little distance.

5*

One of the most ancient as well as favourite recreations of the Hottentots is found in the *gorrah*, which resembles in form a violin bow, but in its use is quite different, combining, as it does, a stringed and a wind instrument. It consists of a slender bow, on which a catgut is stretched. To the lower end of this string is attached a flat piece of an ostrich quill, so as to form part of the length of the string. This quill being applied to the lips, is made to vibrate, by strongly inhaling and exhaling the air. The resulting tunes are said to be powerful, but they are, doubtless, far more agreeable to barbarous than civilised ears.

The old Bushman, represented in the engraving, seated himself on a flat piece of rock, and resting his elbows on his knees, put one forefinger into his ear, and the other into his wide nostril, either as it so happened or for the purpose, it might be, of keeping the head steady, commenced his solo, and continued it with great earnestness, over and over again. The exertion it required to bring out the tones loudly was very evident ; and in his anxious haste to draw breath at every note, there were certain grunting sounds, which, though they afforded no gratification to his European auditors, might, perhaps, have "pleased the pigs."

A Bushman family came for water to a muddy pool where Campbell's wagons were stopping. It consisted of the husband and wife, a younger brother, two daughters, eleven and twelve years of age, and a child of about eighteen months, which the mother continued to suckle.

The man had a bow and a quiver full of poisoned arrows. They had part of the entrails of a zebra filled with water, from which they frequently drank, and then filled five ostrich shells with water to carry home. The traveller gave the man a piece of tobacco, for which he nodded and uttered some words in a low tone, expressive of thanks. But, on giving him the skin of a sheep killed in the morning, he added to his former expressions of gratitude some singular motions by knocking with his elbows against his sides. On being asked how long it was since he had washed his skin, which was exceedingly dirty, he said he could not tell, but that it must have been a long time ago. His wife laughed heartily on hearing the question.

One of the daughters, after grinding the tobacco between two stones into snuff, mixed it with the white ashes of the fire that had been kindled ; the mother then took a large pinch, put the remainder into a piece of goat's skin, among the hair, and folded it up for future use. She had a stroke of dark blue, like tattooing, from the upper part of her brows to the nose, about half an inch broad, and two similar strokes on her temples. The man had several cuts on his arms, and smaller ones on his temples, and so had the children, which they said was done to cure sickness. The dark colour of these cuts was produced by putting into them ground charcoal when the wounds were green.

A notion has prevailed in the South of Africa, that some of the Bush-people can change themselves into animals at pleasure. The following legend will illustrate it :—Once on a time, a certain Namaqua was travelling in company with a Bushwoman, who carried her child on her back. They had proceeded some distance on their way, when a troop of wild horses appeared.

The man now said to the woman, "I am hungry, and know you can turn yourself into a lion ; do so, and catch us a wild horse that we may eat."

The woman answered, " You'll be afraid."

" No, no," said the man, "I am afraid of dying of hunger; but not of you."

Whilst he was yet speaking, hair began to shoot out at the back of the woman's neck; her hands gradually assumed the appearance of claws ; and all her features were altered. She set down the child. Alarmed at the metamorphosis, the man climbed a tree close by ; the woman glared at him frightfully, and going to one side, threw off her skin petticoat. Instantly a perfect lion rushed out into the plain; it bounded and crept among the bushes towards the wild horses, and springing on one of them, it fell and the lion lapped its blood. The lion now came to where the child was crying, when the man called from the tree, "Enough! enough! don't hurt me! Put off your lion's shape;—I'll never ask to see this again."

The lion looked at him and growled. "I'll remain here," said the man, "till I die, if you don't become a woman again."

Then the mane and the tail began to disappear; the lion went to the bush where the skin petticoat lay; in a moment it was slipped on, and the woman in her proper state took up the child. The man now came down from the tree, made a meal from the horse's flesh, but never again asked the woman to catch him any game.

"Poor Bushman!" says Mr. Moffat. "Thy hand has been against every one, and every one's hand against thee. For generations past they have been hunted like partridges in the mountains. Deprived of what nature had made their own, they became desperate, wild, fierce, and indomitable in their habits. Hunger compels them to feed on everything edible. Ixias, wild garlic, mesembryanthemums, the core of aloes, gum of acacias, and several other plants and berries, some of which are extremely unwholesome, constitute their fruits of the field; while almost every kind of living creature is eagerly devoured, lizards, locusts, and grasshoppers not excepted. The poisonous, as well as innoxious serpents, they roast and eat. They cut off the head of the former, which they dissect, and carefully extract the bags, or reservoirs of poison, which communicate with the fangs of the upper jaw."

Yet, degraded as they are, their condition is not hopeless. Dr. Philip, who resided among them, says: "Many of the accounts which have been published in England, respecting the savage, ferocious, untameable character of the Bushman can scarcely be read in Africa without a smile. The civilisation of that degraded people is not only practicable, but might be easily attained ; while they are by no means deficient in intellect, they are susceptible of kindness ; grateful for favours ; faithful in the execution of a trust committed to them ; disposed to receive instruction ; and by the use of proper means, could be easily brought to exchange their barbarous manner of life for one of comfort."

7

CHAPTER IX.

THE different species of termites, or white ants, build nests of various forms. Some construct upon the ground a cylindrical turret of clay, about three-quarters of a yard high, surrounded by a projecting conical roof, so as in shape considerably to resemble a mushroom, and composed within of innumerable cells, of various sizes and figures. Others build their nests—which also vary in size from that of a hat to that of a sugar-cask, and composed of pieces of wood glued together—amongst the branches of trees, often seventy or eighty feet high.

But other nests, found in various parts of Africa, are still more curious. They are formed entirely of clay, and are generally twelve feet high and broad in proportion, so that when a cluster of them, as is often the case, appears, they might be taken for a village, and are, in fact, sometimes larger than the huts inhabited by the natives.

The first process in erecting these singular structures, is the elevation of two or three turrets of clay about a foot high, and in the shape of a sugar-loaf. These, which seem to be the scaffolds of the future building, rapidly increase in number and height, until at length being widened at the base, joined at the top in one dome, and consolidated all round into a thick wall of clay, they form a building of the size already mentioned, and of the shape of a haycock, which, when clothed, as it generally soon becomes, with a coating of grass, it at a distance very much resembles. When the building has assumed this, its final form, the inner turrets, all but the tops, which project like pinnacles from different parts of it, are removed, and the clay employed over again in other services.

The lower part of the building alone is occupied by the inhabitants. The upper portion, or dome, which is very strong and solid, is left empty, serving principally as a defence from the vicissitudes of the weather, and the attacks of enemies, and to keep up in the lower part a general warmth and moisture necessary to the hatching of eggs and cherishing of the young ants. The inhabited portion is occupied by the *royal chamber*, or habitation of the king and queen, the *nurseries* for the young, the *storehouses* for food, and innumerable galleries, passages, and empty rooms, arranged according to a regular plan.

To employ the words of Kirby and Spence : "That the millions necessary to execute such Herculean labours, perpetually passing to and fro, should never interrupt or interfere with each other, is a miracle of nature, or rather of the Author of nature, far exceeding the most boasted works of man ; for, did these creatures equal him in size, retaining their usual instincts and activity, their buildings would soar to the astonishing height of more than half a mile, and their tunnels would expand to a magnificent cylinder of more than 300 feet in diameter ; before which, the pyramids of Egypt and the aqueducts of Rome would lose all their celebrity, and dwindle into nothing."

Some insects of this kind are at present making their ravages at La Rochelle, Rochefort, Saintes, and the neighbouring districts in France. Naturalists have recently taken to

Paris several material proofs of the dangers to which these apparently insignificant enemies are capable of subjecting the inhabitants of these districts. They have described the sudden manner in which the roofs and floors of houses had crumbled to pieces, and how soon buildings were found to be so entirely undermined, that it was necessary either to reconstruct them from the very foundations, or entirely to abandon them.

M. Quatrefages, when residing at La Rochelle, says : "The prefecture and a few neighbouring houses are the principal scene of the destructive ravages of the termites, but here they have taken complete possession of the premises. In the garden not a stake can be put in the ground, and not a plank can be left on the beds, without being attacked within twenty-four, or forty-eight hours. The fences put round the young trees are gnawed from the bottom, while the trees themselves are gutted to the very branches. Within the building itself, the apartments and offices are all alike invaded. I saw upon the roof of a bed-room which had been recently repaired, galleries made by the termites which looked like stalactites, and which had begun to show themselves the very day after the workmen had left the place.

" In the cellars I discovered similar galleries, which were either half-way between the ceiling and the floor, or running along the walls, and extending, no doubt, up to the very garrets, for on the principal staircase other galleries were observed between the ground floor and the second floor, passing under the plaster wherever it was sufficiently thick for the purpose, and only coming to view at different points where the stones were on the surface ; for, like other species, the termites of La Rochelle always work under cover whenever it is possible for them to do so. It is generally only by incessant vigilance that we can trace the course of their devastations, and prevent their ravages. At the time of M. Audouin's visit, a curious proof was accidentally obtained of the mischief which this insect silently accomplishes. One day it was discovered that the archives of the department were almost totally destroyed, and that without the slightest external trace of any damage. The termites had reached the boxes in which these documents were preserved, by mining the wainscoting, and they had then leisurely set to work to devour these administrative records, carefully respecting the upper sheets and the margin of each leaf, so that a box which was only filled with a mass of rubbish, seemed to enclose a file of papers in perfect order. The hardest woods were attacked in the same manner. I saw on one of the staircases an oak post, in which one of the clerks had buried his hand up to the wrist, in grasping at it for support as his foot accidentally slipped. The interior of the post was entirely formed of empty cells, the substance of which could be scraped away like dust, while the layer that had been left untouched by the termites was not thicker than a sheet of paper."

Anxious to observe these creatures minutely, M. Quatrefages obtained from a friend a constant supply of them. It will be readily understood that he took every precaution to prevent their escaping, for had they got abroad they would undoubtedly have destroyed the house, and in the course of time, the part of the city in which it is situated. He kept these insects in a basin that was only half full, and took every precaution to screen them from the light; and as his prisoners were unable to scale their glassy walls, he could observe them at his leisure ; and he was thus enabled to follow in detail the various steps by which they transformed into a regular nest the confused mass of earth and rubbish, in the midst of which they had first been thrown. Their remarkable movements he has described as follows :—

" A very few minutes after the bowl had been placed upon my table, each insect endeavoured to join his companions. Some attempted to climb along the smooth walls of their prison, but after a few unsuccessful attempts, they buried themselves in the midst of the earth. The entire troop was soon dispersed, and I saw them divided into small groups on the darkest part of the bowl. After a few hours the various groups were reunited into one, and from this moment their labours began and were continued in common.

"The first care of the termites seemed to be to lay down a sort of high-road all round the bowl, and as the materials were very unequally distributed, they were obliged to clear away some parts and to fill up others. The first of these tasks was easy, but the second gave them more trouble. The workmen first transported a certain quantity of earth, intended to raise the soil to the required height, and they next constructed an arch above it. I saw them come one after the other, each carrying between his jaws a little mass of earth, which he applied without pausing to the projecting edge of the work; next he descended by a kind of incline which had been expressly constructed for the purpose, and returned underground by a special gallery.

"Some of these insects appeared to me to moisten the materials after they had been put in their right places, with a liquid which was no doubt intended to harden them. During these labours, the soldiers were most evidently engaged in playing the part of leaders and superintendents. I saw one here and there, and always alone, mixing amongst the labourers, but never performing any of the work. At times they made a sort of tremulous motion with the whole of their body, and struck the ground with their forceps, on which all the neighbouring workers executed the same movement and exhibited renewed activity. In twenty hours the gallery was fit for use.

"It must be admitted, however, that the walls of the bowl formed almost half of it. At the same time the earth had been consolidated, and its surface smoothed, while a cork which I had thrown in was half buried. I then gave them three other corks, and added successively a closely compressed paper ball and a large ball of bread-crumbs. These different materials remained precisely in the same position in which they had accidentally fallen, and I thought at first that they had been despised by the termites, but having after a few days turned the bowl completely over, I found that they all remained in their places, notwithstanding their weight. They had, in fact, been cemented together, and I discovered afterwards, on opening them, that the insects had carried their galleries through them, although the work of cementing and boring was not discoverable from the exterior.

"The labours of my prisoners appeared at first to be continued without any intermission, but they were relaxed as soon as the great works were terminated. A few days, however, sufficed for the completion of the nest, and at this time the largest cork had almost entirely disappeared, whilst the earth had been raised to the level of the other two. All the surface of the soil was smooth, without any apparent opening, and the earth, which, at the beginning of the experiment, was as loose as fine sand, had been so well consolidated that only a few particles were detached from it when the bowl was overturned. Under this kind of crust, and at the very bottom of it, there extended all around the bowl a gallery of about half an inch wide and two-thirds of an inch high, in the form of a semi-arch, which rested against the transparent sides of the glass. Several openings issued from this circular road, and gave access into low vaulted chambers, large enough to contain thirty or forty workers. These compartments communicated with other internal cells by means of very low doors, through which five or six workers could pass abreast.

"As soon as this work was completed the termites remained at rest, at least during the day. I generally found them grouped together in the darkest part of the large gallery, or in the adjoining compartments, whilst a few isolated soldiers seemed occasionally to mount guard at the entrance of the empty cells; but as soon as the light struck them they manifested an intense degree of excitement. Labourers and soldiers then performed the singular and tremulous movement of which I have already spoken, and in a few moments all had disappeared into the central apartments, where the light could not penetrate."

A singular animal is a native of South Africa, where, in some districts, it is very common, and where, from its singular habits, it has acquired the name of the Aardvark, or Earth Hog. It is gifted with molar teeth, which are of a cylindrical form, and perforated longitudinally, with an infinite number of minute tubes, closely resembling those in a piece of cane. Their surface is nearly flat, and well adapted for the bruising of soft insects; the nails are hoof-like, strong, and fitted to excavate the ground; the head is elongated; the limbs are short and powerful; the hair is scanty, especially about the head, and approaches bristles in its texture, being coarse and stiff; the tongue is extensible. The food of this animal consists exclusively of the white ants, whose dome-like buildings are so numerous in the places adjacent to the Orange River, and in other localities which are thinly peopled.

The dwelling of the aardvark is a burrow, at a little distance beneath the surface of the ground. A wagon of Burchell's was nearly overturned by one of its wheels sinking into such an abode. During the day the creature is rarely to be seen; but as the dusk approaches it creeps forth intent on its prey, and then proceeds to the ant-hills. Scratching a hole with its fore feet on one side of them, it disturbs the little community; on which the ants, running about in confusion, are easily drawn by its long and slender tongue into its mouth. Without tusks, or any efficient teeth, this animal may appear defenceless, but it is so safe in its concealment that no animal is so seldom seen. It burrows for itself a retreat with astonishing rapidity.

CHAPTER X.

EVENING having come, some families pitched their tents; others,
more vividly impressed with the terror of snakes, scorpions,
tarantulas, and other noxious creatures, of which they had
heard or read, resolved to sleep as they had travelled—above
their baggage in the wagons. Meanwhile the native attendants
adopted due precautions to avert surprise from the more formidable denizens of the forest. In this part of the country
elephants and lions had formerly been numerous, and were still
occasionally, though rarely, met with. To scare away such
visitants two or three large fires were kindled; and the oxen
were fastened by their horns to the wheels of the wagons. The
Dutch-African boors unslung their huge guns from the tilts
of the wagons, and placed them against a magnificent evergreen bush, in whose shelter, with a fire at their feet, they
had fixed their place of repose.

Untying each his leathern scrip, they produced their provisions for supper, consisting chiefly of dried bullock's flesh,
which they seasoned with a moderate dram of colonial *brande-
wyn* from a huge horn slung by each man in his wagon beside
his powder-flask. The slave-men and Hottentots, congregated
apart round one of the watch-fires, made their frugal meal

without the brandy, but with much more merriment than their phlegmatic masters. At the same time the frying-pans and tea-kettles of the emigrants were actively employed; and by a seasonable liberality in the beverage "which cheers but not inebriates," they ingratiated themselves not a little with both classes of their escort, especially with the coloured caste, who prized "tea-water" as a rare and precious luxury.

The characteristic groups of this rustic camp presented an amusing spectacle. The boors, most of them of almost gigantic size, sat apart at their bush, in aristocratic exclusiveness, smoking their huge pipes with self-satisfied complacency. Some of the graver emigrants were seated on the trunk of a decayed tree, conversing in broad Scotch on subjects connected with their intended settlements, and on the comparative merits of long and short-horned cattle. And the livelier young men and servant lads were standing round the Hottentots, observing their merry pranks, or practising with them a lesson of mutual tuition in their respective dialects ; while the awkward attempts at pronunciation on either side, supplied a constant fund of amusement.

Conversation appeared to go on with alacrity, though neither party scarcely understood a syllable of the other's language; while a sly rogue of a Bushman sat behind, mimicing to the very life each one of the party in succession. These groups, with all their variety of mien and attitude, character, and complexion, — now dimly discovered, now distinctly lighted up by the fitful blaze of the watch-fires, the exotic aspect of the clumps of aloes and euphorbias, peeping out amidst the surrounding jungle, in the wan light of the rising moon, seeming to the excited fancy like bands of Kaffir warriors crested with plumes and bristling with assagais, together with the uncouth clucking gibberish of the Hottentots and Bushmen, and their loud bursts of wild laughter, had altogether a very strange and striking effect, and made some of the emigrants feel far more impressively than they had hitherto felt, that they were now indeed pilgrims in the wilds of Africa.

Sleep soon stole by degrees over the motley groups. The settlers retired to their tents or their wagons. The boors, sticking their pipes in the bands of their broad-brimmed hats, wrapped themselves in their great coats, and, fearless alike of snake or scorpion, stretched their huge limbs on the bare ground. The Hottentots, each one drawing himself under his sheep-skin garment, lay, coiled up like so many hedgehogs, with their faces to the ground and their feet to the fire. Profound silence reigned over the wide expanse of wilderness, now reposing under the beams of the midnight moon, only broken by the deep breathing of the oxen round the wagons, and, at times, by the far-off melancholy howl of the hyæna, the first voice of a beast of prey the settlers had heard since they landed.

A settler, intending to rear a cabin, selected an open grass meadow, with a steep mountain behind, and a small river in front, bordered by willow trees and groups of the thorny acacia. It was a beautiful and secluded spot : the encircling hills sprinkled over with evergreens, and the fertile meadow-ground, clothed with rich pasture, was bounded by romantic cliffs, crowned with aloes and euphorbias.

Drawing a circle on the ground of about eighteen feet in diameter, he planted upright round this circle about twenty tall willow-poles, digging, with an old bayonet, holes in the ground, just large enough to receive their thicker ends. He then planted a stouter pole exactly in the centre, and, drawing together the tops of the others, he bound them firmly to this central tree, with thongs of quagga's hide. With the same ligature pliant spars or saplings were bound round the circle of poles, at suitable intervals from bottom to top; and thus the wicker-work frame of a cabin was completed, exactly in the shape of a sugar-loaf, or bee-hive. It was then thatched with reeds, the ends of the first layer being let about a couple of inches into the earth.   Spaces were left for a door and a small window; but neither fire-place nor chimney formed part of the plan.   A convenient door to open in two halves, was soon constructed of the boards of some packing-cases ; and a yard of thin cotton cloth, stretched upon a wooden frame, formed a suitable window.

Assisted by his Hottentot servants, the settler then proceeded to plaster the interior to the height of about six feet. The plaster was formed of fresh cow-dung mixed with an equal portion of sand.   This composition is generally used in the interior of the Cape Colony, as lime is scarce and expensive, and as from the dryness of the climate, it serves every ordinary purpose almost equally well.   When the plaster was dry, the whole was washed over with a sort of size, composed of pipe-clay and wood ashes, diluted with milk, giving the surface a durable grayish stone colour.

The next point was to lay a dry and firm floor under foot, and here the advice of a Hottentot was of service.   He directed a dozen or two of large ant-hillocks, of which there were hundreds within view, to be broken up and brought into the cabin, selecting those which had been previously pierced and sacked by the ant-eater, and which were generally destitute of inhabitants.   This material, from having been apparently cemented by the insect architects with some glutinous substance, forms, when pounded and sprinkled with water, a strong adhesive mortar, which only requires to be well kneaded with trampling feet for a few days, in order to become a dry and compact pavement, almost as solid and impenetrable as stone or brick.

In that serene and mild climate, the cabin thus reared, was sufficient for shelter, but more was desired.   Having luckily a small assortment of carpenter's tools, and having been, when a boy, particularly fond of observing mechanics at work, and amusing himself by cabinet-making on a small scale, the settler contrived, in the course of a few weeks, to

have his cabin commodiously and completely furnished.
First, he partitioned off from the outer apartment a small
bed-room, so contrived that, by drawing a curtain or two, it
could be lighted and ventilated at pleasure. In this he constructed a bedstead ; the frame being formed of stout poles
of wild olive from a neighbouring thicket, with the smooth,
shining bark left on them ; and the bottom to support the
mattress, consisting of a strong elastic net-work, made of
thongs of bullock's or quagga's hide interlaced.

With similar materials he made a sofa for the outer
apartment, which also served occasionally for a sleeping
couch ; together with the frame of a table—the top being of
yellow-wood plank ; a few forms and stools, and, lastly, an
arm-chair, which he considered his *chef-d'œuvre*. Not one of
these, except the table, had the touch of a plane upon it.
But they looked none the worse for that ; and the cabin and
its rude furniture had somewhat the aspect of a rustic sum-
mer-house or grotto. Books, ranged high on a frame of spars
over the bed-room, with a couple of firelocks slung in front, a
lion's and leopard's skin or two stretched along the thatch
above, with horns of antelopes, and other country spoils
interspersed, completed the appropriate decorations of this
African cabin.

A few huts, of a similar, but still ruder construction,
were erected behind this one for the accommodation of the
native domestics and herdsmen, and for a store-room and
kitchen. When these and the folds for the flocks and herds
were complete, the establishment was considered finished
for the time. The work of inclosing, cultivating, and irrigat-
ing a portion of land for a garden, orchard, and corn-crops,
was a task requiring much time and labour.

"Suffice it to say," remarks this settler, "that in this
'lodge in the vast wilderness,' with no other inmates than
my wife, and occasionally another female relative, with only
simple Hottentots for servants and dependents, and in the

6

midst of a wild region, haunted by beasts of prey, and occasionally by native banditti (Bushmen and Kaffir marauders
from the eastern frontier), I spent two years, which, though
clouded by some disappointments and occasional privations,
were, on the whole, among the pleasantest of my life.   The
disappointments we bore as we could ; the privations we soon
learned to laugh at."

The following pleasing verses are from the pen of the late
Mr. Thomas Pringle, a settler for some years in South Africa,
and a poet of no mean fame, to whom many volumes on that
interesting country, as well as the present, are greatly indebted :—

> " First, here's our broad-tailed mutton, small and fine
> The dish on which nine days in ten we dine ;
> Next, roasted spring-buck, spiced and larded well ;
> A haunch of hartèbeest from Hyndhope Fell ;
> A paaw, which beats your Norfolk turkey hollow ;
> Korhaan, and Guinea-fowl, and pheasant follow ;

> " Kid carbonadjes, à la Hottentot,
> Broil'd on a forked twig ; and peppered hot
> With Chili-pods, a dish called Kaffir-stew ;
> Smoked ham of Porcupine, and tongue of gnu.
> This fine white household bread (of Margaret's baking)
> Comes from an oven, too, of my own making,
> Scoop'd from an ant-hill.   Did I ask before
> If you would taste this brawn of forest boar ?

> " Our fruits, I must confess, make no great show ·
> Trees, grafts, and layers must have time to grow.
> But here's green roasted maize, and pumpkin pie,
> And wild asparagus.   Or will you try
> A slice of water-melon—fine for drouth,
> Like sugar'd ices melting in the mouth ?

> " But come, let's crown the banquet with some wine.
> What will you drink ?   Champagne ? Port ? Claret ? Stein ?
> Well, not to tease you with a thirsty jest,
> Lo, there our *only* vintage stands confest,

In that half-aum, upon the spigot-rack;
And, certes, though it keeps the old *Kaap smaak*,
The wine is light and racy; so we learn,
In laughing mood, to call it Cape Sauterne."

On another occasion we find the poet in a very different
vein, suggesting his full preparation not only for tendering
all the rites of hospitality, but for the peculiar perils by
which a settlement amidst the wilds of South Africa was,
and is still, surrounded.   Thus he speaks with a spirit and
energy recalling poets of illustrious name :—

" Mount—mount for the hunting—with musket and spear !
Call our friends to the field, for the Lion is near!
Call Arend, and Ekhard, and Groepe* to the spoor; †
Call Muller, and Coetzer, and Lucas Van Tuur.‡

" Ride up Eildon-Cleugh, and blow loudly the bugle:
Call Slinger, and Allie, and Dikkop, and Dugal ; §
And George with the elephant-gun on his shoulder—
In a perilous pinch none is better or bolder.

" In the gorge of the glen lie the bones of my steed,
And the hoofs of a heifer of fatherland's breed; .
But mount, my brave boys ! if our rifles prove true,
We'll soon make the spoiler his ravages rue.

" Ho ! the Hottentot lads have discovered the track—
To his den in the desert we'll follow him back ;
But tighten your girths, and look well to your flints,
For heavy and fresh are the villain's foot-prints.

" Through the rough rocky Kloof, into gray Huntly-glen,
Past the wild olive-clump, where the wolf has his den,
By the black eagle's rock at the foot of the fell,
We have tracked him at length to the buffalo's well.

* Mulatto, or Bastaard Hottentots, tenants on the lands of the Scottish
settlers at Bavian's River.
† Spoor, the track of an animal.
‡ Dutch African Boors, friends and neighbours of the Scottish settlers.
§ Names of Hottentot herdsmen.

" Now mark yonder break where the blood-hounds are howling·
And hark that hoarse sound—like the deep thunder growling;
'Tis his lair !—'tis his voice !—from your saddles alight;
He's at bay in the brushwood, preparing for fight.

" Leave the horses behind—and be still every man;
Let the Mullers and Rennies advance in the van;
Keep fast in your ranks;—by the yell of yon hound,
The savage, I guess, will be out with a bound.

" He comes ! the tall jungle before him loud crashing—
His mane bristled fiercely, his fiery eyes flashing;
With a roar of disdain, he leaps forth in his wrath,
To challenge the foe that dare 'leaguer his path.

" He couches—ay, now we'll see mischief, I dread
Quick—level your rifles—and aim at his head
Thrust forward the spears, and unsheath every knife—
St. George ! he's upon us !—Now fire, lads, for life !

" He's wounded—but yet he'll draw blood ere he falls—
Hah ! under his paw see Bezuidenhout sprawls—
Now, Diederik ! Christian ! right in the brain
Plant each man his bullet.   Hurrah ! he is slain !

" Bezuidenhout—up man !—'tis only a scratch—
(You were always a scamp, and have met with your match !)
What a glorious lion !—what sinews—what claws—
And seven feet ten from the rump to the jaws !

" His hide, with the paws, and the bones of his skull,
With the spoils of the leopard and buffalo bull,
We'll send to Sir Walter.—Now, boys, let us dine,
And talk of our deeds o'er a flask of old wine." *

An adventure of this kind Mr. Pringle has thus minutely
and graphically described :—

" One night, a lion, that had previously purloined a few

_____

* The skin of this lion, after being rudely tanned by the Hottentots,
was, together with the skull, transmitted to Sir Walter Scott, by Mr.
Pringle, as a testimony of grateful regard from some of his countrymen in
South Africa, and these trophies were subsequently ornaments of the
poet's antique armoury at Abbotsford.

sheep out of my kraal, came down and killed my riding
horse, about a hundred yards from the door of my cabin.
Knowing that the lion, when he does not carry off his prey,
usually conceals himself in the vicinity, and is very apt to be
dangerous, by prowling about the place in search of more
game, I resolved to have him destroyed or dislodged without
delay. I therefore sent a messenger round the location, to
invite all who were willing to assist in the enterprise to
repair to the place of rendezvous as speedily as possible. In
an hour, every man of the party (with the exception of two
pluckless fellows who were kept at home by the women),
appeared ready mounted and armed. We were also reinforced
by about a dozen of the 'Bastaard,' or Mulatto Hottentots,
who resided at that time upon our territory, as tenants or
herdsmen,—an active and enterprising, though rather an
unsteady, race of men. Our friends, the Tarka boors, many
of whom are excellent lion-hunters, were all too far distant
to assist us,—our nearest neighbours residing at least twenty
miles from the location. We were, therefore, on account of
our own inexperience, obliged to make our Hottentots the
leaders of the chase.

"The first point was to track the lion to his covert. This
was effected by a few of the Hottentots on foot. Commencing
from the spot where the horse was killed, they followed
the *spoor* through grass, and gravel, and brushwood, with
astonishing ease and dexterity, where an inexperienced eye
could discern neither footprint nor mark of any kind,—
until, at length, we fairly tracked him into a large *bosch*, or
straggling thicket of brushwood and evergreens, about a mile
distant.

"The next object was to drive him out of his retreat, in
order to attack him in close phalanx, and with more safety
and effect. The approved mode in such cases is to torment
him with dogs, till he abandons his covert, and stands at bay
in the open plain. The whole band of hunters then march
8

forward together, and fire deliberately, one by one.   If he
does not speedily fall, but grows angry and turns upon his
enemies, they must then stand close in a circle, and turn
their horse's rear outward,—some holding them fast by the
bridles, while the others kneel to take a steady aim at the
lion as he approaches, sometimes up to the very horse's heels,
couching every now and then, as if to measure the distance
and strength of his enemies.   This is the moment to shoot
him fairly in the forehead, or some other mortal part.   If
they continue to wound him ineffectually, till he waxes
furious and desperate, or if the horses, startled by his terrific
roar, grow frantic with terror, and burst loose, the business
becomes rather serious, and may end in mischief, especially if
all the party are not men of courage, coolness, and experience.
The frontier boors are, however, generally such excellent
marksmen, and withal so cool and deliberate, that they seldom
fail to shoot him dead, as soon as they get within a fair
distance.

   "In the present instance, we did not manage matters
quite so scientifically.   The Bastaards, after recounting to us
all these and other sage laws of lion-hunting, were themselves
the first to depart from them.   Finding that the few indifferent hounds we had, made little impression on the enemy,
they divided themselves into two or three parties, and rode
round the jungle, firing into the spot where the dogs were
barking round him, but without effect.   At length, after
some hours spent in thus beating about the bush, the Scottish
blood of some of my countrymen began to get impatient, and
three of them announced their determination to march in
and beard the lion in his den, provided three of the Bastaards,
who were superior marksmen, would support them, and follow
up their fire, should the enemy venture to give battle.

   "Accordingly, in they went (in spite of the warnings of
some more prudent men among us) to within fifteen or twenty
paces of the spot where the animal lay concealed.   He was

couched among the roots of a large evergreen bush, with a small space of open ground on one side of it; and they fancied on approaching, that they saw him distinctly lying glaring at them from under the foliage. Charging the Bastaards to stand firm and level fair, should *they* miss, the Scottish champions let fly together, and struck—not the lion, as it afterwards proved, but a great block of red stone, beyond which he was actually lying. Whether any of the shot grazed him is uncertain, but, with no other warning than a furious growl, forth he bolted from the bush.

"The pusillanimous Bastaards, in place of now pouring in their volley upon him, instantly turned, and fled helter skelter, leaving him to do his pleasure on the defenceless Scots, who, with empty guns, were tumbling over each other, in their hurry to escape the clutch of the rampant savage. In a twinkling he was upon them; and, with one stroke of his paw, dashed the nearest to the ground. The scene was terrific! There stood the lion, with his foot on his prostrate foe, looking round in conscious power and pride upon the band of his assailants, and with a port the most noble and imposing that can be conceived. It was the most magnificent thing I ever witnessed. The danger of our friends, however, rendered it at the moment too terrible to enjoy either the grand or the ludicrous part of the picture.

"We expected, every instant, to see one or more of them torn in pieces; nor, though the rest of the party were standing within fifty paces, with their guns cocked and levelled, durst we fire for their assistance. One was lying under the lion's paw, and the others scrambling towards us in such a way, as to intercept our aim at him. All this passed more rapidly than I have described it. But luckily the lion, after steadily surve...ng us for a few seconds, seemed willing to be quits with us ...air terms; and, with a fortunate forbearance (for whic.. .e met with but an ungrateful recompense), turned calmly ..way, and driving the snarling dogs like rats from among his heels, bounded over the adjoining thicket, like a cat over a footstool, clearing brakes and bushes, twelve or fifteen feet high, as readily as if they had been tufts of grass, and, abandoning the jungle, retreated towards the mountains.

"After ascertaining the state of our rescued comrade (who, fortunately, had sustained no other injury than a slight scratch on the back, and a severe bruise in the ribs, from the force with which the animal dashed him to the ground), we resumed the chase, with Hottentots and hounds at full cry. In a short time we came up again with the enemy, and found him standing at bay, under an old mimosa tree, by the side of a mountain stream, which we had distinguished by the name of Douglas Water. The dogs were barking round, but afraid to approach him ; for he was now beginning to growl fiercely, and to brandish his tail in a manner that showed he was meditating mischief. The Hottentots, by taking a circuit between him and the mountain, crossed the stream, and took a position on the top of a precipice, overlooking the spot where he stood. Another party of us occupied a position on the other side of the glen ; and, placing the poor lion thus between two fires, which confined his attention, and prevented his retreat, we kept battering away at him till he fell, unable again to grapple with us, pierced with many wounds.

" He proved to be a full-grown lion of the yellow variety, about five or six years of age. He measured nearly twelve feet from the nose to the tip of the tail. His fore-leg below the knee was so thick that I could not span it with both hands ; and his neck, breast, and limbs, appeared, when the skin was taken off, a complete congeries of sinews."

CHAPTER XI.

THE CAPE BUFFALO.

Appearance of this Animal—Its Great Ferocity—Its Rage when wounded—Dangers of Hunting the Buffalo—Remarkable Courage and Dexterity of the Hottentots in the Chase—A Troop of Buffaloes hunted by a Party of Boors—A Yarn of an Old Hunter—A Buffalo kills a British Officer.

THE Cape buffalo does not exceed the ordinary ox in height, but is much more massively built, and is a far more ponderous animal, with short, thick limbs, and a dense hide nearly destitute of hair. It is a native of the wilds of Southern Africa, where, associated in herds, it frequents the borders of woods and thickets, and the watered ravines and glens among the hilly grounds. It is fond of wallowing in the pools and swamps, and in the muddy ooze, covering its hide with defensive clothing against the attacks of insects. The horns of this species form at their base a solid rugged mass, covering the forehead, from which they bend downwards, and somewhat outwards, gradually diminishing to the points, which suddenly curve upwards. The distance between the points of the horns is frequently five feet, but the massive base of each is in contact, forming an impenetrable helmet. Their colour is black. With these formidable weapons, the Cape buffalo has been known instantaneously to transfix a horse, lift him up, and hurl him with crushing violence to the ground. The eye of this animal is savage and lowering, and indicates great ferocity; the ears are large, and generally observed to be torn, either from combats among the animals themselves, or from being lacerated with spines and thorns, as they force their way through the dense thickets.

6*

When the Cape buffalo is wounded, he ploughs up the ground with his horns, scattering the turf and stones on all sides, and rushes through the thickets and up the rugged sides of the steep ascent with astonishing energy. Often, when urged by revenge, instead of escaping, he returns suddenly to the attack, and appears in the midst of his assailants, one or more of whom often fall victims to his rage : he gores them, tramples upon them, and presses upon them his whole weight, as if to glut his revenge ; bellowing, meanwhile, with mingled pain and fury, until some well-aimed bullet lays him prostrate on the earth. Old solitary bulls are at all times dangerous, and will attack any intruder, even if unassailed.

The Cape buffalo is, at all times, a dangerous animal to hunt ; as, when wounded or closely pressed, he will not unfrequently turn and run down his pursuer, whose only chance of escape, if he be a colonist or European, is in the swiftness of his steed. The Hottentot, light and agile, and dexterous in plunging, like an antelope, through the intricacies of an entangled forest, generally prefers following this game on foot. Like all pursuits, when the spirit of enterprise is highly excited by some admixture of perilous adventure, buffalo hunting•is passionately followed by those who once devote themselves to it. Nor do the perilous accidents that occasionally happen, appear to make any deep impression upon those who witness them. The consequence is, that the buffalo is now nearly extirpated throughout every part of the Cape Colony, except in the large forests or jungles, where, together with the elephant, he still finds a precarious shelter.

On one occasion, a party of boors had gone out to hunt a troop of buffaloes, which were grazing in a piece of marshy ground, interspersed with groves of yellow wood and mimosa trees. As they could not conveniently get within shot of the game without crossing part of the marsh, which did not afford a safe passage for horses, they agreed to leave their steeds in charge of their Hottentot servants, and to advance on foot, thinking that if any of the buffaloes should turn upon them, it would be easy to escape by retreating across the quagmire, which, though passable for man, would not support the weight of a heavy quadruped.

They advanced accordingly, and, under cover of the bushes, approached the game with such advantage that the first volley brought down three of the fattest of the herd, and so severely wounded the great bull leader, that he dropped on his knees, bellowing with pain. The foremost of the huntsmen, thinking him mortally wounded, issued from the ccvert, and began reloading his musket as he advanced to give him a finishing shot. But no sooner did the infuriated animal see his foe in front of him, than he sprang up, and rushed headlong upon him. The man, throwing down his empty gun, fled towards the quagmire ; but the angry beast was so close upon him that he despaired of escaping in that direction, and turning suddenly round a clump of copse-wood, began to climb an old mimosa tree which stood at the one side of it. The buffalo was, however, too quick for him. Bounding forward with a most frightful roar, he caught the unfortunate man with his horns, just as he had nearly escaped his reach, and tossed him in the air with such force, that the body fell, dreadfully mangled, into a lofty cleft of the tree. The buffalo ran round the tree once or twice, apparently looking for the man, until, weakened by the loss of blood, he again sank on his knees. The rest of the party then, recovering from their consternation, came up, and despatched the buffalo, but too late to save their comrade, whose body was hanging in the tree quite dead.

A yarn of an old hunter is thus given by Lieutenant-Colonel Napier :—

" Well, gentlemen, you must know that old dozy there and myself got a fortnight's leave, to have a little 'gunning,' and stole away quietly with a couple of Totties (Hottentots) to a favourite sporting haunt of his, where we bivouacked for the night. The next morning before dawn, my friend took me to a 'vley,' occasionally, as he said, at that time of the year frequented by a strong herd of buffaloes, and judging from the footmarks, some had evidently been drinking there during the night.

"We put the Totties on their trail, and 'spoored' them up rapidly, as long as the dew was on the grass, till we tracked them into the thick bush. Here the spoor continued clear enough, it was all plain sailing; and Mr. Claas, our head Tottie hunter, confidently pronounced the herd to consist of five head, and that one of the lot was a large bull. The trail, which we had now followed some three or four hours with scarcely a check, took us at last over a bare, rocky, dry, and open space of ground, where we soon became completely at fault. However, leaving a handkerchief on the spot up to which we fancied we had brought the spoor, we made several broadcasts to the right and left, when at last Claas succeeded in hitting it off again; and, from its appearance, thought the herd must have passed fully an hour before.

"Well, to make short of a long business, we toiled on, under a burning sun, the greater part of the day; till, emerging from a kloof near some wooded clumps, on a marshy rise, covered with grass, the footmarks became mixed —a sure sign, as you know, of the animals being in search of a place of rest. We therefore dismounted, secured our horses among the bushes of the kloof; and, taking every necessary precaution as to the direction of the wind, crept cautiously forward, at some distance apart. I had taken a sweep to the right; and, whilst passing behind a cluster of tall underwood, which, for a moment, hid my companion, I heard the sharp report of his double-barrelled rifle.

"At this instant, on clearing the intervening space, as the

smoke drifted away, I beheld him crouching on his knee, his rifle half raised, with the blade of a long hunting-knife firmly clenched between his teeth. Whilst, charging down upon him, and when within twenty yards, furiously rushed an enormous bull buffalo, tail on end, and his head—garnished with at least six-foot horns—close to the ground. Next second, as he appeared in the very act of being ground to atoms, and amalgamated with his mother earth (for the brute was now within a yard of the spot where he knelt) the second barrel was discharged; his legs flew up with a summersault into the air, while the infuriated monster apparently missing his mark, passed over him, and dashed headlong through the opposite thicket in the direction of our horses, which, breaking loose in their alarm, wildly scampered away across the open slope of the hill.

"All this, which happened within a few yards of where I stood, was apparently the work of a second. I immediately started up to see what part of our friend remained attached to his exalted legs, when, to my infinite surprise, he got up unscathed, and staring around, asked where the brute had vanished. 'For,' added he, 'I am sure that my last shot hit him between the eyes.' With regard to the latter assertion, I must confess, I entertained many doubts on that subject.

"The first object was to recover our nags, which took us fully a couple of hours to effect, when we returned to the scene of adventure, for the purpose of obtaining, if possible, tidings of the buffalo."

It was soon evident that one of the shots had told. A mass of clotted gore, and what seemed a portion of the brain, adhered to a branch of a dense bush against which the enraged animal had madly rushed. Leaving, therefore, the horses under charge of one of the Hottentots, they cautiously pursued through the bush the bloody traces of the wounded buffalo, which at every step became more evident.

Silently following Claas, they had not proceeded a quarter

of a mile, before he suddenly came to a stand-still, listened attentively for a second, and put his ear to the ground; then, with an expressive gesture, directing them to crouch down and remain where they were, he, without uttering a sound, crept forward like a snake, amid the entangled underwood of thorny briars. On his return, he stated, in a scarcely audible whisper, that he had discovered the carcase of the buffalo, which was being cut up by ten or twelve Kaffirs. Of this they soon had evidence. In an open space, surrounded by thick jungle, lay the remains of the mighty slain, already disembowelled and partly cut up. Some were carving off with their spears long strips of flesh; others were busily preparing fires for the approaching feast; whilst a solitary vulture, soaring far above, and reduced by the great distance to a mere motionless speck, appeared also to wait his share in the entertainment.

In one hunt, a British officer who was pursued by a wounded buffalo, took refuge amidst the branches of a low, stunted tree. The infuriated animal, though unable to reach him with its horns, effectually used its tongue as a weapon of offence, with whose rough, grating surface—by licking the legs and thighs of the unfortunate sufferer—it so completely denuded them of flesh, that although at last rescued from so dreadful a situation by some Hottentot attendants, who shot his tormentor, the colonel only lingered on for a few days, when he died in the most excruciating agonies.

CHAPTER XII.

Origin of the Word Karroo—"Afar in the Desert "—Discovery of Ostrich Nests—Singular Mode of carrying away their Eggs—Instincts of the Ostrich—Ostrich Hunting a Profitable Pursuit—Bushmen disguised as Ostriches—Amusing Adventure of a Hottentot—A Night passed in the Desert, amidst the Prowlings of Lions and Hyænas.

THE word *Karroo*, in the Hottentot language, signifies an arid desert, and is specially applied to the great wilderness, extending between the Zwartzbergen, or Black Mountains, on the one side, and the Nieuwveld and Sneeuwberg ridge on the other. This plain is about three hundred miles in length, and about eighty in breadth. With the exception of a few straggling spots around its skirts, supplied with permanent springs from the adjoining mountains, the Karroo is only fit for human residence a few weeks in the year,—after the fall of the periodical, or rather the occasional rains, for sometimes more than one season intervenes without them. Its principal inhabitants are therefore the wild game, especially spring-bucks, and the beasts of prey who accompany them; and who, as the water and pasturage fail in one quarter, migrate to another.

It is to this Mr. Pringle alludes in one part of his poem " Afar in the Desert:"

> " Afar in the desert I love to ride,
>   With the silent bush-boy alone by my side,
>   O'er the brown Karroo, when the bleating cry
>   Of the spring-buck's fawn sounds plaintively;
>   Where the zebra wantonly tosses his mane

As he scours with his troop o'er the desolate plain:
And the timorous quagga's whistling neigh
Is heard by the fountain at fall of day;
And the fleet-footed ostrich over the waste
Speeds like a horseman who travels in haste,
Flying away to the home of her nest,
Far hid from the piteous plunderer's view,
In the pathless depths of the parched Karroo.
Afar in the desert I love to ride,
With the silent bush-boy alone by my side;
Away—away—in the wilderness vast,
Where the white man's foot hath never passed,
And the quivered Coranna or Bechuan
Hath rarely crossed with his roving clan:
A requiem of emptiness, howling and drear,
Which man hath abandoned from famine and fear;
Where grass, nor herb, nor shrub takes root,
Save poisonous thorns that pierce the foot;
And the bitter melon, for food and drink,
Is the pilgrim's fare by the salt-lake's brink;
A region of drought, where no river glides,
Nor rippling brook with osiered sides;
Where reedy pool, nor palm-girt fountain,
Nor shady tree, nor cloud-capt mountain,
Is found to refresh the aching eye;
But the barren earth and the burning sky,
And the blank horizon, round and round,
Without a break—without a bound,
Spread—void of living sight or sound.
And here while the night-winds round me sigh,
And the stars burn bright in the midnight sky,
As I sit apart by the desert stone,
Like Elijah at Horeb's cave alone,
'A still small voice' comes through the wild—
Like a father consoling his fretful child—
Which banishes bitterness, wrath, and fear—
Saying—'Man is distant, but God is near.'"

Mr. Burchell relates that in passing over a plain he discovered an ostrich's nest, consisting of a bare concavity
scratched in the sand, six feet in diameter, surrounded by a

trench equally shallow, and without the smallest race of any materials, such as grass, leaves, or sticks, to give it a resemblance to the nests of other birds. Within this hollow, and quite exposed, lay twenty-five gigantic eggs, and in the trench were more, intended, as the Hottentots informed him, as the first food of the twenty-five young ones. Those in the hollow, he remarks, being designed for incubation, may often be found useless to the traveller, but the others on the outside will often be found fit for eating. In the present case the whole number were good.

Near a brackish fountain, about the middle of the karroo, called "Rhinoceros·Fountain," where some travellers unyoked their wagons for part of a day, their Hottentot attendants discovered two ostrich nests. In the one all the eggs had been broken, apparently by the birds themselves—such being their practice on finding their nests discovered. In the other nest were twenty-five fine fresh eggs, which the Hottentots took to the wagons by a curious mode of conveyance. Pulling off their leathern trowsers, they tied them tight at the lower extremities, and then, filling the two legs with the eggs, slung them over their shoulders ; and in this plight, without any notion of indecorum, presented themselves with good-humoured smiles at the wagon, claiming as their reward an extra allowance of tobacco—a claim duly allowed.

Their strange device appears not to have been original. Two of Burchell's attendants, who, in the pursuit of game, had deviated from the wagon-road, fell in with an ostrich's nest, containing within it seventeen eggs, and round the outside nine more. This being a greater number than they knew how to carry, and yet not enduring the idea of leaving any behind, they at last hit on a strange expedient : they took off their shirts, and by tying them up at bottom, converted them into bags. But these not holding more than half their number, their trowsers were next stripped off, and, in the same manner, the bottom of each leg being closed, they also were crammed full of eggs, and being then secured at the waistband, were placed on their shoulders. The handkerchief which they wore round the head, was taken to supply ·the place of trowsers. Nothing could be more grotesque than the figure they cut, with the trowsers then sitting on their shoulders, and their heads just peeping out between the legs which projected before them.

The male ostrich of South Africa usually associates to himself from two to six females. The hens lay all their eggs together in one nest ; this being merely a shallow cavity scraped in the ground, of such dimensions as to be conveniently covered by one of these gigantic birds in incubation. An ingenious device is employed to save space, and give at the same time to all the eggs their due share of warmth. The eggs are made to stand each with the narrow end on the bottom of the nest, and the broad end upwards ; and the earth which has been scraped out to form the cavity, is employed to confine the outer circle and to keep the whole in a proper position. The hens relieve each other in the office of incubation during the day, and the male. takes his turn at night, when his superior strength is required to protect the eggs, or the new-fledged young, from the jackals, tiger-cats, and other enemies. Some of these animals, it is said, are not unfrequently found lying dead near the nest, destroyed by a stroke of the foot of this powerful bird.

Some of the colonists on the skirts of the Great Karroo and other remote districts, make the pursuit of the ostrich one of their principal and most profitable amusements. The beautiful white feathers, so highly prized in Europe, are found only in the tail of the male bird. In the market of Graham's Town, South Africa, the average value of ostrich feathers was five pounds per pound ; and two hundred pounds of them were often imported by one trader, Mr. Hume, with two thousand pounds of ivory, average value 3s. 6d., besides numerous native curiosities, and upwards of two hundred native carosses.

Sir J. E. Alexander, observing two light frames covered with gray and black ostrich feathers, on a tree, asked some Bushmen what they were. The reply was, "With these we disguise ourselves as ostriches, and thus get near the kaop (a remarkable species of antelope) to shoot it, as we do the ostrich, with poisoned arrows."

A present of tobacco induced one of the party to put on the disguise. He placed one of the feather frames on his shoulders, and secured it about his neck. Then taking from a bush the head and neck of an ostrich, through which a stick was thrust, he went out a little way from the huts, with a bow and arrows in his left hand. Pretending to approach a kaop, he pecked at the tops of the bushes in the manner of an ostrich, and occasionally rubbed the head against the false body, as that bird does ever and anon, to get rid of flies. At a little distance, and sideways, the general appearance of the Bushman was like that of the ostrich; but a front view betrayed the whole human body. In this way approaching sufficiently near to the kaop, which, of course, has nothing to dread from its feathered companion of the plains, the Bushman slips the ostrich head between his neck and the frame, and cautiously taking aim, discharges his arrows, and makes the deceived kaop his prey.

A Hottentot, at Jackal's Fountain, on the skirts of the Great Karroo, had a remarkable adventure. He was sleeping a few yards from his master, according to the habit of the people, wrapped up in his sheep-skin caross, with his face to the ground. A lion came softly up, and seizing him by the thick folds of his greasy mantle, began to trot away, counting securely, no doubt, on a savoury and satisfactory meal. But the Hottentot, on awaking, though sufficiently astonished, was quite unhurt, contrived slowly to wriggle himself out of his caross, and scrambled off, leaving the lion walking simply away with the empty garment.

Mr. Thompson and his Hottentot guide, Frederick, arrived at a fountain in the desert, where they and their horses quenched their raging thirst. Thus refreshed, they pushed on, and about four in the afternoon obtained a distant view of Cradock River, but remote from the course it was necessary to keep. They continued to observe numerous traces of lions, and began to look forward, with some anxiety, for a place of rest during the night. In passing down a valley, they came on a chain of deep pits dug right across it, and adroitly concealed by reeds slightly strewed over with sand. Happily some of them had been recently broken down, otherwise they would most likely have fallen into them, and been impaled on the sharp stakes fixed in their centres. These are the contrivances of the Bushmen or Corannas, to entrap the larger game.

Soon afterwards they fell in with another fountain; but as there was no wood near, they were forced reluctantly to proceed, after filling with water one of Mr. Thompson's bottles, out of which he poured the brandy to make room for it. Their situation now began to be very unpleasant. No wood was to be seen as far as the eye could reach; and without a fire they would run imminent risk of losing their horses in the night by the hyænas and lions; and might not improbably fall a prey themselves.

Galloping on in this anxious mood, the sun seemed descending with unusual speed. Not a bush appeared over the naked surface of the desert. At length, just as the day was closing, and the sun already sunk below the horizon, they reached a rising ground, and discovered close at hand a clump of camel-thorn trees, a species of mimosa, with beautiful branching top, spreading like an umbrella. No time was now to be lost. The horses were hastily *knee-haltered*—that is, tied neck and knee, to prevent their running off—and turned to graze till the night closed in, while Mr. Thompson and the Hottentots eagerly set about cutting wood to make fires for their protection.

Having chosen their resting-place under a camel-thorn,

they lighted one huge fire there, and others at a little distance on their flanks, front, and rear. " I then began," says Mr. Thompson, "to feel somewhat more comfortable; and overhauling our wallet, we found a small piece of coarse bread and sausage remaining, which Frederick and I divided. With this short allowance, a glass of brandy, and a grateful draught from the bottle of water which I had providently brought from the last fountain, I made my breakfast, dinner, and supper all at once, with a good appetite.

"Our horses, which we had tied up within a few yards of us, seemed to enjoy our company, lying down with the greatest confidence near our fire. Poor animals! we had ridden them above fifty miles this day, and as far on each of the two preceding, so that they stood in great need of rest ; and during the journey they had seldom an opportunity of feeding.

" The ground here I found covered with nitrous particles, like a hoar-frost. Such a couch is considered, I believe, rather dangerous to sleep upon. In India, as I have heard, it often proves fatal to the weary traveller, lying down never more to rise. The soil was also sprinkled with the seed of a plant covered with prickles, making it very unpleasant to sit or lie down. These seeds are jocularly called by the colonists *dubbeltjes*—twopenny pieces. Making my bed as comfortable as circumstances admitted, I wrapped myself in my great coat, with my saddle as usual for my pillow, and my loaded gun by my side. We knew pretty well that the fires were sufficient to scare off the lions, but we had some fears of the crafty hyæna attempting a snatch at our horses. Nor were we altogether without apprehension of the Bushmen, some of whose traces we had seen during the day.

" As I lay thus beside our watch-fire, I could not avoid some sombre reflections upon my present forlorn predicament, uncertain of our route, and surrounded by savage hordes. and ravenous beasts of prey. The flashing of our

9

fires only added to the gloominess of the scene, making the heavens appear a vault of pitchy darkness; nor was there any kind moon to cheer our solitude. Thus ruminating, I unconsciously gave utterance to my feelings—lamenting the uncertainty of our situation, and how unfortunate it was that we did not know our road better.

"This stung poor Frederick, who, with much emotion, exclaimed, 'Oh that I had wings like a bird, that I might fly and bring from the landdrost a better guide than I have been!' Finding him in this disconsolate mood, which was not unmixed with fear for his own safety, I changed the subject, spoke to him cheerfully, and committing my safety to Providence, I turned myself to sleep. After enjoying a couple of hours' refreshing repose, I was awakened by the shrieking of the jackals. I rose and replenished the fires with fresh fuel, and after smoking a cigar, again addressed myself to sleep. Frederick expressed his surprise at my composure in falling asleep in such a hazardous position. For his part, poor fellow! he was too much alarmed to sleep, and comforted himself by smoking away the principal part of the night—a pipe being the Hottentot's usual solace in all his distresses.

"We hailed the first dawn of morning with no common pleasure, and with feelings of thankfulness for our safe preservation during the dreary watches of the night. On looking round our station we perceived, by the fresh traces of lions and hyænas, that numbers of these ferocious animals had been prowling round within two hundred yards of us during the darkness, being evidently prevented solely by our watch-fires from making a supper of us."

CHAPTER XIII.

INCIDENTS OF TRAVEL.

The Wandering Colonist—Wild Mountain Pass and Beautiful Valley—Singular Mode of Watering Oxen—Remarkable Cataract—Oxen in Travelling—Stoppage of Wagons—Trees, Shrubs, and Flowers—Sandstorms and Tornadoes—Remarkable Caverns—Surprise and Terror of a Hottentot Guide—A Night in the Rain—A Night in Savage Solitudes—Astonishment and Alarms of Natives—Story-telling—A Traveller plundered by Bushmen.

A WRITER in the *South African Journal* describes the love of travel displayed by many a wanderer over the colony of the Cape, in the following amusing verses :—

> "Let Englishmen boast of the speed of their steam,
>   And despise the dull life that we drag on ;
> Give me my long roer,* my horse, and my team,
>   And a well-seasoned tight bullock wagon.

> "Through Africa's wild deserts expanding to view,
>   I'm there ever ready to fag on :
> Who's more independent, the Trekboer† or you,
>   As he slowly moves on with his wagon ?

> "The race to the swift isn't always secure,
>   Nor the fight to the strong, who may brag on ;
> The 'Tortoise and Hare,' though a fable, I'm sure,
>   Has a moral that points to my wagon.

> "Full two miles an hour, do not call this dull life,
>   'Tis a pace I'm contented to lag on ;
> For I bear independence, my children, my wife,
>   In my castle, my home, in my wagon.

Heavy gun of great calibre.   † Trek means wagon.

" Should the weather be hot, to forms I'm unbound,
    I may wander with scarcely a rag on ;
In light marching order I'm oft to be found,
    ' Al fresco,' at ease in my wagon.

" If venison is wanted, no license I ask ;
    Quick, presto ! you'll find me my nag on ;
At eve I return, 'tis no difficult task,
    With a spring-buck, or gnu, to my wagon.

" If butter I lack, I have milk at my beck,
    My churn is a goodly-sized flagon ;
'Tis worked without labour whenever I trek,
    Being tied to the wheel of my wagon.

" From the smouch* I obtain coffee, sugar, and tea ;
    As for raiment I scarce want a rag on ;
Then tell me, whose more independent than he—
    The Trekboer confined to his wagon ?

" From Kaffir, or Bushman, no insult I brook ;
    If they steal—they will find me a dragon ;
So long as they're civil they get a kind look,
    And share what I've got in my wagon.

" But my vengeance is quick as the Englishman's steam,
    And gives them few minutes to brag on ;
What matters palaver !—I not only seem,
    But prove that I'm king in my wagon."

Circumstances altogether peculiar to South Africa, occur to the traveller, to a few of which we shall now allude.

About fifty miles from Cape Town stands the valley of the Fransche-Hoek, originally a settlement of French Hugonots, but latterly the inhabitants have been Dutch.

Near the valley is a ravine called the Fransche-Hoek Kloof,† one of the passes through the mountain barrier, that

---

* Trader.

† In the country round the Cape, kloof generally means a pass among the hills and mountains; in Albany, a deep-wooded hollow, frequently the retreat of savage animals.

must be crossed at some point in order to penetrate into the interior of the country. The road, though it is nearly seven miles in length, ascending from the near gorge that opens into the valley, gradually to the summit, and descending on the other side in the same manner ; and in both cases running along the face of one of the steep mountains which form the boundaries of the ravine.

This road was made with great labour : many parts are cut out of the solid rock, whose high gray crags tower above it ; while a parapet wall only separates the travellers from a precipice, in whose shadowy depth a stream winds its way far below, through the rocky defile—so low that even its roar, when the torrents pour down the steep sides of the ravine, swelling the brown rush of its turbid waters, cannot be heard.

"I have been," says Mr. Cowper Rose, "among higher mountains than those of this wild pass ; but, under some effects of light and shade, I know not that I ever saw a scene more gloomily impressive.

"I have ridden through it when the sun stood high in the heavens, and I looked around for shelter from its tremendous power; when objects seem to waver before the eyes in the bright and sultry stillness, and my horse, with drooping ears, and feeble step and frequent halt, slowly and painfully toiled up the steep ascent; while all nature, animate and inanimate, seemed to yield to the scorching influence ; when the stunted shrubs and geraniums that clothe the face of the mountain were parched, and the various proteas that shoot out from the fissures of the rocks were twisted and wreathed into strange fantastic forms, and black as from the effects of fire.

"I have ridden through it when the sun was declining, and one side of the ravine was in gloom, and threw its broad deep shadow over the hollow ; and where it contracted, and the high barriers approached each other, it was strange to

7

mark the mimic resemblance of cliff and pinnacled crags traced in cold gray shade upon the side, whose summits yet shone in the golden light of evening. It was like the dim chillness of age contrasted with the fairy colouring of youth. The only living thing I saw was of a nature to add to the stern solitary character of the scene—a vulture, which, in turning a projection of the rock, I startled from its feast: it rose slowly from the carcase, spreading its broad gray wings, and swept over me with a rushing sound, sailing up the ravine, and disappearing in the deep misty blue of the perspective.

" The valley of the French Hoek is a beautiful and culti-vated amphitheatre, surrounded by mountains—not of one prevailing form, which is so common, but as various as the clouds that rest upon them. Many are clothed at their bases, and half-way up their sides with richest verdure, which sud-denly ceasing gives place to high gray native cliffs; others are wholly bare, except in their shadowy recesses, where the forest trees find shelter and nourishment.

" The valley has many windings, which, during a week's stay that I made with some friends, it was my amusement to penetrate,—into deep hollows or low grounds, in winter flooded, but in the summer covered with the most luxuriant vegetation, with bulbous plants, rare heaths, and bright geraniums, through which my horse with difficulty made his way, startling as we went the fairy sugar birds, that appear to derive their brilliant colours from the blossoms they feed on.

" Then I would trace some mountain river to its source, having, in the attempt, frequently to cross the calm, cool, transparent water, and to break my way through its banks, fringed with high reeds, and shaded with bended willows. In following the course of the stream, I have been much struck with the contrasts exhibited within a distance of a few hundred yards. In one part, the banks are rich with various greens, in glowing orange and yellow tints, in light creepers, which the waters touch, as they ripple by through their leafy and blossomy covert. Go but a short mile, and the scene is changed, and all around bears the stamp of cold decay and death. The barkless trunks of the trees are of a pale gray hue, withered, sun-scorched, and lifeless—the skeletons of what they were; and the river, that everywhere else brings gladness and nourishment, here gloomily wanders through a scene that is beyond its power—a scene over which the fiery breath of desolation seems to have passed, and leaf, and tree, and blossom, to have fallen beneath its blasting influence."

The following is a singular mode of watering the oxen on a journey, as witnessed by a traveller. A well, dug through a chalk rock, about nineteen feet deep, had water at the bottom. In the midst of this one man was standing, another stood on the almost perpendicular sides, about six feet above him, his feet resting in holes cut out of the rock; and about six feet above him stood a third man.

Looking down into the well, the three almost appeared as if standing on one another's shoulders. The lowest man filled a large wooden dish with water, which he handed to the man above him, and he to the other, who emptied it into a little pool, made near the mouth of the well, to which the oxen had access, after which the dish was returned to the man at the bottom. The quickness with which it went down and up was surprising,—perhaps three times a minute.

Though this employed a great part of the day, they could not afford a full draught to each ox once in the twenty-four hours. They admitted four oxen at a time to drink at the little pool; the first time the ox lifted his head from the water, he was considered as having had a sufficient quantity, and was not permitted to put it down again, but was instantly driven away with sticks. About twenty oxen were brought near the well at a time, where they impatiently waited to take their turn; when these had drunk, they walked off to make room for the rest.

Colonel Napier describes himself as travelling considerable distances, on many consecutive days, mounted on one of the little hardy horses of the country, with a Hottentot Cape Corps Orderly as a guide, while another led the sumpter-horse, carrying a small waterproof patrole tent, and a change of linen, together with a few provisions.

"In this manner," he says, "on one occasion did we accomplish the earlier part of our 'trek.' The sun now rides high in the bright unclouded heavens. The Hottentots look anxiously round for the well-known 'vlei,' a pool of water, generally speaking, formed by the rain. But, alas! on reaching the long-expected spot, instead of the wished-for water, rippling under the breeze, nought presents itself to our aching sight save a brown, cracked surface of dry hardened mud!

"The panting steeds have already gone over some twenty or thirty miles of ground ; heavy flanks and drooping heads now bear witness to their toil. Mr. Jacob (for our faithful esquire still rejoiceth in that patriarchal name) looks anxiously about, scratches his woolly head, and appears fairly at his wit's end. 'Farley,' the Cape Corps Orderly, proposes to off-saddle, and try on our nags the effect of half an hour's graze. Although they refuse to feed, they instantly roll on the grass, and appear thence to imbibe renewed spirit and vigour. 'Saddle up' is now the word. We are again on horseback ; but, ere we can raise a canter, the spur is sadly in request ; and Mr. Jacob's horse begins to show increasing and unequivocal symptoms of distress ; he is, in fact, dead beat ; and, stumbling at every step, at last falls on his nose. Jacob shoots over his head, but is on his legs again in a second.

" 'Is the double barrel smashed?'

" 'No, sar ; but horse can never carry me more far ; and pack-horse getting shut up, too.'

" 'You must then just walk, and drive them on before you.' "

An emigrant who resided for a time in the interior of Cape Colony, has described a journey he made through some very striking scenery. His first day's journey, a distance of about sixty-five miles, lay through a rugged and mountainous country, near the banks of the great Fish River. On the second day, accompanied by a friend, at whose house he had stopped the preceding night, he pursued his journey on horseback, guided by a Hottentot servant, over extensive arid plains, and undulating heights, clothed with a brown and scanty herbage, and sprinkled over with numerous herds of spring-bucks. As the traveller galloped on, these beautiful animals bounded off continually on either side, with the light and sportive velocity from which they derive their colonial appellation. Beasts of prey, especially lions, are usually found in the vicinity of these migrating swarms of game, but on this occasion nothing more formidable was encountered than two or three melancholy jackals, and a solitary skulking hyæna.

After passing the flocks of antelopes, the country became still more waste and dreary, and the noon-day sun flamed fiercely down from a cloudless firmament. The monotonous landscape extended around far and wide, enlivened only now and then by a few of the larger fowls of the country, wheeling high overhead in the blue sky, the secretary bird walking about with its long feathered legs like black pantaloons, searching for its favourite prey, the snakes which infest the "dry-parched land," and the stately *paauw*, a species of bustard about twice the size of a turkey, and esteemed the richest flavoured of all the African feathered game. These, and one or two solitary ostriches in the distance, were the only living creatures seen, after the sight was lost of the playful spring-bucks, save and except the numerous lizards, green, brown, and speckled, which lay basking on almost every stone and ant-hill that dotted the sultry waste. The country here was wholly parched up and desolate, and consequently deserted both by the smaller birds and by herbivorous animals. The deep and melancholy silence was unbroken, save by the travellers' voices and the sound of their horses' feet: even the hum of the wild bee and the chirring of the grasshopper were unheard.

At length, after a toilsome ride of about sixty miles, during the latter half of which they had not found a single fountain or pool, or running brook to assuage their burning thirst, they reached, about sunset, the hovel of an African boor, on the side of a river that oozed cool and limpid from a savage-looking chasm of the rugged Zureberg; the mountain towering overhead in precipitous crags, which echoed to the pastoral bleating of the folded flocks, and the loud barking of twenty or thirty watch-dogs. Here they were received with all the hospitality which the inhabitants of a wigwam constructed of a few poles and reeds could exercise. They supped on mutton and potatoes dressed with honey, and slept on a mat of rushes stretched on the clay floor, covered by a blanket of tanned lamb-skin with the wool on it.

Next morning at an early hour they left this hospitable but comfortless "lodge in the lone wilderness," and ascended the first ridge of the Zureberg, by a steep and rugged footpath, worn by the boor's cattle when driven to the upland pastures. On reaching the summit, which at this place is probably not more than 1,500 feet above the level of the plain just crossed, they looked back, and beheld the steep front of the Boschberg mountains, stretching like a huge irregular rampart across the horizon about sixty miles behind; while farther to the north-east, the loftier mountains near the Kaffir frontier, the Cataberg, the Dideina, the Luhèri, and the giant Winterberg, appeared, one behind the other, towering, distinct and well-defined, in the clear blue sky, at the distance of seventy, eighty, and a hundred miles. The atmosphere in this climate is generally so dry and free from vapours, that large objects are seen distinctly at a very great distance, and therefore often appear to European eyes much nearer than they really are. From the summit of the Winterberg, which is one of the loftiest peaks in this part of Africa (probably about 6,000 feet) a traveller has clearly seen the top of a mountain near Uitenhage, at the amazing distance of 150 miles as the crow flies—a fact he would scarcely have thought possible had the testimony of his own eyes not been corroborated by that of an engineer officer who was with him, and who was familiar with every point in the intervening country.

Turning their faces to the southward, the travellers continued their journey across the successive ridges of the Zureberg, which extended before them nearly on the same level, but intersected by deep ravines,·whose broken and stony declivities detained and wearied them exceedingly. The summits of the ridges were often almost flat, and covered with long, coarse, wiry grass, of the sort called *sour* in the colony, being of such an acidulent quality that sheep and cattle will not eat it without great reluctance, nor can they be safely fed on it without frequent changes to more wholesome and nutritious pasturage. From this cause the narrow glens of this range, though sufficiently well watered, are almost wholly uninhabited. In a tract of about twenty miles only one farm-house came into view. Even the larger wild game are somewhat scarce on these elevated pastures ; but this is probably much more owing to the incessant pursuit of the huntsman than their aversion to the coarse herbage.

Unprofitable as these Alpine wastes appear, they have yet their uses, and their features of attraction. They serve to collect the clouds which feed the fountains and streams that water the adjacent plains and valleys, without which the country would be altogether a desert. They are still partially frequented by several species of beautiful wild animals, and in former years must have been so to a much greater extent. Three kinds of partridge, and a variety of smaller birds, frequent the tracts of long, lank grass. On the few straggling trees which grow here and there, by the margins of the brooks in the deep and silent glens, appear the pendulous nests of the loxia and weaver-bird ; and several species of falcons are seen hovering over head, or shooting from cliff to cliff across the valleys. Even the barren tabular summits are frequently covered for an extent of many acres with a profusion of tall lileaceous flowers, which, in spring-time, cover the whole ground with their rich blue or scarlet blossoms. The region, therefore, however unprofitable for the occupation of civilised man, is not without its appropriate inhabitants, nor devoid of utility and beauty in beneficent arrangements of creation where nothing, not even the sterile desert or naked rock, is placed without design, or left utterly unproductive.

The aspect of this mountain scenery, and the obvious similarity of the country generally, in climate and productions, to ancient Palestine, may well suggest to the mind of the traveller the following portions of that sublime sacred poem, the 104th Psalm :—

" He sendeth the springs into the valleys, which run among the hills.

" They give drink to every beast of the field : the wild asses quench their thirst.

" By them shall the fowls of the heaven have their habitation, which sing among the branches.

" He watereth the hills from his chambers : the earth is satisfied with the fruit of thy works.

" The high hills are a refuge for the wild goats (antelopes?); and the rocks for the conies.

" The young lions roar after their prey, and seek their meat from God.

" O Lord, how manifold are thy works ! in wisdom hast thou made them all : the earth is full of thy riches."

As the travellers pursued their journey, the mountains before them became more lofty and desolate, and the rugged path, where there was any, more intricate and difficult.

Often were they forced to alight and to lead their horses, or drive them before them, through the narrow defiles and along the dangerous brink of precipitous declivities. Descending the gorge of a rocky ravine, they then penetrated, as it were, through the bowels of the mountain, following the windings of a narrow, but verdant glen, adorned with occasional clumps of copse-wood and forest trees, and enlivened by a brawling rivulet, the principal source, it was believed, of the White River.

At length this little stream entered a far wider chasm among the rocks, where the foot of man or beast might no further accompany it, and they were forced again to ascend the mountain ridge. Here an extraordinary prospect awaited them, of which no description in words or writing can convey an adequate idea. On the left a wild and billowy chaos of naked mountains, rocks, precipices, and yawning abysses, that looked as if hurled together by some prodigious convulsion of nature, appalled and bewildered the imagination. Let the mind conceive, if it can, a boundless congeries of gigantic crags, or rather the eternal hills themselves, thus tumultuously uptorn and heaved together, with all the veins and strata of their deep foundations disrupted, bent, and twisted into a thousand fantastic shapes; while, over their savage declivities and deep-sunk dells, a dark, impenetrable forest spreads its shaggy skirts, and adds to the whole a character of still more wild and impressive sublimity. Such was the scene now presented to the eye.

Yet this was only the foreground of the landscape. In front, and on either hand, extended, as far as the eye could reach, the immense forest jungle which stretches from the Zureberg even to the sea-coast at the mouth of the Bushman's River. Through the bosom of this jungle might be distinctly traced the winding course of the Sunday River, like the path of some mythological dragon—not from the sight of its waters, but from the hue of its light green willow trees,

7*

which grow along its margin. Beyond, and far to the south, at the distance of sixty miles, appeared the Indian ocean and the bleak shores of Algoa Bay. To the right and west were the Riëtberg mountains and the fantastic peaks of the Winter-hoek. Nearer them, but hidden among the lower hills, and surrounded by dense forests, lay the Moravian settlement of Enon ; but it was far beneath ; for, on this side of the Zureberg, the low country is on a level much inferior to the plains on the northern side, and the front of the mountain was proportionably more imposing.

These rugged ravines and that far-stretched forest are still the haunts of many herds of elephants and buffaloes ; and, in spite of the ardour with which they are pursued both by boors and Hottentots (with whom the hunting of the larger game is not merely a sport, but a passion), it does not seem probable that they will be speedily extinguished ; for, not to mention the enormous extent of the jungle already described —probably averaging seventy or eighty miles in length by thirty or forty in breadth—the chief part of it consists of evergreens and succulent plants, such as milk-wood, spekboom, and euphorbias from fifteen to forty feet high, which cannot be burned down, and which assuredly will never be rooted up by human industry, since the soil from aridity is unfit for cultivation.

After contemplating for a long while this scene of savage magnificence, the travellers descended the long declivities of the mountains, and entered the verge of the forest which spreads half way up its skirts. They entered at the head of a glen by a path that well accorded with the other features of the landscape. It was an alley made by the elephants when they issued forth from their sylvan recesses, as they occasionally are wont, to amuse themselves upon the mountain side. It was about six feet wide and arched over like a summer alcove ; for the elephant, forcing his way through the thickets, tramples down or breaks off the larger

branches that obstruct his passage, while the lighter and
loftier, yielding to the pressure of his huge body, meet again
like a Gothic arch when the monarch and his troop have
passed through.

These animals march always in single file on such occasions ; and a pathway, when once broken out, is soon trodden
by them as bare, if not so regular as a gravel walk. Indeed, but for the services of the elephant as a pioneer, these
dense and thorny forests, choked up with underwood, and
interlaced with rope-like creepers, would be in most places
utterly impenetrable ; and, even with this assistance, it requires some exertion and adroitness to force a passage
through them. In many places limbs of trees half broken
off, and large bushes torn up by the roots, obstruct the passage, and one is every moment in danger of sharing the fate
of Absalom from the numerous boughs that hang across the
path. One of these, as he bent under it on his horse's mane,
has actually caught and pulled a traveller off the saddle.

In many places, too, several of these paths converge or
cross each other, so precisely similar in appearance that,
without an experienced guide, one is almost sure of losing
his way ; and even although the present travellers had a
Hottentot guide (and the memory and adroitness of this race
in such cases is most admirable), yet they lost their road
notwithstanding, and got entangled among the thickets and
gullies of one of these savage ravines. As they toiled and
struggled through the sultry labyrinths of the forest, they
were not without some apprehension at the idea of being
obliged to pass a night in it—not from any anxiety about
shelter, for they had occasionally slept pleasantly enough in
that fine climate, "under the greenwood bough,"—but because they were aware that the elephants and buffaloes,
whose fresh traces they saw everywhere around them, are
peculiarly dangerous in the night. The elephant, indeed,
seeks not for man as his enemy, but, if he accidentally

encounters him, is apt to show him little reverence. The buffalo is scarcely less dangerous; the rhinoceros is also found in this vicinity; and leopards and hyænas are numerous. At length they threaded their way out of the forest, and reached, before the night closed in, the place to which they were destined—the valley of the White River.

This valley lies at the bottom of the Zureberg mountains, which rise on this side to an elevation of about 3,000 feet above the level of the subjacent country. The declivities of the mountain, and the whole of the subsidiary hills which encompass this glen, are covered with the clustering forest jungle already described; but the banks of the stream are comparatively level and open, and covered throughout their whole extent with luxuriant pastures of sweet grass. The whole length of the vale may be altogether, probably, about ten or twelve miles from the spot where the little river emerges abruptly from the savage mountains to where it joins the Sunday River.

The scenery of the upper part of the dell is much the most striking and picturesque. Accompanying the course of the stream, as it meanders through the grassy meadows, there appear, on the right, lofty hills covered with woods of evergreens, and broken by *kloofs*, or subsidiary dells, filled with large forest timber. On the left the hills are lower, but also covered with copse-wood, and in many places diversified by rocks and cliffs of deep red, and other lively colours, overhanging the green pastures, or the deep pools which the river leaves here and there as it bends from side to side. The valley, winding among these woody hills, spreads out occasionally to a considerable breadth; and then again, the hills converging, appear to close it in entirely with huge masses of rock and forest. At every turn the outline of the hill varies, presenting new points of picturesque scenery; while, scattered carelessly through the meadow, or bending peacefully over the river margin, appear little clumps of evergreens, willows, and acacias; and sometimes groves of lofty forest trees (chiefly yellow-wood or Cape cedar) enrich the vale with a stately beauty not always to be met with in a South African landscape.

This combination of the wild, the grand, and the beautiful is heightened in its imposing effect by the exotic appearance of the vegetation : the lofty candelabra-shaped euphorbias towering above the copses of evergreens ; the aloes clustering along the summits or precipitous fronts of the 'weather-stained rocks ; the spekboom, food for the elephant, conspicuous everywhere amidst the mass of foliage, with its light green leaves and lilac blossoms ; the more elegant-shaped mimosa, with its yellow-tufted flowers, diffusing a faint scent of the primrose ; the baboon's ladder, wild vine, and other parasitical plants and creepers that climb among the crags, and festoon in grotesque exuberance the branches of the loftiest trees, intermingled with clustering jessamines and superb geraniums. These, and a thousand other shrubs and flowers, of which only a few are known to our green-houses, cover the barren rocks, and fill up the interstices of the forest jungle.

The meadows, too, or savannahs, along the river banks, are brilliantly embellished, at least in the spring and early summer, with the large purple flowers of a species of amaryllis, which has a very splendid appearance. As it was now the autumn of the southern hemisphere, the vale was thickly overspread with a small, white, delicate flower, somewhat resembling the snow-drop. The river itself is but a large mountain torrent, bursting down, after heavy rains, in floods which swamp over a great part of the level meadows above described, and which fling up, in their violence, immense quantities of large rolled stones and gravel into banks, through which the stream, when diminished by the summer heats, filtrates silently and unperceived. The current, however, even in the greatest droughts, is never entirely interrupted, though sometimes invisible ; but always fills the large pools, or natural tanks which spread out like little lakelets along its channel, and which its temporary floods serve to sweep and purify. The waters of this stream, though perfectly sweet and salubrious, have a certain opaque and milky appearance, from a mineral solution which they bring down from the mountains, and from which the stream obtains its name of Witte Rivier, or White Water.

On approaching the Sunday River, the environs of the White Water gradually lose their more striking and distinctive features, and at length merge themselves into the dreamy and monotonous stormy wilderness which extends, with little variation, from the Zureberg to the sea-coast.

A forest grows in a narrow glen or *kloof*, running up between the subsidiary ridges abutting from the Zureberg, and was accessible only by a narrow wagon path cut through the thickets from the White River valley. It was choked up, as the woods of South Africa generally are, by a rank exuberance of undergrowth and creepers, to such a degree as to appear quite impenetrable until a path had been opened into its recesses by the axe.

Among other parasitical plants, the baboon's rope protruded itself in all directions in a wild web of tangled vegetation. Climbing, like ivy, the trunks of the loftier trees, it coiled its snake-like creepers along the branches, stretched them from tree to tree like the cordage of a ship, or flung them dangling in the air like ladders of ropes—fitting ladders for the monkeys which inhabit these woods, and from which adaptation the plant derives its colonial name. This plant is sometimes called the wild vine, from its berries resembling clusters of purple grapes ; and in summer, when it is in bearing, these clusters have a very tempting and beautiful appearance, hanging in rich festoons in the bosom of the wild woods ; but though wholesome, this fruit is too acidulent to be eaten in any quantity, unless when freed from the stone, and sweetened with sugar as a conserve, as it is found occasionally in the houses of colonists.

The clumps of forest, comprising a great variety of fine large wood, are scattered throughout the vast jungle along the whole southern front of the Zureberg mountains; but the best timber is frequently inaccessible from the position in which it grows in the recesses of rugged ravines, or on the steep front of dangerous precipices. Such situations appear favourable in this climate to the growth of large trees, owing to the more abundant moisture which the porous crevices of the rocks convey to the roots, and the mists that roll over the summits of the foliage. At this particular spot, however, a sufficient supply of timber grew on tolerably level ground, where it could be readily cut and drawn out with oxen. The most common species was a tree greatly resembling the cedar in its general aspect, but belonging to a quite different genus, termed by the colonists geelhout, or yellow wood.

A handsome tree grows wild in the damp rocky places, with fine shining green foliage, contrasted by numerous dense, elongated bunches of small milk-white flowers, and twigs of a red colour. Its colonial name means the Red Alder, although the tree has no resemblance to the alder of Europe; but the wagon-makers say there is some similarity in the wood. The name of the former was derived probably from the two trees growing in similar situations. The Cape acacia is often met with. The name of acacia is correctly applicable to this tree, because of its great affinity to the tree acacia of the ancients, or gum-arabic tree of Egypt. It is very different from that which in England is commonly, but improperly called acacia. Innumerable straight white thorns, from two to four i⌁ ⌁s long, cover every branch and twig; and the foliage is ⌁ fine and thin as to afford a remarkable example of a ⌁ ⌁ furnished with a profusion of leaves being neither dens⌁ ⌁or umbrageous. These two generally grow in a sandy soil, on the banks of rivers, along the dry beds of periodical streams, or in hollow spots that receive water in the rainy season.

On the branches of the acacias large lumps of very good clear gum may be frequently observed. Wherever the trees have been wounded by the hatchets of the people, there, most commonly, the gum exudes. What a quantity of this substance might be obtained from these trees only, which line the banks of the Orange River and its branches, amounting to a line of wood, reckoning both sides, of more than 2,000 miles! Yet to the acacias of this river may be added the myriads which crowd almost every river in extra-tropical Southern Africa.

The Baobab is a tree of enormous size and noble appearance. Its trunk, which is scarcely ever known to exceed fifteen feet in height, often measures no less than eighty feet in circumference. The lower branches, which are adorned with tufts of leaves, extend from its sides horizontally, and, bending by their great weight towards the earth, form a mass of verdure no less astonishing in. size than beautiful in appearance. The circumference of a full-grown tree, measuring the circle which surrounds the branches, is said to be as much, in some cases, as 450 feet; when of this size, its bulk is so enormous that, at a distance, it bears a greater resemblance to an overgrown forest than a single tree.

The blossoms are as gigantic in proportion as the tree which 'bears them. The fruit differs greatly in its shape. Sometimes it is found of an oblong form, pointed at both ends; at other times it is said to be perfectly globular; and it often bears a shape which is between the two. In its size it differs as considerably as it does in shape. It is covered with a green rind or skin, which, however, as it dries, becomes of a dark fawn colour, and often assumes a deep brown. It is very prettily marked and ornamented with rays, and is suspended from the tree by a stalk, the length of which is nearly two feet. The fruit, when broken, exhibits to the eye a spongy substance of a pale chocolate colour, containing much juice. The bark of the tree is nearly an inch in thickness, of an ash-coloured gray, greasy to the touch, and very smooth; the exterior is adorned with a description of varnish; while the inside is of a brilliant green, beautifully speckled with bright red. The wood itself is white, and very soft and penetrable.

A large tree, of picturesque growth and thin foliage, is called by the Hottentots Red Leaf, on account of the beautiful crimson colour which the leaves assume at the season of fading; in which circumstance it remarkably agrees with the Indian Almond, a well-known tree of the same genus. It grows to the height of forty feet, with several crooked spreading trunks, from one to two feet in diameter, covered with a smooth white or pale greenish bark.

The oak, transplanted from Europe—where it is nearly the last tree of the forest which assumes its vernal garb—is almost the earliest to be covered with foliage in South Africa. These tall, wide-spreading oaks, however, have not the appearance of strength or the gnarled tortuous branches with which England is familiar; for they droop, as if unable to support the weight of their foliage and the hanging nests, around which their yellow inmates are twittering. That clump of tall, thin, graceful stems, gradually and beautifully diminishing, covered with light flexible branches, thinner even than the slender willow-like leaves with which they are covered, glancing in every ray of light, and quivering in every breeze —that is the bamboo. There stands the orange tree, where the fruit and the blossom mingle; the lemon, the plum, the pomegranate, the peach, the almond; while that thinly-leaved tree should not be despised, nor its black shrivelled fruit—for it is the fig—which, it is said, is only eaten in perfection in the morning, when it has not been touched by the sun. The long regular lines of stumps, in winter bare and black, and in summer thickly covered with leaves and purple clusters, are vines.

Mr. Galton, in one of his expeditions, emerged on a plain, everywhere covered with thin grass, and studded over with stunted thorn trees   The Hakis, or Fish-hook thorn, as the Dutch call it, begins to grow at Tsobis; but the land more to the westward is too barren to give even sustenance to that; and from this point to the borders of Ovampo-land, the traveller has to tear his way through its cruel and tangled branches.

Not a tree grows that does not bear thorns, and there are very few in which the thorns are not hooked ; and their sharpness and strength are such as to throw a most serious difficulty in the way of exploring, especially as, when travelling with a wagon, the oxen will not face them, and in difficult parts it is often quite impossible to get through the bushes, round to the struggling and fighting oxen.   Cruel as the Hakis thorn is, there is yet another and much more severe opponent in a smaller, but sharper and stronger thorn. Mr. Galton has often tried the strength of all these with a spring weighing machine, by tying a loop of string to one end of it, which he hooked round the thorn, and then steadily pulled at the other end till the thorn gave way, marking the number of pounds' resistance that the scale indicated at the moment when the thorn broke.   The Hakis thorn stood a pull of four or five pounds, and the other one about seven, but often much more, and on one occasion he registered a strain of twenty-four pounds.   Now, as several of these thorns generally lay hold of the traveller's clothes or person at once, it may easily be conceived the cruel laceration they cause.

Mr. Burchell, on meeting, for the first time, with a thorny bush about five feet high, wished to cut some specimens of it, which the Hottentots observing, warned him that if he did not take great care, he was sure to be caught in its branches. "In consequence of this advice," he says, "I proceeded with the utmost caution, but, with all my care, a small thorn caught hold of my sleeve. While thinking to disengage it quietly with the other hand, both arms were seized by these rapacious thorns; and the more I tried to extricate myself, the more entangled I became; till at last it seized hold of my hat also; and convinced me that there was no possibility for me to free myself, but by main force, and at the expense of tearing all my clothes. I therefore called out for help, and two of my men came and released me by cutting off the branches by which I was held."

The rhinoceros bush burns while green as freely as the driest fuel; whole plants thrown into the fire blaze up in an instant, the larger stems giving a very strong heat and flame. The wood called Assagai-hout, of which the Kaffirs most commonly make the shafts of their assagais, possesses the valuable property of extreme toughness. The pole of a wagon bent to an angle of about 150°, exhibited scarcely any transverse fracture, but appeared split into a number of longitudinal splinters, which still held the two parts strongly together.

One of the commonest of Cape heaths grows luxuriantly, and is covered with a profusion of pink flowers. The Cape misletoe, a very curious parasitic plant, bears small white berries, is without leaves, and exceedingly brittle. A kind of wild cucumber spreads itself over the bushes and along the ground, bearing a small yellow oval fruit, and called Poison-apple, because of its extreme bitterness. The African sage is an ornamental flowering shrub, of very frequent occurrence. A curious shrub, from eight to ten feet high, is armed at all points with exceedingly strong branched thorns. It produces little bunches of small white flowers, having both the form and the scent of the jessamine, and are succeeded by berries resembling those of the berberry. A very extraordinary grass grows in some places. Its panicle of flowers forms a bunch of strong, sharp thorns, so rigid and pungent, that no animal can graze near it; nor will naked-legged Hottentots venture to walk amongst it, although it may not be more than a foot and a half high.

Mr. Burchell had pointed out to him a small shrub, the flowers of which are used by the people as a dye for giving a yellow colour to their leather. He found, by experiment, that the corollæ of the dried flowers, being infused in a small quantity of warm water, gave out very readily a strong colour, approaching the one called Raw Terra Sienna. It flows freely from the pen or pencil; and some trials he made during his travels, remained for ten years without fading, or losing any of their original brightness. The inhabitants of some districts, when in want of resin, use as a substitute, a gum which exudes from different species of shrubs, to which, therefore, they give the name of Resin-bush.

A beautiful parasite grows on a thorny bush. It grows without a root, out of the very substance of the branch which supports it, exactly in the same manner as the misletoe; and, like that, is also disseminated by birds, which, after eating sweet viscous berries, wipe their beaks on the branch of some tree, to which the seed adheres, and where, if the bark be smooth and full of sap, it soon thrusts out a large gum radicle, which gradually pierces the outer rind, and fixes itself as firmly as if it were naturally a branch of the tree. The flowers grow several together at every leaf; and their tubular shape, half split open, red without and white within, might well cause it to be compared with the honeysuckle; but then it wants all the fragrance of the English favourite. It may also be stated that between the trees and bushes which clothe the bank of the Orange River, a species of asparagus is everywhere found climbing and entwining, so that the traveller cannot without difficulty force his way through them.

Storms of sand have sometimes to be endured, attended,

too, by tornadoes that are really dreadful. Wagons are overturned, men and horses thrown down, and the shrubs torn out of the ground. The dust and sand are whirled into the air in columns of several hundred feet in height, which, at a distance, look like water-spouts seen sometimes at sea, and with those, they are equally, if possible, avoided; all that falls in their way being snatched up in their vortex. Sometimes dust and small pebbles are hurled into the air with the noise and violence of a sky-rocket; rain and thunder generally succeed these heated winds and gradually bring about a decrease of temperature.

One of these is described as about 1,000 feet high, and extending in breadth nearly four miles. The dust having a reddish hue, and being brilliantly tinged by the sun, while this glowing colour was strongly contrasted with the gloomy blackness of those parts in shade, the vast volumes of fire and smoke that proceed from a volcanic eruption, was naturally recalled by the spectator. Though it was known to consist only of dust, it rolled on towards him and his party with a terrific grandeur that awakened sensations of awe and wonder. On its first reaching them, it merely resembled a thick mist; but quickly increasing in density, it became impenetrable to the light of the sun, and surrounded them with midnight darkness. Standing in the open air, they could only discover objects at the distance of ten yards. Within the houses persons could not see each other, it being as dark as in a closed room at night with the light out.

Mr. Thompson was much amused by the curiosity and wonder of the people, when he placed his map, compass, and thermometer on the table, and proceeded to fill up his daily journal—all gathered round him, and staring open-mouthed, as if he had been a magician or an astrologer.

"After shaving in the forenoon," says Campbell, "I happened to show a person himself in the looking-glass which was in the lid of my box, and this gave me employment

enough, for he ran off to bring his wife and other friends to
see themselves. Every one was afraid at the first sight
obtained, starting back from the glass ; most of them looked
behind it to see that there was no deception. The crowd
increased every minute, and the press to get forward was so
great, that the tent was often in danger of being overturned.
They all touched some part of their face with the finger, to
ascertain whether it was really themselves that they saw in
the glass When both my arms were completely tired of
holding it before them, I was obliged to request a respite to
some future time, and on laying it aside, they walked away,
greatly entertained."

Mr. Rose says of some Kaffir women : " They brought us
sweet milk in baskets, and stood around, anxiously examining
every part of our travelling equipment ; nor shall I easily
forget the terror, half feigned, half real, excited by my pocket
compass, from which they shrank as if its movement was
life ; at length one mustered courage enough to take it in her
hand, and then, placing it to her ear, repeated 'Tic, tic, tic.'
This act of daring was imitated by the whole circle, who had
made up their minds it was a watch."

In like manner some Bushmen were greatly amused with
Campbell's compass. A Hottentot, without being desired, told
them it would always direct the owner to the way which led
to his home. They attempted by turning the compass, to
force the needle to point another way than towards the north,
but not being able to effect it, they held up both hands,
laughed heartily, and looked upon the traveller as a most for_
tunate person, in the possession of such a treasure.

Some of the people by whom he was beset, at another
time, asked to have his seal, and others, the keys attached to
his watch-chain, that they might suspend them to their ears.
To convince them he could not spare these articles, he took
out his watch to explain their use, when, by pushing the pin
that pressed on the spring, the watch instantly opened as if

of its own accord, which spread so great an alarm, that the whole party fled to the distance of thirty yards. Observing that the traveller only smiled at their fears, they gradually returned, and cautiously viewed the inner works, the motions of which excited great astonishment.

When presenting his gifts to the king of the Mashows, a white night-cap led to the question : "What is its use ?" This being explained, his majesty immediately put the night-cap on his head, and wore it throughout the interview. On receiving a looking-glass he viewed himself in it for a long time, but without any signs of emotion. He could not conceive the use of the scissors, till Campbell, with his consent, clipped off a small part of his beard. He knew nothing of the uses of needles, thimbles, or a pincushion with its pins, till these were severally explained. He had to be shown twice how to open a snuff-box he received. How soon a gimlet made a hole through a stick filled the whole company with amazement.

Methuen says : " The Griquas were enchanted by the notes of an accordion, which we had with us : the night had begun ; it was extremely cold ; we all sat in a circle round the fire, and never were flames reflected in more brilliant black eyes than in those of the children, whose glances were intensely fixed on the mysterious instrument. One man sagely remarked on hearing it, 'Well, the English will always be masters !' "

While walking along the side of a low hill, three women approached and called to Campbell and his party to stop, that they might get a sight of the white people. The number soon increased to twenty or thirty. As he had a magnifying-glass, he let them feel the effects of collecting the rays into a focus. All seemed to doubt its power, but they generally screamed when they felt the first impression; they were, how-ever, greatly amused, and evidently considered it a most mysterious operation. During the entertainment, some of them said the whites, they thought, were lovers of mankind.

They minutely examined Campbell's dress, but were most diverted by finding hair instead of wool on his head.

In another instance, the sight of white men threw a large crowd into fits of convulsive laughter; but the young were more seriously affected, they screamed, and in the utmost horror, fled to the first place of concealment they could find. The noise, meanwhile, was tumultuous.

As Mr. Thompson was travelling, he observed his Hottentot guide, Frederick, looking out for the *spoor* or track of human feet, being exceedingly anxious to get to some kraal before night; but the only tracks he could discover were those of quaggas, gnus, and antelopes of various kinds, and of their pursuer, the lion. The footprints of the latter were so frequent and so fresh, that it was evident these tyrants of the desert were numerous and near. Frederick added, too, the *cheering* remark : " Wherever such numbers of the large game may be seen, we may be sure lions are not far distant." It was confirmed by numerous skeletons of animals scattered over the plain.

Mr. Thompson says : " We were jogging pensively along, the Hottentot with two horses, about ten yards before me, I following with the other two ; Frederick was nodding on his saddle, having slept little, I believe, during the previous night. In this posture, happening to cast my eyes on one side, I beheld, with consternation, two monstrous lions reclining under a mimosa bush, within fifteen yards of our path. They were reclining lazily on the ground, with half-opened jaws showing their terrific fangs. I saw our danger, and was aware that no effort could save us if these savage beasts should be tempted to make a spring.

" I collected myself, therefore, and moved on in silence ; while Frederick, without perceiving them, rode quietly past. I followed him exactly at the same pace, keeping my eyes fixed upon the glaring monsters, who remained perfectly still. When we had got seventy or eighty yards from them, I rode gently up to Frederick, and, desiring him to look over his shoulder, showed him the lions. But such a face of terror I never beheld, as he exhibited on perceiving the danger we had so narrowly escaped. He was astonished, too, that he had not previously observed them, being, like most of his countrymen, very quick-sighted.

" He said, however, that I had acted very properly in not speaking or evincing the least alarm while passing the lions ; for, if I had, they would probably not have let us pass so quietly. Most likely we owed our safety to their hunger being satiated—for they appeared to have been just devouring some animal they had killed ; a quagga, as it seemed to me, from the hurried glance I had in passing."

Mr. Thompson, accompanied by a guide and some Corannas on foot, determined on visiting a remarkable cataract. As they approached it, the sound began to rise on their ears like distant thunder. It was still, however, a work of some exertion to reach the spot, from which they were divided by a part of the Orange River, and beyond that by a tract of wild woodland several miles in extent. The main, or middle branch of the river, which forms the cataract, traverses a sort of island of large extent, covered with rocks and thickets, and environed on all sides by streams of water. They crossed the southern branch, which at that season was but an inconsiderable creek, and proceeded for several miles through the dense acacia forests, while the thundering sound of the cataract increased at every step.

At length they reached a ridge of rocks, and Mr. Thompson found it necessary to dismount and follow the rest on foot. It seemed as if they were now entering the untrodden vestibule of one of nature's most sublime temples. The Corannas repeatedly requested him to keep behind and follow them softly, for the precipices were dangerous for the feet of men, and the sight and sound of the cataract were so fearful that they regarded the place with awe, and ventured but seldom

8

to visit it. They now bathed, and requ...ted him to do the same ; one of them stepped forward to the brink of the precipice, and, having looked cautiously over, beckoned him to advance. He did so, and witnessed a curious and striking scene, but it was not yet the waterfall. It was a rapid formed by almost the whole volume of the river, compressed into a narrow channel of not more than fifty yards in breadth, whence it descended at an angle of nearly forty-five degrees, and, rushing tumultuously through a black and crooked chasm among the rocks, of frightful depth, escaped in a torrent of foam.

"My swarthy guides," says Mr. Thompson, "although this was unquestionably the first time that they had ever led a traveller to view the remarkable scenery of their country, evinced a degree of tact as *ciceroni*, as well as natural feeling of the picturesque, that equally pleased and surprised me. Having forewarned me that this was not yet the waterfall, they now pioneered the way for about a mile further along the rocks, some of them keeping near, and continually cautioning me to look to my feet, as a single false step might precipitate me into the raging abyss of waters,—the tumult of which seemed to shake even the solid rocks around us.

"At length, we halted as before, and the next moment I was led to a projecting rock, where a scene burst upon me, far surpassing my most sanguine expectations. The whole water of the river (except what escapes by the subsidiary channel we had crossed, and by a similar one on the north side), being previously confined to a bed of scarcely 100 feet in breadth, descends at once in a magnificent cascade of fully 400 feet in height. I stood on a cliff nearly level with the top of the fall, and directly in front of it. The beams of the evening sun fell full upon the cascade, and occasioned a most splendid rainbow ; while the vapoury mists arising from the broken waters, the bright green woods which hung from the surrounding cliffs, the astounding roar of the waterfall, and the tumultuous boiling and whirling of the stream below, striving to escape along its deep, dark, narrow path, formed altogether a combination of beauty and grandeur, such as I had never before witnessed.

"As I gazed on this stupendous scene, I felt as if in a dream. The sublimity of nature drowned all apprehensions of danger; and after a short pause, I hastily left the spot where I stood, to gain a nearer view from a cliff that more immediately impended over the foaming gulf. I had just reached this station, when I felt myself grasped all at once by four Corannas, who simultaneously seized hold of me by the arms and legs. My first impression was, that they were going to hurl me over the precipice; but it was a momentary thought, and it wronged the friendly savages. They are themselves a timid race; and they were alarmed lest my temerity should lead me into danger. They hurried me back from the brink, and then explained their motive, and asked my forgiveness. I was not ungrateful for their care, though somewhat annoyed by their officiousness. I returned to my station to take a sketch of the same; but the attempt was far too hurried, and too unworthy of its object, to please myself. The character of the whole of the surrounding scenery, full of rocks, caverns, and pathless woods, and the desolate aspect of the Gariepine mountains beyond, accorded well with the wild grandeur of the waterfall, and impressed me with feelings never to be effaced.

"The river, after pouring itself out in this beautiful cascade, rushes along in a narrow chasm or canal, of about two miles in length, and nearly 500 feet in depth, apparently worn in the solid rock in the course of ages by the force of the current. In the summer season, when the river is in flood, the fall must be infinitely more magnificent; but it is probably at that season altogether inaccessible; for it is evident that the mass of waters, unable to escape by this passage, then pour themselves out in mighty streams by the two subsidiary canals, which were now almost dry, and at the same time overflow nearly the entire tract of forest land between them, which forms at other seasons a sort of island, as we now found it."

Campbell and his party reached a point of the Maklareen River where it forms a lake of great extent, covered so profusely with rushes and reeds that they completely conceal the water. It was about a quarter of a mile across. His wagon happened to enter first, and got over without any material difficulty, only the hind leg of one ox sank so deep that he fell, but, immediately recovering himself, he went on briskly.

The two other wagons were not equally fortunate : both stuck fast in the middle in consequence of some of the oxen in each sinking into the mire up to their bellies. After a long and severe struggle, one of the two got over; but they were obliged to take out the two oxen that were yoked to the shafts of the wagon, and then, with about sixteen or eighteen oxen, they succeeded in dragging it to the side also; but still there remained one ox which had sunk so deep that no part of him was visible from the side. As his legs were so benumbed that he could not use them, they found his extrication a very difficult business. By tying several ropes, made of buffalo skins, to his horns, and holding him by the tail, they got him turned upon his side, after which, with great exertion, they dragged him to the edge of the lake, when he instantly recovered, and ran to take his place in the yoke.

Meanwhile loud peals of thunder were rolling over the heads of the travellers, attended with vivid lightning, and a heavy storm was fast approaching. When they had got about two hundred yards from the lake, a deluge of rain began to descend which obliged them to halt for two hours under the bushes.

Another incident called for greater endurance.—" Both

our wagons," says Captain Harris, " stuck fast in the Sant
River, and were with difficulty extricated by the united
efforts of the teams. The heat was intense, not a breath
stirred, and heavy black clouds fast collecting bade us prepare for a deluge. We therefore formed the camp in an
elevated position, under the lee of a high stone inclosure,
which only required the entrance to be closed with bushes to
make a secure pound for the cattle.

" Scarcely were these arrangements completed, when a
stream of liquid fire ran along the ground, and a deafening
thunder-clap, exploding close above us, was instantly followed
by a torrent of rain, which came ' dancing to the earth,' not
in drops, but in continuous streams, and with indescribable
violence, during the greater part of the night; the thunder
now receding, and rumbling less and less distinctly, but
more incessantly among the distant mountains—now pealing
in echoes over the nearest hills, and now returning to burst
with redoubled violence above our heads

> ' Far along
> From peak to peak, the rattling crags among,
> Leapt the wild thunder, not from one lone cloud,
> But every mountain soon had found a tongue.'

" The horses and oxen were presently standing knee-
deep in water ; our followers remained sitting all night in
the baggage-wagon, which leaked considerably, but our now
being better covered, fortunately resisted the pitiless storm.
Sleep was, however, out of the question, the earth actually
threatening to give way under us, and the lightning being
so painfully vivid that we were glad to hide our heads under
the pillow. Those only who have witnessed the setting in
of the south-west monsoon in India are capable of fully
understanding the awful tempest I have attempted to
describe."

When travelling in Sneuberg, Campbell went with some
of the people to examine a remarkable cave. It was on the
11

side of a high cliff, separated from another equally high only by a few yards. For about two hundred yards they had to walk on projecting rocks near the middle of the opposite cliff. They were soon obliged to take off their shoes lest they should slide down the rocks, and, advancing a few yards further, they took off their stockings as more likely to prevent their sliding down.

On coming opposite to the cave they cautiously descended to the bottom of the cliffs; then two Hottentots went into a pool formed by the river, on purpose to sound it, as this had to be crossed in order that the cave might be reached. They found it two feet and a half deep till within two yards of the other side, over which they placed a ladder which had been brought with them. One Hottentot mounted first, but, when climbing the rock, he slipped and rolled down into the water completely overhead; but this appeared to the rest only a trifle; for they only smiled, and instantly pressed onwards. A friend who was tall and strong carried Campbell over on his back.

It proved no easy matter to climb up to the cave's mouth from the steepness and smoothness of the rock. A light being struck, the party entered it with three candles. On the roof of the cave, which resembled that of a cathedral in miniature, hundreds of bats were hanging fast asleep. The lights woke many of them, and they flew around the visitors, endangering their being shrouded in darkness. After viewing the different apartments of the cave, which appeared singularly gloomy and dismal, they found their return not a little difficult.

Directly across the Black Mountain ridge lies the small secluded tract called the Cango, containing some remarkable caverns. They were discovered in the year 1780, by a boor, who was out hunting among the mountains. On Mr. Thompson's arrival at a farmer's of the name of Botha, in the district of George, who resides a few miles from them, he made arrangements with the farmer to accompany him to the caverns.

Accordingly he proceeded to the grotto early in the morning, attended by Mynheer Botha, three of his sons, two neighbours, and five Hottentots. It is in the side of a rocky hill which forms part of the black mountains. The mouth has the appearance of an irregular dark-looking gateway, of about twenty feet in height, and enters the rock about one hundred feet above the level of a brook, which has its source in some desolate ravines to the eastward.

Advancing from the entrance about two hundred feet, in a crooked but horizontal direction, they came to an abrupt precipice of about thirty-three deep, which they descended by the aid of a ladder brought for the purpose. On reaching the bottom several lighted torches, borne by the Hottentots, disclosed a magnificent scene. They found themselves in an apartment about 600 feet in length, by a hundred broad, and varying in height from sixty to seventy feet. This hall was adorned with the most splendid stalactites. These are produced from the whinstone rock, which forms the walls and roof, being hard and compact, but penetrated in many places by fissures, through which the water oozing after heavy rains, and strongly impregnated with calcareous matter, from the superincumbent strata through which it is filtered, forms them as it trickles down drop by drop, assuming an infinitude of singular and grotesque figures. Some in the shape of columns, rising to the height of forty feet, and one majestic one not less than sixty ; others assuming the fantastic forms of cauliflowers, festoons, and a variety of grotesque figures. Many of these stalactites were quite transparent, and reflected the glare of the torches with a very brilliant and enchanting effect. This apartment was called Van-Zyl's-Hall, after the name of its first discoverer.

From thence, a long range of apartments extend, one beyond another, which the boors and other visitors have distinguished by names of their own choice. The first is called the Registry, from the walls being inscribed with the names of many visitors. It is about forty feet in diameter, and in height apparently about thirty feet. It serves as a vestibule for a noble apartment, about 140 feet in length and breadth, and fifty in height, ornamented also, though not so splendidly as the first, by many gorgeous stalactites. A sort of gallery leads out of this, about fifteen feet in breadth, and twenty in height at the entrance, but narrowing as it penetrates inward, till, at the distance of about sixty feet, it is terminated by another abrupt descent.

No one had hitherto explored the cavern beyond this spot; and as the ladder at the entrance could not be conveniently brought forward, Mr. Thompson contrived to scramble down the precipice, which was about forty-four feet in depth. Three of the Hottentots followed, but so confusedly, that all their torches were extinguished in coming down. His, happily, was not, and relighting theirs, he proceeded to explore the recesses of this furthest grotto. Finding the atmosphere very oppressive, and being somewhat apprehensive of foul air, he directed the Hottentots to keep at a good distance behind, in order that their lights might burn, should his be extinguished. Proceeding in this manner, he fully examined this chamber, and found it to be about 500 feet in length, by fifty broad, and varying in height from twenty to forty feet. At the extremity he was stopped by a wall or rock, in the middle of which, about fifteen feet high, appeared another opening. Fancying that this might be a continuation of the cavern, he contrived to clamber up, in the manner of a chimney-sweep, between two columns of spar, and examined this excavation also; but he found it to be merely a narrow chasm, neither remarkable in extent nor decoration. Beyond this he discovered no opening, and at this spot he calculated that he was about 1,500 feet from the entrance of the grotto.

Retracing his steps, and again ascending the precipice,

not without difficulty, Mr. Thompson returned to his companions, who were waiting with some anxiety for his safety
at the last descent. " I was congratulated," he says, "on my
success ; and Mynheer Botha, the guardian of this pande-
monian palace, did me the honour to confer my name on the
chamber I had now explored."

He then examined in detail the whole of this immense
cavern, and was shown a variety of smaller chambers or
recesses, opening out of the great gallery, or range of state
apartments. One of the smaller grottoes is called the *Tskegel
Kamer*, from its being hung round with stalactites resembling
icicles. Another very beautiful one is called the Bath, from
its containing some curious natural cisterns, formed by petri-
factions, and resembling marble basins hollowed by art in the
living rock. These basins were full of fresh water, delight-
fully cool and limpid.

In some parts of the caves the roof and the walls were
covered with myriads of bats, many of which, awakened by
the unwonted light and clamour, began to fly about, and it
was with difficulty they were prevented extinguishing the
lights. The floor was in many places covered several feet
deep with their excrement, dry as chaff ; but it is remarkable
that the Bath-room, probably from being moister than other
parts of the cavern, was entirely free from this nuisance.

"Having once more surveyed Van-Zyl's-Hall," says Mr.
Thompson, " I ascended the ladder, requesting the rest of the
party to fall back a little into the cavern, while I took a
hasty sketch of them from the top of the precipice. The
effect was strikingly picturesque. The glare of the torches
held by the Hottentots, showing dimly the bandit-looking
forms of the boors, grim and fierce as Dirk Hatteraick himself—and the strange, grotesque, unearthly shapes of the
stalactites, half-hidden, half-revealed, formed altogether
one of the most extraordinary scenes I ever witnessed, and
vividly called to my imagination some of the descriptions of

8*

caverns in the works of the ancient poets, probably suggested by actual scenery of the same character as that which I now contemplated."

A night in savage solitude is thus described by a traveller :

" The stars shone in brightness and beauty through a dark blué sky : I listened, and at times caught wild remote sounds —the nameless sounds of night. Who that has passed a night in savage solitudes has not felt how distinct its sounds are from those of day—has not discovered a voice and a language in the night-wind as it moaned by, different from the rush of any wind on which the sun ever shone—like spirit-warnings from the past ? I listened, and could imagine in the distant booming hollow noises, that hundreds of elephants were crossing the hills ; and again all was as still as death : then would come the wild melancholy howl of the wolf, and its short whoop, the next nearer than the first ; then, by sending a brighter flame from the fire, all would again be hushed ; and then the stillness would be interrupted by the croak of the night-raven, as it sailed down the ravine, catching the scent of the dead elephant ;—that ceased, and I heaped more wood upon the fire, until it threw up its bright flames, gleaming with a distinct and lurid light on the surrounding bushes. Then came a strange noise, as of some animal that was approaching us ; it came nearer, and roused my companion, who said it was the hyæna with its hideous laugh and chatter—the most wild, unnatural sound that breaks the silence of night in those tremendous solitudes."

Mr. Moffat says that when parting with his friend Mr. Anderson, he remarked that the weather to the westward looked like a storm, " but as these appearances often pass over without a drop of rain, we set off, and trusting to the strength of our recruited horses, we hoped to pass through the desert to the Orange River without much suffering.

" Mr. A. had provided us with some biscuit, which one of the men placed in a sack also containing tobacco. We

intended to sleep at Witte Water that night, but long before
we reached that place, we were overtaken by an awful storm
of thunder. The peals were deafening, and our horses frequently started from each other, at the vivid glare of the
lightning. It poured torrents, so that by the time we reached
the spot where we intended to halt, we were drenched to the
skin.

" We let our horses go, and sat down like half drowned
cocks, at a bush which could afford us no shelter, either from
wind or rain. After the vehemence of the storm had abated,
we began to think what must be done, for by the falling hail
and the piercing wind, we trembled as if we should die with
cold. After much patient search, we found a very few substances capable of ignition, and struck a light in the only box
where the tinder was dry, but in vain we looked for fuel to
supply our fire ; we threw most of our clothes off, for the
suffering with them on was unbearable, and leaving one to
blow the fire, we sallied forth in quest of materials to burn.

" At some distance we succeeded in gathering a few small
branches, where we found at least four hyænas looking on in
a most daring manner, and resolved to attack us. Such as
had both hands occupied, soon relieved one, and with stones
scared them a little. But, alas ! the light of a little fire we
had left, had disappeared, and we knew not the direction
from which we had come. We shouted to the man who had
remained with it, but no answer, save the ugly howl of the
hyænas. Now every one was pointing in a different direction
as that by which we had come, and we were completely
bewildered.

" A second storm pelted us most unmercifully, and the
wind seemed to penetrate through and through our almost
naked frames. After a long search, we found the little bush,
the man asleep, and the fire out. We threw down our crow's
nests which we had gathered for fuel, resolving to brave it
out; but the prospect was horrible—of shivering till the next

day's sun should warm us. Each lay down in a lump, on a
goat-skin, which had served as a saddle-cloth. Two of us
tried to get down to dry earth, for though there had been a
stream on the ground, it was scarcely six inches deep.
Beyond our expectations we fell asleep, and as I lay rather
lower than some of my comrades, the rain and sand buried
nearly half of my body.

"It would be vain attempting to describe my feelings on
awaking at daybreak, stiff, cold, and dizzy; my hair clotted
with mud. We crawled off to the pool of rain-water, and
though very thick, we enjoyed a thorough ablution; after
wringing the water out of our clothes, we put them on as
they were, being obliged to proceed. Before starting, we
resolved to have a delightful taste of our biscuit, but, alas!
when the contents of our bag were turned out, we found
that the rain having saturated the tobacco and biscuit, the
latter was reduced to a dark-brown paste; smokers as we
were, this dish was too unpalatable for us, and a good
draught of muddy water had to supply the deficiency. As
the sun arose towards the meridian, the heat became exces-
sive; and if we had been nearly frozen at night, we were
almost scorched during the day; and before we reached
water the following night, we would have given a crown for
a bottle of that in which we had washed in the morning."

Lieutenant-Colonel Napier thus describes the "tedium of
a darksome march" as pleasantly whiled away. "One of
the party—a man from infancy devoted to the chase, whose
youth and manhood were passed in its pursuit, who had
marked down the last elephants in these their once favourite
haunts—entered most enthusiastically on the theme. Striking
on an elephant's 'spoor,' he soon eloquently led away his
audience through deep and rocky valleys, and dense thorny
jungles; threading the narrow elephant path amidst all the
intricacies of wooded kloofs; tracked the noble animals to
where they fed; pointed out their gigantic forms, looming

like dark ocean-rocks above a green glittering sea of bright 'spekboom'—the elephant's favourite food—aloes, euphorbias, and other strange and fantastic shrubs. Next would he tell of the stealthy, snake-like approach, the moment of breathless suspense, the sharp crack of the rifle, the fall of the huge patriarch of the flock, the wild crashing charge of the survivors, arrested in mid career by the ignited bush blazing up into a secure rampart of smoke and flame. The lifeless prostrate victim is next approached; then would follow the process of 'marking' the tusks, to be carried off at some future time; the tail docked in token of triumph; the amputation of the trunk, of a foot, or extraction of the heart; part of which, wrapped in a flap cut from one of the fallen monster's ears, would form, at the bivouac, the evening repast of the tired and famished hunter.

"This old hunter had associated with, and well remembered, the famous and intrepid Thwackray (a settler some forty years ago), who, after slaying I forget how many hundred elephants, was, as our friend related, at last trampled to death by one he had unfortunately wounded without disabling."

The reader will doubtless be amused by the following story of the sporting doctor of the party, which we shall slightly abridge:—

"Whilst jogging quietly along the edge of the Kowie Bush, the dogs suddenly gave tongue, and I 'yoiked' them forward through the covert, the increasing thickness of which compelled me to dismount; whereupon, tying up my nag to the stump of a tree, I followed up the chase on foot. The dogs soon brought their quarry to bay; and, fancying it must be a porcupine, I boldly advanced, flourishing aloft the aforesaid hunting-whip.

"Scarcely had I approached the scene of action—a thick wait-a-bit bush, around which the dogs were loudly baying —than a canine yell of agony, then two or three grunts, and a heavy crash amongst the underwood, announced the presence of a wild hog.   Before I had made up my mind what to do, an immense boar, with bristles like toothpicks, all standing on end, rushed at me through the intervening scrub.   Of course, I turned tail, and never ran so quick in all the course of my life, clearing, at a single bound, the clumps of brambles and shrubs which came in my path.

"Spite of numerous tumbles, from my spurs catching in the creepers, I still kept ahead; but piggy perseveringly forcing his way through the underwood, which I had to jump over, was soon close at my heels; and at every purl I got, I fancied I felt his tusks grinding against my ribs.   The pace we were both going was too quick to last; and, just as I found myself quite done up, fortunately for me, a thick spekboom bush stood in my way.   With a last desperate effort, I made a spring which carried me into the midst of its soft fleshy foliage and flowering boughs.   The latter, fortunately, did not give way under my weight; there, like King Charles in the oak, I looked down—though in no comfortable mood— upon my baffled and angry foe, who trotted round and round my place of refuge, sniffing the stems of the bush, and ever and anon casting up towards me his little twinkling, blood- shot eyes, at which—for so close was I to the brute—I kept striking with the butt-end of the whip, whilst getting up my legs in the best way I could to keep them out of his reach.

"As you may readily fancy, I was in no little stew, lest the tender, pulpy branches should give way, and leave me to the tender mercies of Mr. Piggy, who, maddened at not being able to reach me, and at the baying of the dogs around, every now and then would make a sudden dash at some of the boldest of his assailants, and, with a side-thrust of his formidable tusks, send them off howling with fearful wounds. I had thus the mortification of helplessly witnessing the destruction of many of my favourites.   A poor little wretch of a pup happened to be of the party, and, probably not knowing its danger, was foremost in the attack. The boar, suddenly turning on his diminutive opponent, seized him in his foaming mouth, placed him on the slope of a bank, and appeared determined to disembowel him in the most scientific and approved of fashion.

"At this critical moment for poor puppy, a powerful bloodhound rushed to the rescue; and though in so doing he was badly ripped in the shoulder, succeeded in laying fast hold of the boar by the end of his snout, and thus pinned him to the ground. 'Now,' thinks I to myself, 'is my sole chance.' The only weapon I had with me, was a small mother-of-pearl penknife I had bought in the Quadrant for a shilling, when on the coach by which I left London to start for this country; it was my last purchase in Old England, and never was a shilling better laid out."

"But come to the point, doctor; and don't keep us in suspense."

"That's just what I did: for seeing that this was my only hope of escape, I opened the mother-of-pearl knife, jumped out of the bush, and, seizing the boar by the ear, whilst the bloodhound was pinning his nose to the ground, I—thanks to some little knowledge of anatomy—thrust it into what I knew to be an artery, left it firmly sticking there, and quickly scrambled back again into my former place of refuge. The boar, on finding himself wounded, made such a violent effort that he shook off the dog; and to my inexpressible delight, was followed by a plentiful stream of blood. In a more or less disabled state, my bristly acquaintance had full leisure to indulge in his rude meditations. He after a while trotted off some twenty or thirty yards; stopped again; remained a few seconds quite motionless; assumed rather a sentimental look; staggered, fell forward, and rolled over on his side. Still, I could not believe that the grim monster was really dead. For a moment longer I therefore remained ensconced amongst the branches of my leafy castle, in a state of the most anxious suspense; till, seeing no signs of returning life as the dogs approached and sniffed the carcase, I slid cautiously down, picked up the bloody knife; crept on tip-toe towards my fallen enemy; touched him first gingerly with my foot, and then, finding him *really* dead—and no mistake—in the ecstasy of the moment I took off my cap, and gave three hearty cheers."

" Bravo, doctor ! a capital *finale !* and all owing to your unrivalled anatomical knowledge, and being able to discover the carotid artery under the bristles of a wild boar."

One other incident ought not to be passed over; for the traveller may be plundered, as Captain Harris was, by Bushman hordes, and left a wreck in the greatest necessity. "Here then, like sailors," he says, "who have foundered upon a rock when within sight of their destined haven, were we, after weathering many a storm, and accomplishing the most hazardous part of our journey—left at last, a wreck in the desert. The spirit of Ethaldur groaned within him, when he thus saw his prediction on the eve of being verified, and the lower jaw of Cœur-de-Lion dropped until his beard was dangling at his girdle. To add to *our* misfortunes, the scanty pool upon which our supply of water depended, being drained to the dregs, it had become necessary to perform a journey of *six miles* over an enemy's country, in order to replenish the tea-kettle."

CHAPTER XIV.

HUNTING THE ELEPHANT.

The difference between the Elephants of Africa and India—An Elephant Hunt and its Results—Adventure of Mr. Cowper Rose—Carl Krieger, the Hunter—Temerity of a Boor—Unnatural Parents—The Flesh of the Elephant.

It was not till the days of Cuvier that naturalists were aware of the specific distinction that exists between the elephant of India and that of Africa. Nor can this excite surprise when it is known that no living African species had appeared in Europe, since the year 1681, until the Pasha of Egypt presented a young female to the King of France, in 1826.

The characteristic differences are briefly these :—In the African the head is rounder, the tusks larger, the ears of enormous magnitude, sometimes covering the shoulders, and used by the natives as a sort of truck on which to drag various loads. The molar teeth also in the African have thin flat surfaces marked with làrge irregular lozenge-shaped ribands, passing from side to side, while in the Asiatic, these transverse ribands are narrow, with indented edges, and fold upon each other in parallel lines.

" Wisest of brutes, the half-reasoning elephant,"

when contemplated in his native forests, presents no ordinary spectacle.

" Trampling his path through wood and brake
    And canes, which crackling fall before his way,
    And tassel-grass, whose silvery feathers play,
        O'ertopping the young trees,
On comes the elephant, to slake

His thirst at noon in yon pellucid springs.
Lo! from his trunk upturned, aloft he flings
   The grateful shower ; and now
   Plucking the broad-leaved bough
Of yonder plume, with waving motion slow
   Fanning the languid air,
He waves it to and fro."

Formed, as it were, for the service of man in warm
climates, the elephant possesses every quality that can render
it useful.   Strong, active, and persevering, it is so gentle in
disposition, as well as docile and sagacious, as to be trained
to almost any service.   Its large head, small eyes, broad and
pendent ears, thick body, arched back, clumsy legs, and skin
generally of a deep brown, approaching to black, have all
been long familiar.   When first born, the elephant is about
three feet high ; it continues to grow till it is sixteen or
eighteen years of age.   It is very playful, delighting in
gambols and frolic, and displays its exuberant feelings in a
thousand buoyant antics.   The tusks are not visible in the
young animals, but when they are mature, they project, in some instances, several feet.   The usual height of
the adult elephant is from eight to ten feet, but instances
have occasionally occurred in which it has reached fifteen or
sixteen.   The standard of the East India Company for
serviceable animals was seven feet and upwards, measured
at the shoulder, which is several inches lower than the
back of the elephant.

The wonderful facility with which the elephant can apply
his trunk to so many purposes of a hand, is one great reason
of his superiority.   Not only does he possess the power of
moving it, but he can bend it, shorten it, lengthen it, bend it
back, and turn it in every direction.   The extremity of this
trunk is furnished with a rim, lengthened in front into the
form of a finger, and it is by this means that he is able to
pick up the smallest piece of money, gather flowers one by

one, untie knots, and open and shut doors, turning the keys and forcing back the bolts. The muscular structure of the trunk is extremely curious. Cuvier states that the muscles, contained in it, which have the power of distinct action, are not far short of forty thousand. The delicacy of the organ is shown in case the elephant becomes blind, when it is projected as far as possible, so as to avoid actually touching the ground, and then lets the finger, which is curved inward to protect the nostrils, skim along the surface of uneven ground, to the inequalities of which it adjusts itself with great exactness. In circumstances of danger the elephant takes great care of its trunk, and then, when attacked by a tiger, he carries it as high in the air as he can. If it becomes wounded in the conflict, the rage of the animal is almost inexpressible. On this account he rarely uses the trunk as a weapon, though he sometimes hurls missiles by it.

As a colonist, attended by a guide, was penetrating into the recesses of a woody wilderness, the fresh traces of a troop of elephants appeared on their path ; and the guide, after carefully inspecting their footprints, declared that they had passed this way to the eastward only about an hour or so before. Eager to have a sight of these extraordinary animals, which he had not yet seen in their wild state, he followed on their route as fast as the Hottentot could keep pace with him. For four or five miles they pursued their track in this manner through the mazy glades of the jungle, the Hottentot warning the colonist, every now and then, as the lofty evergreens crowded more densely around the path, to proceed with caution ; and at every new opening among the thickets they glanced eagerly forward and around, in the expectation of coming plump on " a covey of elephants." Their expectations were, however, fruitless, and on gaining an elevation where the jungle opened up and admitted a view of the country for many miles before them, saw clearly that they were too late. The sagacious animals had retreated, as they usually do, just before sunrise, to their less accessible haunts, in all probability concealed in some of the more lofty woods or wild ravines that run up to the skirts of the savage Zureberg. Further pursuit, therefore, was utterly vain.

Elephants live in herds in remote and secluded districts, especially where large streams or rivers flowing through a wild and level track are bordered by a luxuriant vegetation. One of these, browsing in majestic tranquillity amidst the wild magnificence of the African landscape, is a very noble sight, but many of them may, not unfrequently, be observed. "We suddenly found ourselves," says Mr. Pringle, "on issuing from a wooded defile, in the midst of a numerous herd of these animals. None of them, however, were very close to us; but they were seen scattered in little clumps over the bottom and sides of a valley two or three miles in length; some browsing on the spekboom which clothed the skirts of the hills on either side; others at work among the mimosa trees sprinkled over the low and grassy savannah. As we proceeded cautiously onward, and some of these parties came more distinctly into view (consisting, apparently, in many instances, of separate families, the male, the female, and the young of different sizes), the gigantic magnitude of the leaders became more and more striking. The calm and stately tranquillity of their deportment, too, was remarkable. Though we were a band of about a dozen horsemen, including our Hottentot attendants, they seemed not to observe, or altogether to disregard, our march down the valley."

Some remarkable qualities of the elephant are graphically described by the same writer in the following terms :— "As we pursued our route down the valley of the Koonap River, we became aware that a numerous troop of these gigantic animals had recently preceded, as foot-prints of all dimensions from eight to fifteen inches in diameter were everywhere visible; and in the swampy spots on the banks of the river it was evident that some of them had been

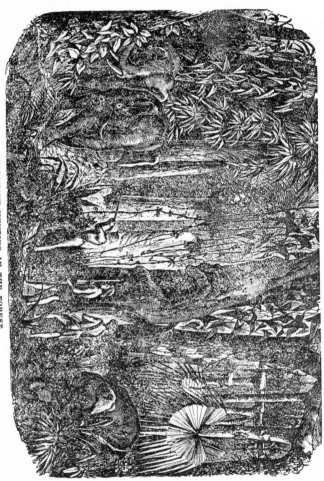

ELEPHANT HUNTING IN THE FOREST.

laxuriantly enjoying themselves by rolling their unwieldy bulks in the ooze and mud. But it was in the groves and jungles that they had left the most striking proofs of their recent presence and peculiar habits. In many places paths had been trodden through the midst of dense thorny forests otherwise impenetrable.

" They appeared to have opened these paths with great judgment, always taking the best and shortest cut to the next savannah or ford of the river ; and in this way these were of the greatest use to us by pioneering our route through a most difficult and intricate country, never yet traversed by a wheel carriage, and great part of it, indeed, inaccessible even on horseback, except for the aid of these powerful and sagacious animals. In such places (as the Hottentots assured me) the great bull elephants always march in the van, bursting through the jungle as a bullock would through a field of hops, treading down the thorny brushwood, and breaking with his proboscis the larger branches that obstruct his passage ; the females and younger part of the herd follow in his wake in single file ; and in this manner a path is cleared through the densest woods and forests, such as it would take the pioneers of an army no small labour to accomplish. Among the groves of mimosa trees, which were thinly sprinkled over the grass of meadows along the river's margin, the traces of the elephants were not less apparent. Immense numbers of these trees had been torn out of the ground and placed in an inverted position, in order to enable the animals to browse at their ease on the soft and juicy roots, which form a favourite part of their food. I observed that in numerous instances, where the trees were of considerable size, the elephant had employed one of his tusks exactly as we should use a crowbar, thrusting it under the roots to loosen their hold of the earth before he could tear them up with his proboscis. Many of the larger mimosas had resisted all these efforts, and, indeed, it is only after heavy rains, when the soil is soft and loose, that they **can** successfully attempt this operation."

A troop of elephants came down one dark and rainy night close to the outskirts of a village. The inhabitants heard them bellowing and making an extraordinary noise for a long time at the upper end of an orchard ; but knowing well how dangerous it was to encounter these animals in the night, they kept close within their houses till daybreak. Next morning, on examining the spot where they had heard the elephants, they discovered the cause of all this nocturnal uproar. There was, at this spot, a ditch or trench about four or five feet in width, and nearly fourteen in depth, which some of the people had recently cut through the bank of the river, on purpose to lead out the water to irrigate some part of their garden ground, and to drive a corn mill. Into this trench, which was still unfinished and without water, one of the elephants had apparently fallen, for the marks of his feet were distinctly visible at the bottom, as well as the impress of his huge body on the sides. How he had got in was easy to conjecture ; but how, being once in, he had ever contrived to get out again was the marvel. By his own unaided efforts it was obviously impossible for such an animal to have extri- cated himself. Could his comrades, then, have assisted him ? There can be little question but they had ; though by what means, unless by hauling him out with their trunks, it would not be easy to conjecture. And in corroboration of the sup- position, on examining the spot, the edges of this trench appeared deeply indented with numerous vestiges, as if the other elephants had stationed themselves on either side, some of them kneeling, and others on their feet, and had thus, by united efforts, and probably after many failures, hoisted their unlucky brother out of the pit.

The visitor of a solitary dwelling in the White River Valley, heard the farmer's wife complain bitterly of the annoy- ance that she and her family received from the nocturnal visits of the elephants. They were "ugly customers," she said, "and too big to wrestle with." They came out of the forest by night, trod down her little corn field, devoured her crop of maize, pulled up her fruit trees, and tossed about and injured, as if in wanton malice, articles that they could neither devour nor destroy; and only a few days previously, her husband, on returning home at a late hour, had made a narrow escape from one of these animals, which met him in the wood, and chased him several times round his wagon. She added, however, that they were far less dangerous than they had been when she and her family came first to reside in this wild, though beautiful valley; and, pointing to a rocky mound at a little distance, which rose abruptly from the grassy meadows, and overhung a part of the river, she said that on the summit of that rock, not many years before, her husband used to lie concealed among the brushwood, and shoot the elephants as they passed down the glen in numerous herds, even at mid-day.

Lieutenant Moodie had recently joined the semi-military settlement of Fredericksburg, on the Gualana, beyond the great Fish River, where his party had already shot many elephants, with which the country at that time abounded. On one occasion he witnessed an elephant hunt for the first time, when a large female was killed, after some hundred shots had been fired at her. At first the balls seemed to produce little effect, but at length she received several shots in the trunk and eyes, which entirely disabled her from resisting or escaping, and she then became an easy prey to her assailants.

On the following day one of the servants stated that a large troop of elephants was in the neighbourhood of the settlement, and that several of the people were on their way to attack them. Moodie instantly set out to join the hunters; but from losing his way in the jungle through which he had to pass, he did not overtake them till after they had driven

9

the elephants from their first station. On getting out of the jungle he was proceeding through an open meadow on the banks of the Gualana, to the spot where he heard the firing, when he was suddenly warned of approaching danger by loud cries of "*Pas-op!*"—"*Take care!*"—in Dutch and English, coupled with his name; and at the same moment he heard the crackling of broken branches, produced by the elephants bursting through the wood, and the tremendous screams of their wrathful voices resounding among the precipitous banks.

Instantly a large female, accompanied by three others of a smaller size, issued from the edge of the jungle which skirted the river margin. As they were not more than two hundred yards off, and were proceeding directly towards him, Moodie had not much time to decide on his motions. Alone, and in the middle of a small open plain, he saw that he must inevitably be caught if he fired in this position, and his shot did not take effect. He therefore retreated hastily out of their direct path, thinking they would not observe him, until he should find a better opportunity for the attack. But in this he was mistaken, for, on looking back, he perceived to his dismay, that they had left their former course, and were rapidly pursuing and gaining ground on him. He now determined to reserve his fire as a last resource; and turning off at right angles, in the opposite direction, he made for the banks of the small river, intending to take refuge among the rocks on the other side, where he felt he should be safe.

But before he got within fifty paces of the river the elephants were within twenty paces of him—the large female in the middle, and the other three by her sides, apparently with the intention of making sure of their victim; all of them screaming so tremendously that he was almost stunned with their noise. Immediately he turned round, cocked his gun, and aimed at the head of the largest elephant. But, unfortunately, as the powder was damp, the gun hung fire, till he was in the act of taking it from his shoulder, when it

went off, the ball grazing merely the side of her head.
Halting only for an instant, the elephant again dashed
furiously forward. He fell ; but could not remember whether
he was struck by her trunk or not. She then made a thrust
at him with her tusk. Luckily for Moodie, she had only
one, which, still more luckily, missed its mark ; but it
ploughed up the earth within an inch or two of his body.

She then caught him with her trunk by the middle, threw
him between her fore-feet, and knocked him about for some
time. Once she pressed her foot on his chest with such
force that he actually felt, as it were, the bones bending under
the weight; and once she trod on the middle of his arm,
which, fortunately at the time, lay flat on the ground. In
these critical circumstances, he happily never entirely lost
his recollection, or they would most likely have proved fatal.
But owing to the roundness of her foot, he generally managed,
by twisting his body and limbs, to escape her direct tread.

At this crisis, Lieutenant Chisholm and Diederik, a
Hottentot, came up, and fired several shots at the elephant,
one of which hit her in the shoulder ; and at the same time,
her companions retiring and screaming to her from the hedge
of the forest, she reluctantly left Moodie, giving him a cuff or
two with her hind feet, in passing. He now got up, picked up
his gun, and staggered away as fast as his aching bones would
allow ; but observing that she turned back and looked towards him before entering the bush, he lay down in the long
grass, and by this means escaped her observation.

On reaching the top of the high bank of the river, he met
his brother, who had not been at this day's hunt, but had run
out on hearing one of the men say he had seen Moodie killed.
His brother was not a little surprised at meeting him alone
and in a whole skin, though plastered with mud from head
to foot. While the two brothers and Mr. Knight, of the
Cape regiment, were talking of the adventure now related,
McClane, a soldier of the Royal African Corps, attracted the

attention of a large male elephant, which had been driven towards the village. The ferocious animal gave chase, and caught him immediately under the height where the three persons were standing, carried him some distance in his trunk, then threw him down, and bringing his four feet together, trod and stamped upon him till he was quite dead. Leaving the corpse for a little while, he again returned, as if to make quite sure of McClane's destruction, and kneeling down, crushed and kneaded the body with his fore-legs. Then seizing it again with his trunk, he carried it to the edge of the jungle, and threw it among the bushes. While this tragedy was proceeding, Moodie and his brother scrambled down the bank as far as they could, and fired at the ferocious animal, but, unhappily, they were at too great a distance to render the unfortunate man any service.

Shortly after this, a shot from one of the people broke this elephant's left fore-leg, which completely disabled him from running. Seeing the danger and distress of her mate, the female, who had been Lieutenant Moodie's personal antagonist, regardless of her own danger, quitted her shelter in the bush, rushed out to his assistance, walked round and round him, chasing away the assailants, and still returning to his side, caressing him, and, when he tried to walk, she placed her flank under his wounded side, and supported him. These attentions were continued for about half an hour, until the female elephant received a severe wound from Mr. Mackenzie, of the Royal African Corps, which drove her again to the bush, where she speedily sank exhausted from the loss of blood ; and the male soon after received from the same officer a mortal wound.

An adventure of Mr. Rose is thus related : " The search was becoming hopeless, when the leader pointed to a distant hill. There was a consultation, in which it was decided that a troop of elephants was passing over it. I looked, and could see nothing. But now we went on with fresh vigour, and

ELEPHANT HUNTING IN THE PLAIN.

gained the hill opposite to that at which they were ; we
halted and watched ; and few words passed between the hunter
and Skipper, and we descended silently the ravines that
divided us.

"Again they whispered; marked from which point the
light breeze came ; and we commenced the steep ascent in a
direction that the wind might come from the animals to us ;
for we were now so near them, that their quick scent would
have discovered us. Skipper led, while we followed in Indian
file, threading a narrow rocky path, which skirted one bank
of a small hollow, while the huge beasts were feeding on the
opposite one.

"The leader halted, the hunter gave my companion and
myself lighted sticks, and whispered directions to fire the
bush and grass, and to retreat in the event of the animals
charging. It was a strange feeling to find myself within
twenty yards of creatures whose forward movement would
have been destruction ; but they stood browsing on the
bushes, and flapping their large ears, pictures of indolent
security. We were taking our stations, when we heard a shot,
and then another, and of the eight elephants, seven fled.

"We went forwards to see the effect of the shots.
Skipper's had carried death with it ; the elephant had fallen,
but rose again.   I never heard anything like its groans ; he
again fell, and we went up to him ; the ball had entered
behind the shoulder, and reached the heart.

"In looking at the mighty monster, I could not help saying, 'Poor beast ! and were it not for these ivory tusks, you
might live happy and unmolested, and they appear given but
for your destruction, for of what use are they ?'—'Defence,'
answered my companion.—'No,' said the hunter ; 'for the
most dangerous among them is a breed that the Dutch
call Koeskops, and they have no tusks.'

"We cut off his tail in token of triumph ; and then followed the troop that had fled down the hill ; we saw them

cross the ravine, and traced their downward course by the destruction and uprooting of everything that had impeded it; branches were strewed around ; and the large palm-like euphorbias, so common in these wild regions, were broken like twigs.

"In our pursuit, we crossed the lairs of the buffalo and elephant, and gained the ravine ; when I, who had walked full twenty-four miles over the rough ground, with a gun that weighed twenty pounds, found it impossible to keep up with my more active companions ; and seating myself on the ground, told the hunter to go and leave me ; and on reaching the bivouac, to send my Hottentot and my horse ! 'It is impossible,' he replied, 'it will be a dark night, and even in the day, no one would find you here !'—'It is of no conse- quence ; I do not wish to spoil your sport ; but I can go no further. I stretched myself on the ground, indifferent to the result. 'Were a rhinoceros to come down, I think you would find your legs.'—'No ; nothing could make me mount that hill.'

"There was a consultation which I scarcely heard, and it was resolved that the little boy should remain with me ; and that when I had rested, we should ascend the hill, light- ing fires as we went, to mark our course ; the remainder of the party followed the elephants.

"In half an hour I again took my gun, which had been changed for one that would scarcely fire, and began to ascend the hill by an elephant path ;—the valley we had just left, and the side of the hill were thickly covered with high dark bush,—on my right so close as to prevent my seeing any object in that direction. We were slowly rising the ascent, when I heard a heavy gallop of a large animal approaching. My little companion was at some distance from me, blowing a lighted stick. 'Listen,' I said, the boy's eyes looked wild and he fled from the sound, while I ran up the hill, not doubting it was a rhinoceros ; the heavy tramp was close to me, and I scarcely saw a large dark animal burst through the

bush within a few yards of me—in the spot I had just quitted,
and in the very path I was following. I did not stop ; for,
from the glimpse I caught, I believed it to be a rhinoceros;
my young companion fired the bush, which I heard crackling,
and in a few minutes came up to me.

"'What a narrow escape,' said he. 'What was it?'—
'The rhinoceros.' 'Did you not see it close to you?—it
turned from the lighted bush.' It was certainly a situation
of danger ; yet without affecting any particular courage, I
trusted rather to my heels than my gun."

Carl Krieger was an indefatigable and fearless hunter;
and being also an excellent marksman, often entered into the
most dangerous situations. One day, having with his party
pursued an elephant which he had wounded, the irritated
animal suddenly turned round, and, singling out from the
rest the person by whom he had been wounded, seized him
with his trunk, and lifting him high in the air, dashed him
with dreadful force to the ground. His companions, struck
with horror, fled precipitately from the fatal scene, unable to
turn their eyes to witness what might follow. But, on the
following day, they returned to the spot. They collected the
few bones that could be found, and buried them. The enraged animal had not only literally trampled Carl's body to
pieces, but pounded the very flesh into dust.

On New Year's day a party of boors got heated with
liquor, when each begun boastingly to relate the feats of
hardihood they had performed. One of them, who had been
a great hunter of elephants, having killed in his day above
forty of these gigantic animals, laid a wager that he would go
into the forest, and pluck three hairs out of an elephant's tail.
This feat he actually performed, and returned safely with the
trophy to his comrades. But not satisfied with this daring
act, he laid another bet that he would go back and shoot the
same animal on the instant. He went accordingly ; approached the elephant too incautiously, when his first shot

not proving effective, the enraged animal rushed on him before he could reload, or make his escape, and having first thrust his tremendous tusks through his body, trampled him to pieces.

Two settlers, a man and his wife, one day walking along, were terribly frightened by a troop of elephants. Seeing these enormous animals suddenly emerging from an adjoining copse-wood, they fled in the utmost alarm, and to aid their speed, popped their little infant child which they were carrying into an ant-eater's hole. The elephants, however, happily took another direction, and the selfish parents recovered the poor child uninjured from its dismal bed.

Captain Harris remarks : "It is said that the epicures of Rome esteemed the trunk of an elephant an extraordinary luxury ; and descending to more modern times, we find our brother traveller, Le Vaillant, feasting upon the foot with extraordinary relish. To the attention of the city alderman, however, I must be allowed to recommend the slice round the eye, which appears to have been hitherto overlooked by *bon vivans.* Upon this dainty morsel, roasted upon a stick before a blazing fire, or singed among the embers, so as to come under the Hottentotish denomination of *carbonaadtje,* or devilled grill, we frequently feasted ; and I can aver, without the smallest fear of contradiction, that the dish rather resembled the fragment of a shoe, picked up after a conflagration, than the meat which could boast of having been subjected to a culinary process."

Another traveller says : "Would you form an idea of what elephant's flesh actually is, take the toughest beef-steak you ever tasted, multiply it by five hundred, and subtract the gravy !"

CHAPTER XV.

THE CORANNAS.

Oppression of the Native Tribes—The Corannas defended by the Great Karroo—Their Dwellings, Dress, Utensils, and Habits—Visit of Corannas to Burchell—He draws the Portrait of their Chief—He paints a Fish—Great Astonishment of his Visitors—Their Singular Method of crossing the Orange River—Jan Kapetein, a Coranna Chief and a Lion.

WHEN the Dutch had possession of the Cape Colony, the various native tribes suffered greatly from their cruel oppression. One tribe, the Corannas, or Korahs, were protected to a considerable extent, by the wide desert Karroo, situated between them and the colony. Hence they displayed more civilisation than the general race of Hottentots who lived on its skirts. They are now widely dispersed over the country on the northern side of the Gariep or Orange River ; but it is not easy to define the boundaries of their country, as they constantly shift their quarters, and the villages of two or three tribes are so intermingled that it is difficult to decide to which the territory belongs. They never consider the soil as worth claiming, or even disputing about. The water and the pasturage are all they esteem, and when these are exhausted, the land is abandoned as useless.

In their persons the Corannas are more cleanly than the Hottentots, arising probably from the abundance of water with which the Orange River, whose banks they frequent, is supplied at all seasons, and more especially in the summer, and which is scarce in almost every other part of the southern angle of Africa. Their dress and domestic utensils are neater and constructed with more care. Their dwellings, which are

DWELLINGS OF CORANNAS.

formed with great skill, are in the shape of hemispheres, generally about six feet high and eight in diameter, and are covered with several folds of neat matting, made of rushes, or coarse grass. Their water or milk-vessels, are sometimes made of clay, baked in the sun, sometimes of gourds, and at others of wood, hollowed out from blocks of willow. Their possessions of horned cattle, sheep, goats, and dogs, are sometimes considerable. They have no kind of carriages ; but on removing from place to place, their mats, furniture, and utensils are packed on oxen, which also usually carry the women and children.

Their dress consists of skin cloaks, similar to those of the other Hottentot tribes. When visited by Barrow, the women wore square ornamented aprons, suspended from the waist, with copper chains, and beads of glass around the neck, wrist, and legs. These chains he supposed to have been procured from the Damaras, a tribe of Kaffirs to the north-westward, dwelling at the foot of the Copper Mountains.

Four Corannas paid Burchell a visit, and he purchased of them a fresh ostrich egg, for a small piece of tobacco. They belonged to a neighbouring kraal, of which one was the chief. Of this man he drew a portrait. After making the bargain to give him a large piece of tobacco, he stood patiently and still, till the drawing was finished, but as it was only in black-lead pencil it did not produce any extraordinary impression. It is by the imitation of the lively colours of nature, far more than by exactness of forms, that drawings afford delight to the far greater number of those who view them ; the more valuable part of the art being generally underrated.

This Coranna wore on his head a piece of leather bound round in the form of a cap, and was clothed with a leathern cloak or caross, which, together with his whole body, was so covered with red-ochre and grease, that the part of the wagon against which he leaned to have his portrait taken, was soiled with a red stain, not easily removed. From his

13

neck hung a number of bead-necklaces of various colours, to which were appended a Bechuana knife, and the shell of a small tortoise, to hold snuff or tobacco. His wrist and forearm were ornamented with bracelets of beads, cords of acacia bark, and a broad ivory ring. Although perfectly friendly in all their intentions, these men were armed with spears, and some with a bow and arrows. The countenance and manners of this chief were expressive of a good, natural, quiet disposition; his behaviour was even respectful; and he was less troublesome in the way of begging, than the generality of his countrymen.

At another time a party of Corannas, attracted by the provisions of the travellers, took up their abode with them. One of them having struck a yellow-fish, Burchell borrowed it that he might finish a drawing he had previously made. As soon as this was done he called the Coranna to the wagon, to take his fish again; when, catching sight of the drawing, he was instantly struck with a most laughable degree of astonishment, and for a minute, stood with his mouth and eyes wide open, dumb with wonder. At last, without taking his eyes off the picture, he called to his companions to come and see.

A crowd now being collected, astonishment was general, and the various expressions of it not a little entertaining; none ever having imagined that objects could be so imitated by art as to exhibit the colour and appearance of life, they seemed to believe that it had been done by magic; while others supposing it to be the fish itself fastened to the paper, asked where was the wound with which it had been struck. Curious were their looks of incredulity and amazement, as they examined the back of the drawing, and actually felt the thinness of what they supposed to be a solid fish. There was but one way in which the mystery could be unravelled; so Burchell showed them his brushes and colours, and in their presence, laid some of the same tints on a piece of paper. After this, they all retired satisfied and greatly pleased; the wonders they had witnessed forming for a long time the topic of conversation.

In crossing the Orange River, which is both wide and rapid, the Corannas adopt a curious contrivance to transmit their sheep and other property. They take a log of wood, from six to eight feet in length, and at a few inches' distance from one of its ends, fix a wooden peg. On this log the person intending to cross the river stretches himself at full length, and holding fast by the peg with one hand, while with the other, and occasionally with his feet, he strives to keep the end of the log at an angle of about forty-five degrees with the stream, when the obliquity of the log opposed to the current causes it in floating down the stream, to push gradually over to the opposite side.

Jan Kapetein, a Coranna chief, set off on a hunting expedition, and came just before sunset to some old cattle-folds, which the party thought to be a proper place to unpack their oxen, and tarry for the night; when they saw an enormous lion, which they determined to kill, as otherwise their lives would be in great danger. Jan, with a number of his companions, mounted their horses, and approached the lion ; and, always noted for his extraordinary courage, he now dismounted, giving the reins of his bridle to his brother Jacob, while the others waited the result.

Jan fired at the lion, but missed him, when the animal made a bound towards him. Jacob cried, "Spring on your horse ; he is coming on;" but before Jan was fairly mounted the lion sprang on his horse, and with his left paw fastened upon the thigh of the docile animal, while he put his right paw on the saddle. The horse instantly gave a tremendous kick, extricated himself as in a fright from the lion's hold, and threw Jan to the ground. The lion then seized his powder-horn, which was buckled round his loins, then attempted to grasp Jan's head, which, however, he defended with his left arm ; but its sinews and arteries were bitten through.

Jacob could afford him no assistance, for his horse ran away at the sight of the lion, while the others made off absolutely scared by its first approach. One intrepid youth alone remained. He ran to Jan's assistance, and on his approach the lion left his antagonist. No medical aid was near ; Jan had to subsist wholly on animal food, and as his wounds were exposed to a very severe frost, mortification ensued, which soon terminated his life.

CHAPTER XVI.

SERPENTS.

The Boomslange not a Poisonous Reptile—Formidable character of the Cobra da Capello—A Snake in the Grass—Extreme Peril of Mr. Moffat—The Puff Adder—The Bushman extracting and using the Venom of destructive Reptiles—Why do Serpents assail Men?—Adventure of Captain Harding.

THE Boomslange, though regarded as poisonous by the Hottentots, is not so; it has no poison-fangs, but the posterior teeth are somewhat like fangs, for they enable the reptile to seize birds with more security. It has large and full eyes, and is subject to great variety of colouring. Some of these snakes are very beautifully variegated with olive or yellow; some with pale brown, pink, and yellow; while some are plainly brown.

This creature is generally found in trees, to which it resorts for the purpose of catching birds, on which it delights to feed. As soon as it is discovered by the birds of the neighbourhood, they collect around it and fly to and fro, uttering the most piercing cries, till one, more terror-stricken than the rest, actually scans its lips, and, almost without resistance, becomes a meal for its enemy. During this proceeding the snake is generally observed with its head raised about ten or twelve inches above the branch round which its body and tail are intertwined, with its mouth open, and its neck inflated, as if anxiously endeavouring to increase the terror which, it would almost appear, it was aware would, sooner or later, bring within its grasp some one of the feathered group.

The Cobra da Capello is a most formidable serpent,

characterised by the head being covered with large plates,
and by the skin of the back being dilatable, or capable of
such expansion as to form a sort of hood, impres-ed with a
mark somewhat like a pair of spectacles. The bite of this
creature is deadly in the extreme. It often exceeds six feet
in length. It was doubtless one of these which alarmed the
servant of Sir James Alexander, by glaring at him with his
fiery eyes, and made him declare that its hooded head was as
large as a teapot.

When irritated, these serpents rise on their tail, or the
posterior portion of their body, elevate their head, expand
their hood, the scales being forced to a great distance asunder,
hiss loudly, and by their actions and the bright glance of
their eye, evince boldness and resolution. They then look
very beautiful ; and were no danger connected with their
threatening, might be contemplated with pleasure. They
will, however, not only make an assault, but repeat the
attack, pursue their assailant with great fury, and spring
upon him with wonderful velocity. *

Moffat, in one of his early journeys, left the wagons,
and wandered to a distance among the coppices and grassy
openings in quest of game. He had on his shoulder a small
double-barrelled gun, which was loaded with a ball and small
shot ; and an antelope passing, he fired at it, and slowly
followed the course it took. After advancing a short distance, he saw a tiger-cat staring at him between the forked
branches of a tree, behind which his long spotted body was
concealed, twisting and turning his tail like a cat just going
to spring on its prey.

He felt this to be a critical moment, for he had not now a
ball in his gun. He moved about as if in search of something on the grass, taking care to retreat at the same time.
After getting, as he thought, a suitable distance to turn his
back, he moved somewhat more quickly ; but in his anxiety
to escape what was behind, he did not see what was before,

until startled by treading on a large cobra da capello, asleep in the grass. It instantly twisted its body round his leg, on which he had nothing but a pair of thin trowsers, when he leaped from the spot, dragging after him the venomous and enraged reptile, and while in the act of throwing itself into a position to bite, without turning round, he threw his piece over his shoulder, and shot the cobra. Taking it by the tail, he now took it to the people at the wagons, who, on examining the poison-bags, asserted, that had the creature bitten him, he could never have reached the wagons. This cobra was six feet in length.

The puff adder is so called from its mode of inflating itself when irritated. It is extremely venomous, but sluggish in its movements, and easily avoided ; it is, however, capable of throwing itself backwards with a sudden impulse. Its body is thick in proportion to its length, and its tail is remarkably short.

With the venom obtained from this and other poisonous snakes, the Bushmen prepare a glutinous substance, in which they dip the points of their arrows, and thus render even a slight wound from them fatal. The boldness and dexterity displayed by these wild huntsmen, and by many, also, of the colonial Hottentots, in searching out and seizing alive the formidable cobra da capello and puff adder, are truly astonishing. Still more amazing is it to witness the snake-hunter extracting from the yet living and writhing reptile, held fast by his naked foot planted on its neck, the little bag containing the secreted venom, which the animal, in its rage, injects into the wound made by its fangs, at the moment it strikes its victim ; to see him take this, and fearlessly drink its contents, as schoolboys in England would suck the blob of the honey-bee !

The swallowing of this venom, they conceive, renders them in time proof against its deleterious effects, when it is brought into immediate contact with the blood, whether by the bite of a snake, or the point of an arrow.

The more usual object, however, of the Bushman in catching serpents, exclusive of their value to him as an article of food, is to procure poison for his arrows. The animal venom, too thin and volatile to preserve its efficacy long unimpaired, when used alone, is skilfully concocted into a black glutinous consistency, by the admixture of powerful vegetable and mineral poisons ; the former being generally the juice of a root of a species of amaryllis, called from this circumstance the "*gift-bol*," or poison-bulb ; the latter a bituminous or unctuous substance, which is said to exude from certain rocks and caverns. With this deadly mixture the dwarfish and despised African anoints the desperate weapons with which he resists, though unavailingly, the aggressions of the colonists, and sometimes cruelly revenges the injuries they have inflicted.

It should, however, be remembered, that it is from apprehension of danger, or the instinct of self-defence, far more than from any peculiar fierceness or innate malignity, that the serpent-race ever assail man or any of the larger animals. They turn, of course, against the foot that tramples, or the hand that threatens them ; but, happily, Providence has not armed them, in addition to their formidable powers of destruction, with the disposition of exerting those powers from motives of mere wanton cruelty, or for purposes connected with their own subsistence or security. Were it otherwise, countries like the Cape would be altogether uninhabitable.

Captain Harding relates the following fact :—" Being on a military expedition across the frontiers, I had slept one night, as usual, wrapped in my cloak, beneath a tree. On awaking, at daybreak, the first object I perceived, on raising my head from the saddle which served for my pillow, was the tail of an enormous puff adder lying across my breast, the head of the reptile being muffled under the folds of the cloak, close to my body, whither it had betaken itself apparently for warmth, during the chilliness of the night.

There was extreme hazard, that if I alarmed it by moving, it might bite me in a vital part. Seizing it, therefore, softly by the tail, I pulled it out with a sudden jerk, and threw it violently to a distance. By this means I escaped without injury; but had I unwittingly offended this uninvited bed-fellow before I was aware of his presence, I might, in all probability, have fatally atoned for my heedlessness."

CHAPTER XVII.

NATIVE ARTS.

The Art of the Skinner—The Tailor—The Mat-maker—The Rope-maker—
The Potter—The Smelter—The Smith—The Cord Twisters—The
Wooden Bowl-maker—The Maker of Ivory Rings.

THE skinner takes a sheep's skin, reeking from the back of
the animal, and rubs into it as much fat as he can. So
carefully does he conduct this process, that the skin becomes tough and smooth, and the wool or hair is secured
from falling off. He does no more if he dresses a skin for
an European ; and Kolben describes it as " a very curious
piece of work." But if he dresses a skin for the use of one
of his countrymen, to rub it alternately with cow-dung and
fat has been the usual practice, the skin being then dried in
the sun.

Wood-ashes are plentifully rubbed into the hair when
the hide of an ox, a bull, or a cow is tanned. After this it
is sprinkled with water. Should the hair be only loosened
by this process, the ashes and water are plied again until
the skinner can pull it off. On the removal of the hair he
rubs in all the fat he can, and curries the hide with all his
might.

A Hottentot skinner generally practises as a tailor too.
When he cuts the several parts of a caross out of a skin
he follows neither line nor pattern, but only his eye, yet he
works quickly and exactly. When all the parts are cut out,
he squats down to stitch them together, using the bone of a
bird as an awl, and the split sinews of beasts as thread, with
no little dexterity.

When he has a hide to cut into straps, he makes holes here and there on its edges, and in every hole ties a string. To each string he fastens a peg, and by these pegs stretches out the hide fully on the ground. Then, with a knife following his eye, he cuts out a strap, however long, with great precision, the strap being of the same breadth even when taken from the whole length of the hide. Such straps are of great service. With these the people tie up the materials of their huts and their hut furniture when they remove their kraals; girding them on the backs of their oxen. They answer also many other purposes.

The mat-makers are mostly women. They go out in bands to gather flags, reeds, and bulrushes. These, when they have brought them home, they lay in the sun to dry. When dry enough they are woven, simply with the fingers, into mats. If they are too dry, the women moisten them slightly with water before they are used, and so close is their weft that neither light, nor wind, nor rain can penetrate it. As the mats that cover the huts decay, their place is supplied by fresh ones; the people generally providing themselves with a good stock.

Of the same materials ropes are made; the flags, reeds, and bulrushes being separately twisted up into small strings, which are tied together to the length of about four yards. When a sufficiency of these four-yard strings are provided, they twist them very tightly one round another to the thickness of about an inch; such are the ropes commonly used. The whole work they do with their hands only; but so good is it that oxen can rarely break a rope when it is sound. The Europeans at the Cape often purchase these ropes of the people, and use them for their ploughs, and in various other ways. When required, they can make ropes, by the same process, of any length.

Earthen pots are made by each family, only, however, of the mould of ant-hills. This mould they take off even with the surface of the ground, and, having cleaned it from every particle of sand or gravel, knead it tightly, bruising and incorporating with it the ant-eggs that are scattered up and down in it. The ant-eggs act as a cement. Of this mould, now a clay or dough, they take the quantity that will make a pot of the required size, shaping it on a smooth, flat stone, with the hand only, into the form of the Roman urn.

The vessel is then carefully smoothed inside and out, and set, on the stone, for two days in the sun. As it is now thoroughly dry, it is detached from the stone by drawing a dried sinew to and fro, between the stone and the bottom of the pot. The pot is then put into a hole as deep as the pot is high, but of twice or more of its circumference ; while over and about it they make a quick fire, which they leave to burn till it goes out of itself. The people say that while the pot is baking in this primitive oven, the substances of the ant-eggs spread through it, and give it the great solidity which characterises all their earthen vessels.

To melt iron from the ore they make a hole in a raised ground, large enough to contain a good quantity of ironstones, which are found in abundance, and kindle a fire about them up to its mouth. About a foot and a half from this hole, on the descent, they make another, and much less, to be the receiver of the melted iron. As soon as the iron in the receiver is cold, they take it out, and break it to pieces with stones, to be, in their turns, heated in other fires, and beaten out to the desired shape with other stones.

Vogel, omitting the action of the fire, says : " They take a piece of new or old iron, and without any other implement than stone, make a weapon of it. They get the hardest flat stone they can ; and, putting the iron upon it as an anvil, bend it with a roundish stone, which serves for a hammer, into the desired form. They then grind it on the flat stone, and afterwards polish it so nicely that it comes out a very valuable piece of work both for beauty and service, and which no European smith could, perhaps, produce the like to, by the like means."

A traveller observed a smith who made knives and as-sagais, or spears. His implements were few. He had a stone for an anvil, a rough-made iron hammer, the head of which might weigh about a pound, and two small bellows made of skin, with a piece of cow-horn at one end, through which the blast went, the other end being open like a purse and sewed to two round pieces of wood. These bellows were laid upon the ground opposite the fire, with a heavy stone to keep the under side steady. He effected a blast by quickly raising and depressing the upper side of the bellows, and, with great ease, blew both at the same time.

The Hottentot women, sitting in the shade, often employ themselves in twisting cord from the acacia bark, while others chop down the branches, or strip off long pieces of it from the stems. Some engage in an occupation of a double nature: for, instead of dividing the fibres by pounding them on a large stone, they perform the operation by chewing, as they fancy the juice to have an agreeable taste.

Considering the mode in which it is manufactured, this cord is made very expeditiously. The workwoman being seated on the ground, and having a quantity of prepared bark at hand, spins two yarns at once, by the simple process of rolling them down her thigh with her palm, and then, by bringing them close together and rolling them upwards, with a turn in the contrary way, they are neatly twisted into a strong single cord.

Wooden bowl-makers display their industry and skill in carving out bowls and jugs from the green wood of the willow; while, perhaps, at a distance a large willow-tree may be seen falling to the ground, hacked through by hatchets, so weak and small, that nothing but perseverance and much time could enable the people, with such tools, to sever trunks above a foot or eighteen inches in diameter. These are cut

10

into convenient lengths, according to the utensil intended to be made; and the soft, tough nature of the wood renders it peculiarly fit for the purpose.

After the rough log has been chopped with the hatchet or adze nearly to the required shape, a common knife is the only tool employed to smooth and complete the outside; and another knife, having its top bent literally into a semicircular hook, is used, with great dexterity and neatness, to hollow out the inside. As soon as this is done, the whole is thoroughly smeared with fat, to prevent it splitting from the heat and dryness of the weather. The bowls are of various sizes, but most frequently from twelve to eighteen inches across, shallow, and mostly oval. The jug or jar is made in the form of ·a short cylinder, having the mouth or neck contracted generally to about two-thirds. Their usual capacity is about a gallon, but they are made of all sizes, from a pint to five gallons.

A Hottentot makes ivory rings to be worn upon the arms by way of ornament. From the moment he lays his hand on an elephant's tooth to cut out a ring, to its completion, he makes use of no other instrument than a knife, yet is the ring round, smooth, and bright. The manufacture is, of course, proportionally tedious.

HUNTING THE RHINOCEROS.

CHAPTER XVIII.

HUNTING THE RHINOCEROS.

Peculiarities of the African Rhinoceros—A huge Animal shot—Cooking of the Legs and Feet—The Three Perils of Mr. Andersson—Most marvellous Escape.

THE African Rhinoceros differs materially from that of India, in the appearance of his skin, which is devoid of the large folds and wrinkles of that species, having merely a slight plait across the shoulders, and some fainter wrinkles on the sides. It is, also, when compared with the Indian animal, comparatively smooth, having no hair on any part of it, except at the edge of the ears, and the extremity of the tail.

A rhinoceros shot by Campbell's party was eleven feet long; six feet in height; four feet broad; three feet from the tip of the nose to the ear; the circumference of the body about eleven feet. The skin was dark brown, resembling tanned leather, about an inch in thickness, and smooth, without hair. The front horn was about fourteen inches long, the other considerably shorter.

The natives were delighted by the sight of so huge a carcase. Four different parties began to cut it up, each carrying portions to their respective heaps as fast as they could. Some being more expeditious than others excited jealousy, and soon caused a frightful uproar. Twenty tongues were bawling at one time, one of which seemed sufficient to deafen an ox. Not a word was spoken in jest, all were deeply serious. Some severe strokes with sticks were dealt among them by the leaders of the parties. But now a circumstance occurred which instantly produced silence and

14

amazement.   A Mashow happening to pierce through the animal's side with his knife, the fixed air rushed out from the swollen carcase with great noise and violence.   The

HEAD OF A RHINOCEROS.

terror thus produced soon, however, subsided, and in less than an hour every ounce of the rhinoceros was carried off.

The legs and feet were cooked by a singular process. As the ants' nests are composed of hard clay, several of

them were dug up by the people early in the morning, and
their populations destroyed. The space thus obtained was
filled up with lighted fuel till the bottom and sides within
became red hot. The embers of the wood were then removed, the leg or foot of the rhinoceros introduced, and the
door closed up with heated clay and embers. Fire was also
made on the outside over the nests, and the flesh was allowed
to remain in it for several hours. Food cooked in this way
is highly relished by all the tribes.

Mr. Andersson, though anxiously desirous to reach a
distant spot, seemed not very well prepared for the journey.
"My leg," he says, "had in some degree recovered its
strength ; but, unobserved by me, it had received a somewhat ugly twist. Little George first drew my attention to
the fact : 'Sir,' said he, 'your leg has grown crooked.'

" ' Crooked!' echoed I, somewhat angrily. 'What do you
mean ? '

" ' Only,' he wickedly replied, ' the calf is nearly where
the shin ought to be.'

" The boy's remark was not without foundation, but in
time the leg assumed its proper shape.

" I determined, before finally leaving Kobis, to devote
one more day, or rather night, to the destruction of the
denizens of the forest. But the adventure nearly terminated
fatally; and the night of the 15th of July will ever be
remembered by me as one of the most eventful epochs of
my life ; for, in the course of it, I was three several times
in the very jaws of death, and only escaped destruction by a
miracle.

" From the constant persecution to which the larger
game had of late been subjected at Kobis, it had become
not only scarce but wary ; and hearing that elephants and
rhinoceroses still continued to resort to Abeghan, I forthwith
proceeded there on the night in question. Somewhat incautiously I took up my position—alone, as usual—on a

narrow neck of land dividing two small pools ; the space on either side of my skärm* being only sufficient for a large animal to stand between me and the water. I was provided with a blanket and two or three spare guns.

" It was one of those magnificent tropical moonlight nights, when an indescribably soft and enchanting light is shed over the slumbering landscape ; the moon was so bright and clear that I could discern even a small animal at a considerable distance.

" I had just completed my arrangements, when a noise, that I can only liken to the passage of a train of artillery, broke the stillness of the air ; it evidently came from the direction of one of the numerous stony paths, or rather tracks, leading to the water, and I imagined it was caused by some wagons that might have crossed the Kalahari. Raising myself partially from my recumbent posture, I fixed my eyes steadily on the part of the bush whence the strange sounds proceeded ; but for some time I was unable to make out the cause. All at once, however, the mystery was explained by the appearance of an immense elephant, immediately followed by others, amounting to eighteen. Their towering forms told me at a glance that they were all males. It was a splendid sight to behold so many huge creatures approaching with a free, sweeping, unsuspecting, and stately step. The somewhat elevated ground whence they emerged, and which gradually sloped towards the water, together with the misty night air, gave an increased appearance of bulk and mightiness to their naturally giant structures.

" Crouching down as low as possible in the ' skärm,' 1 waited, with beating heart and ready rifle, the approach of the leading male, who, unconscious of peril, was making straight for my hiding-place. The position of his body,

* A " skärm " is a small inclosure, six or eight feet in diameter, the walls (usually consisting of loose stones) being about two feet in height.

however, was unfavourable for a shot ; and, knowing from
experience that I had little chance of obtaining more than
a single good one, I waited for an opportunity to fire at his
shoulder, which is preferable to any part when shooting at
night.   But this chance, unfortunately, was not afforded till
his enormous bulk towered above my head.   The consequence was, that, while in the act of raising the muzzle of
my rifle over the 'skärm,' my body caught his eye, and,
before I could place my piece to my shoulder, he swung
himself round, and, with trunk elevated and ears spread,
desperately charged me.   It was now too late to think
of flight, much less of slaying the savage beast.   My
own life was in imminent jeopardy ; and seeing that, if I
remained partially erect, he would inevitably seize me with
his proboscis, I threw myself on my back with some violence ;
in which position, and without shouldering the rifle, I fired
upwards at random towards his chest, uttering, at the same
time, the most piercing shouts and cries.   The change of
position, in all human probability, saved my life ; for, at the
same instant, the trunk of the enraged animal descended
precisely on the spot where I had previously crouched,
sweeping away the stones (many of a large size) that formed
the fore part of my ' skärm ' like so many pebbles.   In another
moment his broad fore-feet passed directly over my face.

" I now expected nothing short of being crushed to death.
But, imagine my relief, when, instead of renewing the charge
he swerved to the left, and moved off with considerable
rapidity—most happily without my receiving other injuries
than a few bruises, occasioned by the falling of the stones.
Under Providence, I attribute my extraordinary escape to the
confusion of the animal caused by the wound I had inflicted
on him, and to the cries elicited from me when in my utmost
need.

" Immediately after the elephant had left me I was on
my legs, and snatching up a spare rifle lying at hand, I

pointed at him as he was retreating, and pulled the trigger; but, to my intense mortification, the piece missed fire. It was a matter of thankfulness to me, however, that a similar mishap had not occurred when the animal charged ; for had my gun not then exploded, nothing, as I conceive, could have saved me from destruction.

" During this incident, the rest of the elephants retreated into the bush ; but by the time I had prepared my skärm, they reappeared with stealthy and cautious steps on the opposite side of the pool, though so distant that I could not fire with any prospect of success. As they did not approach nearer, I attempted to stalk them, but they would not allow me to come to close quarters ; and after awhile moved off altogether.

" Whilst pondering over my late wonderful escape, I observed, at a little distance, a huge white rhinoceros protrude his ponderous and misshapen head through the bushes; and presently afterwards he approached to within a dozen paces of my ambuscade. His broad side was now fully exposed to view, and, notwithstanding I felt a little nervous from my conflict with the elephant, I lost no time in firing. The beast did not at once fall to the ground, but from appearances I had every reason to believe he would not live long.

" Scarcely had I reloaded when a black rhinoceros (a female, as it proved) stood drinking at the water ; but her position, as with the elephant in the first instance, was unfavourable for a good shot. As, however, she was very near me, I thought I was pretty sure of breaking her leg, and thereby disabling her ; and in this I succeeded. My fire seemed to madden her ; she rushed wildly forward on three legs, when I gave her a second shot, but apparently with little or no effect. I felt sorry at not being able to end her sufferings at once ; but as I was too well acquainted with the habits of the rhinoceros to venture on pursuing her under the circumstances, I determined to wait patiently for daylight, and then destroy her with the aid of my dogs. But it was not to be.

"As no more elephants or other large game appeared, I thought after a time it might be as well to go in search of the white rhinoceros, previously wounded ; and I was not long in finding his carcase ; for my ball, as I supposed, had caused his almost immediate death.

"In heading back to my skärm, I accidentally took a turn in the direction pursued by the black rhinoceros, and by ill luck, as the event proved, at once encountered her. She was still on her legs, but her position, as before, was unfavourable; hoping, however, to make her change it for the better, and thus enable me to destroy her at once, I took up a stone and hurled it at her with all my force ; when, snorting horribly, erecting her tail, keeping her head close to the ground, and raising clouds of dust with her feet, she rushed at me with fearful fury. I had only just time to level my rifle and fire before she was upon me ; and the next instant, whilst instinctively turning round for the purpose of retreating, she laid me prostrate. The shock was so violent as to send my rifle, powder-flask, and ball-pouch, as also my cap, spinning in the air ; the gun, indeed, as afterwards ascertained, to a distance of fully ten feet. On the beast charging me, it crossed my mind that unless gored at once by her horn, her impetus would be such (after knocking me down, which I took for granted would be the case) as to carry her beyond me, and I might thus be afforded a chance of escape. So, indeed, it happened ; for having tumbled me over (in doing which her head, and the fore part of her body, owing to the violence of the charge, was half buried in the sand), and trampled on me with great violence, her fore-quarter passed over my body. Struggling for life, I seized my opportunity, and as she was recovering herself for a renewal of the charge, I scrambled out from between her hind legs.

"But the enraged beast had not yet done with me.

Scarcely had I regained my feet before she struck me down a second time, and with her horn ripped up my right thigh (though not very deeply) from near the knee to the hip : with her fore-feet, moreover, she hit me a terrific blow on the shoulder near the back of the neck. My ribs bent under the enormous weight and pressure, and for a moment, I must, I believe, have lost consciousness—I have at least very indistinct notions of what afterwards took place. All I remember is, that when I raised my head, I heard a furious snorting and plunging amongst the neighbouring bushes. I now arose, though with great difficulty, and made my way, in the best manner I was able, towards a large tree, that was near at hand, for shelter ; but this precaution was needless. The beast, for the time at least, showed no inclination further to molest me. Either in the *mêlée*, or owing to the confusion caused by her wounds, she had lost sight of me, or she felt satisfied with the revenge she had taken. Be that as it may, I escaped with life, though sadly wounded, and severely bruised, in which disabled state I had great difficulty in getting back to my skärm." For other most remarkable adventures, we must refer the reader to Mr. Andersson's recent and valuable volume.

CHAPTER. XIX.

THE KAFFIRS.

Characteristics of the Kaffirs—Their Dress, Food, and Mode of Life—Amusing Incident—Bartering at a Fair—Right against Might—Rain-makers and their Impostures—Controversy with one of them—The War-dance—Irruption of Kaffir Clans—Attack on a Moravian Village—Story of the Slagt-boom, or Slaughter Tree—Perfidious Outrage—Surrender of 'Kaffirs to the Colonial Authorities.

The Kaffirs living beyond the Fish River, on the eastern boundary of the colony, form one tribe of the great Bechuana family. Their national character is bold, warlike, and independent. From these qualities, as well as from the cast of their countenance, some have conjectured that they are of Arabian origin. The men are extremely tall and well-proportioned, many being six feet and more in height; the women are said to be good-tempered, animated, and cheerful, with teeth beautifully white and regular, and without the thick lips or flat noses of most of the natives of Africa; but they form a strong contrast to the men in the lowness of their stature, their figures being short and sturdy. Their name of Kaffir, or unbeliever, was originally given to the inhabitants of the south-eastern coast of Africa by the Moors, and, being adopted by the Portuguese, it became the common appellation of all the tribes occupying that region.

The following sketch was from the life :—

> " Lo ! where he crouches by the Kloof's dark side,
>   Eyeing the farmer's lowing herds afar ;
>   Impatient, watching till the evening star
>   Lead forth the twilight dim, that he may glide

Like panther to the prey.   With freeborn pride
    He scorns the herdsman—nor regards the scar
Of recent wound—but burnishes for war
    His assagai and targe of buffalo-hide.
'He is a robber ?'—True ; it is a strife
    Between the black-skinned bandit and the white.
 'A savage ?'—Yes ; though loth to aim at life,
    Evil for evil fierce he doth requite.
 'A heathen ?'—Teach him, then, thy better creed,
    Christian, if thou deserv'st that name indeed ! "

The manner of life of these people is, in general, extremely simple.   Their diet mostly consists of milk, which is
kept in leathern bottles until it is sufficiently thick and
acidulous.   They eat also boiled corn, which is usually served
up in small baskets, from which each one helps himself with
his hands.   They sometimes make of their corn a kind of
pottage; at other times they form it into thick cakes, which
are baked on the hearth.   They lay up provisions for winter
use, either in pits or subterranean granaries.   An occasional
feast of animal food, with the articles now mentioned, are
sufficient for the support of this hardy race.

The apparel of the Kaffirs consists wholly of the skins of
beasts, so prepared as to render them perfectly soft and
pliable.   Sometimes they are long enough to reach to the
feet, hang loosely from the shoulders in the manner of a
cloak, and are, in general, the only covering adopted by the
men.   To protect themselves from the parching effect of the
sun's rays, they anoint themselves from head to foot with
some unctuous substance.   The same materials are used by
the women, but their dress is of a different shape.

The chief wealth of the Kaffir consists in his herds of
cattle.   Nothing affects him more than an injury done to his
horned creatures, whose increase and prosperity appear to
occupy the chief place in his thoughts, and to be the ruling
motive of his actions.   The more laborious occupations of
tillage, of felling wood, and of building dwellings, are per-

GROUP OF KAFFIRS.

formed by the women, whose life, after marriage, is indeed one of bondage.

Of one Kaffir group Mr. Rose says :—"There was one young and finely-formed girl, with her wild expressive eyes, and beautiful teeth, on whom I flatter myself with having made an impression. Her mode of showing it was singular. She picked some vermin from the hairy side of her caross, and offered them to me; and on my exhibiting some symptoms of disgust, laughed most heartily at my fastidiousness, and put one in her mouth, to show that it was good. It was the first mark of attachment which I had received since I left Cape Town, and I was affected accordingly; and had but the refinement of sentiment been added to so touching a proof of love—had she but sung—

> ' I give thee all, I can no more,
> Though poor the offering be,'

I know not what the consequences might have been."

The bartering said to be practised at a fair is worthy of notice. The Kaffir having articles to dispose of, sits down amidst his comrades, waiting the approach of a colonial dealer, who produces his beads and other species of traffic. Neither party understands the other's language, yet it seldom happens that an interpreter is present, and the negotiation is therefore carried on by signs.

Should the beads or other commodities offered not be considered by the Kaffir sufficient for the transfer of his own produce, a shake of the head adequately denotes his dissatisfaction. More beads, perhaps, are then added on the one side, dissent being still manifested on the other, until, as the dealer is not disposed to make any further advance, the affair terminates, without agreement, to the vexation of the bead-merchant, whose time and patience have been so unprofitably exhausted; but to the utter indifference of the Kaffir, whose imperturbable coolness is an additional source of chagrin to the unsuccessful bidder. A second and a third dealer often display their ornamental treasures with similar failure, and it not unfrequently happens that the tenacious Kaffir departs without disposing of his commodity, which he brings to the next fair, and perhaps exchanges ultimately for articles of less number and value than had previously been offered.

When a bargain of any magnitude is concluded, the chief is generally at hand to substantiate his claim, considering himself entitled to a certain portion of the profits as his tribute, in consequence of his territory having been made the scene of traffic. His retainers are therefore dispersed throughout the fair, to watch the various negotiations, and summon their chief at the close of any considerable bargain, no fraction of the payment being touched by the salesman before his arrival. The chief is sometimes extortionate. A traveller having expressed to an interpreter his surprise that on one occasion a Kaffir should have submitted, without remonstrance, to the greedy demands of the chief Gaika, he shook his head significantly, and, showing his mutilated hand, replied, "I once ventured to remonstrate with him myself, when he flew into a rage, and would have thrust his assagai through my body, had I not parried the javelin with my hand, and luckily escaped with the loss of my thumb."

A different story is told of the chief Macomo. An Englishman, being dissatisfied with the conduct of a slave he had brought into Kaffraria from the Cape Colony, after some altercation and a few strokes from his whip of rhinoceros hide, carried him before Macomo, the chief of a tribe near the river Keissi. Here the master and slave filed cross bills against each other. The slave produced witnesses to prove that his master had abused and struck him without cause; and the master accused the slave of laziness, insolence, and disobedience, and demanded that he should be punished by a severe flogging.

Macomo, having heard both parties, informed them that

BIVOUAC OF KAFFIRS

in Kaffraria there are no slaves, and that he must therefore consider them merely as two men who had made a bargain with each other. "Now, it appears," said he to the Englishman, "that you have struck this man, and otherwise ill-treated him; but you can show no proof that he had injured you by offering you violence. I therefore declare your bargain at an end. He is free to go where he pleases, and you shall pay him an ox for the wrong you have done him."

The decision highly incensed the Englishman, who refused to submit. "He deserved punishment, not reward," said he, "for his insolence." "You have not proved that," said Macomo; "but had it been so, you should have brought him to me. Why do I sit here, if need be, from sunrise to sunset? It is to decide between man and man in cases where their anger blinds them, and hinders their judgment. If men use their hands in secret, instead of their tongues before the judge or the old men, whose life would be worth a husk of corn?"

The traveller replied that he would not argue the matter with Macomo, "as he was ignorant of the usages of civilised life, and did not understand the rights of property. I will complain of your conduct," he added, "to Major Somerset, the commander of the frontier, who will soon show you the difference between an elephant and a deer." To this taunt Macomo calmly replied, "I know that Somerset is stronger than I am. He is an elephant, but neither I nor my father has been called a deer. You say that your people are wiser than ours. You do not show it in appealing from reason to force. When you return to the colony, the landdrost will decide between you; here it can go no further. Give him the ox," he added; "it will be better for you." The ox was given.

The tribes of South Africa, like the Mandans of North America, the natives of Ceylon, and many other widely separated people, have their rain-makers, who pretend to

15

command the clouds by means of certain magic charms of which they have the secret.

These impostors have most power in countries which are subject to frequent droughts, and where the people depend for subsistence on corn or cattle. Such is the case with the Kaffirs, among whom the belief prevails that rain can be withheld or granted at the will of their Igiaka-lumsulu, or rain-doctor.

They therefore seek the aid of one of them with much ceremony. The chief and his attendant warriors proceed in state to his dwelling with presents of cattle ; and after signifying their request, they institute a feast, which often lasts many days, during which the impostor pretends that he is using his magic charms.

One of the devices is to collect a few leaves of each kind of tree from a neighbouring forest, to be simmered in large pots over a fire, and then to kill a sheep by pricking it in the heart with a long needle, while the range of superstitious ceremonies is passed through. As the simmering goes on and steam arises, it is supposed to ascend and render the clouds propitious, so that the needed showers descend. Meanwhile the dance is joined in by all the tribe; it is continued throughout the day, and when midnight comes it still goes on ; it may be accompanied with songs, in which the praises of the rain-maker are shouted in a long-continued chorus.

This act, however, is often premature ; for the rain-maker fails ; the young corn often withering for want of the genial and refreshing showers. Other expedients are then tried. Thus, a large circle is formed of young men ; they encompass the side of a mountain which the klif-springer loves to haunt, and, gradually contracting their range, they commonly succeed in taking captive several of these little antelopes. The voices of these animals are supposed to attract rain. The cunning practitioner, trusting not to any natural sounds, urges them round the kraal, and calls forth their screams by pinchings and other tortures. Should all his efforts prove abortive, he seeks safety, like other impostors, in flight, when, on the continuance of drought, the aid of some other of his tribe is eagerly coveted.

When visitors arrive wanting aid, he often amuses them by pretending to work his witcheries, and they are, at length, dismissed with a variety of instructions, on the due observance of which the expected boon is made to depend. These instructions are generally of the most trivial nature : they are not to look back on their journey home; or they are not to speak; or they are to compel every one they meet to return home with them ; and so on. If rain occurs, the credit, of course, is assumed by, and conceded to, the rain-maker ; if disappointment ensues, they blame themselves for not having adequately carried out the instructions they received. The idle ceremony is again repeated ; the poor people have again to make presents, to feast, and to receive instructions ; thus much time is consumed, during which the season of drought frequently passes away. One of the most intelligent of the Kaffirs once visited a missionary, Mr. Shaw, and said he was determined to have the question set at rest, whether or not the rain-maker could produce rain. "We will have our rain-maker summoned to meet you in an open plain, where all the Kaffirs of the surrounding kraals shall be present to judge between you and him."

This was agreed to, and at the appointed time and place thousands of Kaffirs from the neighbouring country appeared in their war-dresses. Mr. Shaw being confronted with a celebrated rain-maker, declared openly that God alone gave rain ; and offered to present the rain-maker with a team of oxen if he should succeed in causing any to descend within a certain specified time. This was agreed to ; the rain-maker commenced his ceremonies, which are said to have been well calculated to impose on an ignorant and superstitious people. The time having expired without any signs of rain, the chief who had convened the meeting inquired of the rain-maker why he had so long imposed upon them? The rain-maker evaded the question, and complained that he had not been paid well enough for the rain, and he appealed to all present to say whether rain had not always been forthcoming on proper remuneration.

Mr. Shaw now pointed out some half-famished cattle belonging to the rain-maker which were to be seen on an adjacent hill starving for want of pasturage : thus clearly proving that had he possessed the skill to which he pretended, it was not likely he would have neglected his own interests. To this the rain-maker adroitly replied, addressing the people : " I never found any difficulty in making rain, till *he* came among us" (pointing to Mr. Shaw); " but now, no sooner do I collect the clouds, and the rain is about to fall in copious showers on the dry and parched soil, than there immediately begins a sound of *ting, ting, ting*" (alluding to the chapel bell), " which puts the clouds to flight, and prevents the rain from descending on your land." Mr. Shaw could not decide as to the effect of this ingenious plea on the majority of the Kaffirs; but he had the satisfaction of knowing that the intelligent native who consulted him on the subject never made any more presents for rain.

Steedman describes an occasion when Gaika, the Kaffir chief, accompanied by his wives, and a large retinue of attendant warriors, had been permitted to enter Fort Wiltshire, on the Keiskamma River, and were exhibiting to its inmates the peculiar and terrific war-dance of his tribe.

" This," he says, " was a performance, indeed, far more adapted to astonish than to please, exciting alarm rather than admiration, and displaying in rapid succession the habits and ferocious passions of a savage community. Let the reader picture to himself a hundred or more unclad Africans, besmeared and disfigured with copious defilements of red clay, and assuming with frantic gestures all the cha-

racteristic vehemence of a furious engagement. **The dance**
commenced with a slow movement to a sort of humming **noise**
from the women in the rear, the men stamping and **beating**
time with their feet, until the gradual excitement occasioned
a simultaneous spring with corresponding shouts, when **the**
action proceeded to an unnatural frenzy, and was calculated **to**
produce in the mind of a stranger the most appalling sensations. The dusky glare of the fire blazing in front of **these**
formidable warriors, during their wild and unearthly evolutions, gave an additional degree of awful effect to **this**
extraordinary scene ; and all that I had ever read in **poetry**
or romance of the Court of Pandemonium, or the Hall **of**
Eblis, fell infinitely short to my imagination, compared with
the realities before me. It was indeed a most seasonable
relief amidst the bewildering fancies of the moment, to **hear**
the gratifiying sound of ' All's well ' from the sentries on **the**
outposts of the fort, which imparted to the mind a feeling **of**
security and composure that, as may well be conceived, **was**
truly welcome."

A traveller, wishing to survey the scenery in the vicinity
of the White River, started one morning before sunrise, **and**
set out on horseback on an exploratory ramble, accompanied **by**
a Hottentot guide on foot, equipped with his gun and hunting
gear. The sun had not yet risen over the bushy hills as **they**
proceeded down the valley, and every tree and flower **was**
bright and sparkling with dew, diffusing a grateful feeling **of**
freshness in this thirsty land, where rain is precarious **and**
often long denied. The rich fragrance of the wild African
jessamine, clustering with its white flowers around the **rocks**
and aged trees, agreeably attracted attention, and recalled **the**
thoughts of the traveller to far distant scenes, where he **had**
seen the same beautiful shrub, or a species nearly resembling
it, naturalised in the rigorous clime of Britain. Blue-bells,
too, almost precisely similar to those of the Scottish braes,
were growing among the tangled brushwood through **which**

11

they wound their way; and a small bird now and then
chirped a few wild notes, which so much resembled the pre-
luding quiver of the wood-lark, as to be almost startling
But the song died away in a feeble trill, and all again was
silent, save the cooing of turtle doves, which, even in the
autumn of South Africa, is continually to be heard at early
morn, in a woodland country, and which produces a soothing
though somewhat monotonous effect.

After proceeding a mile or two down the river, they
struck into a path on the left hand, which led into the
bosom of a jungle, behind the woody heights which bound
the White River on the south.   The path on which they now
entered led them along a sort of valley, or rather avenue,
through the forest of evergreens and brushwood, which
covered the undulating country as far as the eye could reach
This avenue consisted of a succession of grassy savannahs,
often of large extent, opening into each other through the
jungle, and affording a wide range of excellent pasturage for
the herds of the settlement.   It had, however, the disadvantage of being destitute of water, excepting after heavy
rains ; and another serious drawback was the extreme hazard
to which the cattle pastured in it, as well as their keepers,
were exposed during the disturbances with the Kaffirs, in
consequence of the extent of jungle that surrounds it.   Of
this danger sufficient demonstration was exhibited to the
traveller by his guide pointing out, as they passed along, the
spot where, a few years before, nine of his comrades were
slaughtered, and of which he gave the following account.

During the irruption of the Kaffir clans, after the inva-
sion and devastation of their country by the colonial government in 1819, the mountains and forests of the Zureberg
were occupied by numerous marauding bands of these barbarians, who poured themselves into the colony in a state of
great exasperation, resolved either to recapture the cattle of
which they had been plundered, or to indemnify themselves

by carrying off those of the colonists. They had already several times menaced the Moravian village of Enon with nightly attacks; and as it was well known that parties of them were lurking in the vicinity, the cattle of the community were constantly guarded by ten or twelve of the most courageous and steady Hottentots armed with guns. The Kaffirs have no other arms than *kirries* and *assagais*, that is, clubs and javelins; and they knew from experience, that these herdsmen were unerring marksmen, and that their own weapons and mode of warfare were but ill-fitted to compete with the firelock. They had determined, however, at all hazards, to possess themselves of the fine herd of cattle belonging to the settlement, and they proved successful.

The Hottentots had one day driven the cattle up this avenue into one of the open spots, or woodland prairies, already described, and observing no fresh traces of the enemy, seated themselves in a group, about a hundred paces from the side of the jungle, and began to smoke their pipes, each with his loaded gun lying down beside him on the grass. The Kaffirs, who were eagerly watching all their motions from the neighbouring heights, judged that this was a favourable opportunity to attack them. Creeping through the thickets, with the stealthy pace of the panther, they advanced cautiously to the skirts of the copse-wood nearest to the herdsmen; and then crouching in silence till they observed them eagerly engaged in conversation, and with their faces turned in a different direction, they burst out upon them suddenly, with their frightful war-whoop. Pouring in a shower of assagais as they rushed forward, they almost instantly closed, club in hand, with the few not already transfixed by their missiles. So sudden and unexpected was the onset, that only two of the ten Hottentots had time to fire. Two of the assailants fell; but their loss was bloodily avenged by the slaughter of nine of the herdsmen, one of their number escaping by flying to the jungle, with two assagais sticking in his body ; and the cattle of the settlement, to the amount of upwards of a thousand head, became a prey to the enemy.

The men thus slain were among the best and most industrious of the little community, and all of them left wives and families to deplore their untimely fate. The event overwhelmed the settlement with lamentation and dismay ; and as the cattle were the chief support of the inhabitants, and as an attack on the village was nightly anticipated, the Moravian institution was soon afterwards abandoned, and its inmates took refuge in the district town of Uitenhage, where they were received with much sympathy, and treated with great kindness both by the inhabitants and the government functionaries. From this place of refuge they subsequently returned.

As a rude wagon track approaches a glen, the path is closed in on either side for a considerable distance by the tall jungle, so luxuriant in its growth that one would suppose even a wolf or a leopard would scarcely be able to find a way through it. The path itself, originally tracked out by the elephants, appears to have been widened by the axe just sufficiently to allow a single wagon to pass along, and it now formed the only access on this side to the upper part of the glen. This pass is called the *Slagtboom;* and it is said to have acquired its name from the following occurrence :— Many years before the Kaffirs were dispossessed of this part of the country, and finally driven over the Great Fish River, the chief Congo and his clan occupied the White River valley and the fastnesses of the adjacent mountains in great force. During one of the struggles that ensued, in consequence of Congo's attempt to maintain himself in possession of this district, a party of seventy or eighty boors were sent to occupy this glen, while other troops environed the Kaffir camp from the opposite side. The boors rode in without opposition through this pass ; but, finding the enemy stronger than they expected, they became alarmed, and attempted to retreat by the same road. The Kaffirs, however, who on this occasion showed themselves to be not destitute of military skill, had in the meantime blocked up the narrow path, by stretching a large tree across it near the centre, and fastening it with thongs and wattles at either end ; and then stationing themselves in strong bands among the copsewood, they attacked the boors on all sides, as soon as they had fairly entered the defile, with showers of javelins, and slew a great number of them before they were able to force a passage through. From this bloody catastrophe the spot obtained the name of *Slagtboom* or *Slaughter Tree*.

In 1811 a great effort was made by the colonial government to expel the Kaffirs from this quarter of the country, which they claimed as their own, having occupied it, in fact, for the greater part of a century, and having, as they alleged, and it is believed truly, twice purchased it—first from the Hottentots, and afterwards from the boors. Their claim of possession, however, whether just or otherwise, the colonial government had determined not to recognise, and orders were suddenly issued to *invite* them to evacuate this territory, and, if they refused immediate compliance, to drive them by fire and sword across the Great Fish River. At the time when the colonial troops assembled to carry this order into execution it was in the summer, when the corn and vegetables of the Kaffirs were not fully ripe ; and the hardship of their being obliged to abandon their crops, and, consequently, to suffer a twelvemonth's scarcity, during which many must perish of absolute famine, was urgently pleaded to obtain a short respite. Their remonstrances, however, were not listened to ; the peremptory mandate was given to remove instantly.

During these transactions, while the Kaffirs were highly exasperated by what they considered cruel and oppressive treatment, and were beginning to assume a very hostile attitude, the chief magistrate of the district, old Landdrost

Stockenstrom, sought a conference with some of the principal chiefs, with the benevolent purpose of endeavouring to persuade them to evacuate the country peacefully, in order to avoid the devastation and bloodshed that must otherwise ensue. Mr. Stockenstrom was much respected by the Kaffirs, on account of the justice and humanity he had displayed when disputes had occurred between them and the colonists ; and, trusting to their characteristic good faith, he had repeatedly ventured among them with a very slender escort.

It was reported that on the present occasion, for an interview was not declined, a message was secretly sent him by one of the chiefs warning him not to trust his safety at that time among them. This warning, however, as well as the earnest dissuasions of some of his own people, Stockenstrom, though a cautious as well as a brave man, disregarded, and met the Kaffirs in the forest of the Zureberg with only about a dozen or fifteen attendants. Whether the chiefs who acceded to this meeting were accessory to any premeditated plan of treachery does not appear to have been clearly ascertained, but certain it is that Stockenstrom and his party were suddenly attacked in one of the dangerous defiles of the forest, near the spot appointed for the conference, and most of them massacred. One of the few who escaped saved his life by flying into the forest and creeping through the thickets "like a jackal," as he expressed it, until he reached a place of safety.

This perfidious slaughter appears, on satisfactory evidence, to have been perpetrated by a band of the Ammadankee tribe, a broken clan, who entertained an inveterate, deadly animosity towards the colonists, of the origin of which the following account is given.—About the year 1770, the boors of Bruintjes-hoogte invited the Ammadankee clan of Kaffirs, of whom Jalumba was then chief, to meet th m on the western bank of the Great Fish River, for the purpose of holding a consultation on some public matters. The Am-

madankee attended the meeting, where a peaceable conference was held, and they were entertained with brandy
and tobacco. After which the boors said they had brought
a costly present for their good friends the Kaffirs ; and,
having placed some rush mats on the ground, they spread
upon them a profusion of beads, and invited their visitors to
make a scramble and display their activity in picking them
up on a signal being given. The boors then retired a little
distance to where their guns were lying loaded with two or
three bullets each. The promised signal being given by the
Veld-cornet Botman, the Kaffirs, dreading no guile, rushed
upon the beads, overturning one another in their eagerness
to seize a share of these tempting trinkets. At this instant
the boors, seizing their firearms, poured in a volley on their
unsuspecting visitors with so destructive an aim that very
few, it is said, escaped the massacre. The residue, having
lost their chiefs, and their principal men, became a " broken
clan," abandoned the banks of the Fish River, and sought
refuge in the Zureberg with their chief Congo and their
countrymen of the tribe of Tinde ; and it was some of the
descendants of this unfortunate family, who, remembering
that day of treachery and murder, now seized the opportunity of revenging the wrongs of their race on the colonists. A son of their old oppressor, Botman, was among the
slain.

War with the Kaffirs has, unhappily, been long familiar
to the English mind, but on this painful subject we do not
intend particularly to enter. It must suffice to say that this
race of people has been greatly diminished in number, and is
likely, before long, to become less and less. At the commencement of the present year, some 30,000 or 40,000 of
them gave themselves up to the colonial authorities at the
Cape, and are, at the present time, largely employed as
servants and labourers.

In the review of the past, it is pleasant to record that

Sir George Grey, the Governor of the Colony, has lately proceeded, with the consent of the Colonial Legislature, beyond
the limits of his government, on a mission of benevolence
and peace. At the earnest request of all parties concerned,
he has undertaken a mediation between a Free State which
has been established north of the Orange River, and Moshesh,
the formidable chief of the Basutas. In this resolution it is
easy to recognise the operation of a becoming and judicious
policy.

When the Cape Colony, by the events of war, passed
finally into British hands, it was, as we have seen, occupied
by a Dutch population, beyond the limits of whose somewhat
circumscribed settlements resided various tribes of native
origin, thinly scattered and curiously mixed. The Bushman
was probably the earliest tenant of the soil; but he had
receded before the Hottentot, and the Hottentot before the
Kaffir ; until the actual occupation of the country had come
to be determined by a species of conquest not differing greatly
from our own. About thirty years ago the frontier of
the colony was defined towards the north-east by the course
of the Orange River, beyond which the jurisdiction of our
government was not presumed to extend.

Although the European settlers were but thinly planted
on the territory, yet the irresistible exigencies of pastoral life
induced a few of the colonists as early as 1825 to struggle
across the Orange River in quest of fresh fields and more
productive pastures ; but it was not till eleven years later
that the emigration in this direction assumed any serious
proportions. Then, however, occurred an exodus which, in
relation to the numbers of the colonial population, was really
considerable, and in its character and consequences more
important still.

The Dutch farmers, or boors, had become actively hostile
to British rule. Without speculating on the cause of this
enmity, it will be enough to say that a large body of them

crossed the frontier, and fought their way through dangers and difficulties, until they reached Natal, where they proceeded to establish a Batavian Republic. Such an event naturally demanded the attention of the British Government, for the boors were British subjects, and their migration had been accompanied by alarming disturbance on the colonial border.

It was at that time, as it always has been, our professed policy to put limits on our territorial progress, to avoid, if possible, the extension of our dominion, and to preclude the risks of war and its results by cultivating the goodwill and amity of the chiefs beyond the frontier. But our precautions in this respect were utterly nullified by the proceedings of the boors, who, assuming, as was in fact the case, that the tribes claiming a general ownership in the soil had little better title than themselves, showed small scruple or consideration in selecting their new settlements, and the result appeared accordingly in confusion, discord, bloodshed, and peril. To extirpate these elements of danger we followed the boors to Natal, asserted our sovereignty in that province, and left Natal to become a British settlement, dependent on the Crown Colony of the Cape. Upon this, the boors, animated by an invincible fanaticism, wheeled off to the west, crossed the Drachenberg range of mountains, and established themselves in the spacious district to the north of the British possessions between the Orange and Vaal rivers.

In this region they maintained their institutions for some time, though always under the same conditions of conflict and with similar liabilities on the part of the colonial government. At length, in the year 1848, when Sir Harry Smith was Governor of the Cape, another step was taken. In the exercise of his administration he discovered a disposition on the part not only of the native chiefs, but, as it appeared, on that of the boors also, to place themselves immediately and actually under British sovereignty.

11*

At that time the boors seem to have acquired the ascendancy, and to have alarmed the chiefs for the safety of their possessions, though the contest was still stubbornly maintained on both sides; but the upshot of the negotiations was that the supremacy of the British Government was definitely and directly proclaimed. These measures were but half agreeable to the authorities at home, who were impressed with a laudable horror of extending obligations which had already been found to carry with them so heavy a charge. However, as it was represented that our supremacy would be sincerely welcomed by both parties, and that its exercise would cost us nothing, the position was accepted, and the settlements of the boors became attached to the Cape Colony as the Orange River Sovereignty.

Six months sufficed to show that the misgivings of the Home Government were well founded, for in August, 1848, Sir Harry Smith was suddenly called upon to quell something like an insurrection in the new sovereignty. In this he succeeded, but when, some two years later, a fresh Kaffir war broke out, it became presently evident that the Orange River Sovereignty would aggravate our troubles. The chiefs quarrelled with each other, and all quarrelled with the boors, while both sides, instead of deferring to our authority, found their sole ground of agreement in caballing against the protectorship they had invited. Into the events of the Kaffir war, commenced by Sir Harry Smith, and concluded by General Cathcart, we do not enter; but one of the consequences of the contest was, that after a demonstration of our power we retired from the Orange River Sovereignty, evacuated the country, and left the boors to establish there a "Free State," adjacent to which, and beyond the river Vaal, there has also been erected a "Trans-Vaal Republic."

The former of these communities is that on behalf of which the good offices of the Governor has been invoked. Of late years the relative strength of the boors appears to have declined, while that of their antagonists, and especially of the Basuta chief Moshesh, has very considerably increased. This man, indeed, is no common character. In carriage, aspect, and deportment, he is said to be far superior to any other native chief; he can bring several thousand fighting men into the field, and he has recently engaged the forces of the Free State to such purpose as to establish his ascendancy beyond all question. In fact, from all we learn, it seems as if the very existence of the emigrant boors now depended on the protective arm of the British Government.

It is instructive to observe that now, almost for the first time, a considerable European community proves to be no match for the savages who environ it, and that, except for the interference of a stronger power, it might be threatened with actual extinction. The boors appear to have asserted under their free government all the pretensions of a superior race, but to have failed in enforcing them, until at length the war, which perhaps their own assumption provoked, was found likely to be their ruin. There is therefore a loud call for the operations of an irresistible law. Nothing is likely to put any permanent check upon the excursions of pastoral settlers over a half-occupied territory, nor is it probable that any consideration will restrain the advances of the more civilised race. The disputes between the Free State and Moshesh are exactly analogous to those which have recently arisen between our own colonists and Sandilli, another chief, which have only died out from the pure exhaustion of our adversaries under the ravages of a self-inflicted famine; but on the Kieskamma the Europeans were the stronger, whereas on the Orange River that advantage lies with the natives.

It is difficult to see how the colony could long succeed in maintaining a neutrality in such affairs. It was indeed impressed on the authorities before the abandonment of our sovereignty that no wars, however sanguinary, between tribes and settlers beyond the boundary were to be considered as calling for our intervention ; but this indifference, however justifiable in theory, would be difficult in practice. The spectacle of a European community perishing under the hands of savages would scarcely be endurable by those from whose homes the emigrants had proceeded, not to mention that the enhancement of native power, and the encouragement of barbarian insolence, might be discerned among the probable consequences. These embarrassments, indeed, are exemplified in the actual policy of the colonial government, which, after abstaining some time from interference, has at length assumed the office of mediator.

CHAPTER XX.

A LARGE fly, with four long wings, like those of the common dragon-fly, is found in South Africa, as it is in most of the tropical countries. Its egg is laid on the surface of the ground, or just below it, in sandy or loose soils; where the heat of the sun soon causes it to hatch and produce a caterpillar. This creature, at first sight, appears singularly unfitted for the capture of prey; not only is its pace slow, but it can walk in no other direction than backwards. And yet its sole food is the juices of other insects, particularly ants; they are obtained by a very peculiar and remarkable process.

This creature first traces in the sand a circle, the destined limit of its future abode; and then, placing itself inside the circle, it thrusts the hinder part of its body into the sand, and with one of its fore-legs, acting as a shovel, it puts a load on its flat and square head, and then immediately discharges it on the outside of the circle. Walking backwards, and repeating this process, it soon arrives at the part of the circle from which it started; it then traces a fresh circle within the first, and excavates a second furrow; then a third within this, and so it proceeds, repeating these operations, until it arrives at the centre. After the first series of circles is completed, a second, of less diameter and deeper, is begun

16

within it ; and so on with others, until the hole assumes
the appearance of an inverted cone.

Throughout, the power of instinct is clearly observable.
Thus, were all the work done by one leg, the animal would
lose time in recovering from its fatigue, but it avoids this evil.
Having excavated the first circle with one foot, it turns
completely round, so that the second is excavated with the
opposite foot ; and this change takes place during the successive stages of the work. Small stones are jerked out by
its head, just as the sand is, but larger ones cause more
trouble. When the ant-lion meets with one too heavy to
jerk out, it poises the stone on its back, keeps it steady by
moving the segments of its body, and carefully walking up
the ascent, lays down its burden on the outside of the
margin. Should the stone slip off the bearer, and roll
down the side of the hole, it is picked up again, however
often the accident may occur ; but should there be a stone
too large to be removed, the creature abandons the spot, and
finds another that is more suitable.

The pit thus formed is rather more than two inches
deep. When it is ready the ant-lion buries itself at the
bottom in the sand, its jaws alone being visible, and here it
quietly keeps a good look out. Before long some insect,
perhaps an ant passing that way, steps on the margin of the
pit, it may be by accident, or just to see what it is, when the
sand sliding from under its feet, and its struggles hastening
its fall, it drops into the jaws of the ant-lion. If, however,
the particles of sand adhere to each other, in consequence of
rain, and the creature can stop its downward progress, or
even scramble upwards, the ant-lion no sooner perceives this
than he shovels load after load of sand upon his head and
throws them at it so skilfully that it is soon overcome and
falls to the bottom.

The prey has its juices sucked out until only an empty
shell is left. This is jerked out of the pit to a considerable

extent, as if to give no warning of danger to any heedless or curious passer-by. The ant-lion thus catches its food for nearly two years, when the caterpillar sinks deeper into the sand, spins a silken cocoon, changes into a chrysalis, and in about three weeks comes forth a perfect insect.

The bees in Namaqua Land make their nests in the clefts of the rock, and the natives are exceedingly expert in finding them, and extracting the honey, which they keep in leather bags made for the purpose. "I was one day travelling," says Mr. Shaw, "with old Keudo Links, and remarked that he frequently held up his hand above his eyes, and looked towards the sun, which was then descending near the horizon.

" Astonished at the repetition of the act so many times, I inquired of him at what he was looking, when he replied that he had seen some bees flying in the air, and that they were going to their nests, as it was almost sunset. He continued to watch them, and eventually led me to the very place where they deposited their honey. He then lighted his pipe and smoked a little, putting it to the hole at which the bees had entered. On asking him as to his reason for so doing, he said, 'I will make them a little drunk, and then they will not sting.' By this simple process he obtained the honey, and presenting me with the most delicious part, retained for himself the comb containing the young bees, which he ate with high relish, pronouncing it, at the same time, exceedingly rich."

The natives of Africa are often led to the nests of bees by the honey-bird, as it is consequently called. Its instinct leads it, on discovering a nest, to look out for some one to attack it. Known by its piercing notes, it will fly before the person it finds, and rest for him at intervals. By fresh notes it leads him to follow, short ng its strains as they approach the nest; reproving, howev my slowness by its redoubled cries. Having arrived at t nest, it rests quietly on a rock or a bush, till the honey ha een removed, when the comb containing the young bees is left for its portion. Sparrman offered some natives an ample reward if they would assist him in catching a honey-guide, a specimen of which, as a naturalist, he would have highly valued; but they said, "The bird is our friend," and refused to have it betrayed.

Mr. Burchell found a species of the *Gryllus* tribe among the stones, and so exactly like them in colour, and even in

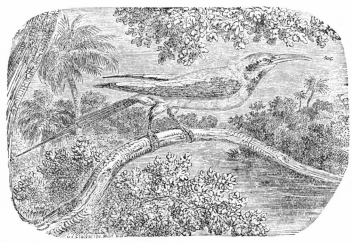

THE HONEY-BIRD.

shape, that it could never have been discovered, had it not been observed just at a moment when in motion; and as if more completely to elude notice, it seldom stirred, and even then but slowly. "The intention of Nature," he remarks, "in these instances, seems to have been the same as when she gave to the chameleon the power of accommodating its colour, in a certain degree, to that of the object nearest it, in order to compensate for the deficiency of its locomotive powers.

By its form and colour, this insect may pass unobserved by those birds which otherwise wou   soon extirpate a species so little able to elude its pursuers."

The Mantis is remarkable for the grotesque forms it assumes. Its resemblance to a portion of a plant is often so great that it is only by its motions its true character is discoverable. Hence it has been called "the walking leaf." The eggs are deposited upon plants, and are covered with a glutinous substance, which soon becomes hard and forms a kind of case, in which they are arranged in a symmetrical manner. The form of the case varies according to the species.

CHAPTER XXI.

THE Secretary bird, which is upwards of three feet in height, is a native of the deserts and mountain gorges of this region. Its name is derived from a tuft of several feathers springing from behind the head, and from some fancied resemblance to pens stuck behind the ear. It has great address in destroying snakes; and hence is often called the "snake-eater."

It is said first to oppose one wing and then the other, to avoid the bite of a snake, as well as to bruise it; it then spurns the reptile with great violence, or takes it in its claws, and dashes it to the ground so forcibly, as often to kill it at a single blow. It has also the power of striking or kicking forwards with its leg, so that with the blow it throws its adversary before it, thereby securing the advantage of keeping the foe fully in sight, and of being prepared to receive and parry its attack. It finishes the struggles of its victim by crushing the skull with its sharply-pointed bill.

The Cape Turtle is a pretty bird, the great length of the tail giving it an appearance of bulk which it does not possess, for the body scarcely exceeds that of a common lark.

A large bird has been met with beyond the Orange River,

sometimes called the Kori Bustard. It measures not less
than seven feet in extent of wing, and is remarkable also for
its bulk and weight. The under part of the body is white,
but the upper part is covered with fine lines of black on a
light chestnut-coloured ground. Its body is so thickly protected
with feathers that the largest sized shot make no impression ;
and hunters, taught by experience, never fire at it but with a
bullet. It is reckoned the best of the winged game in the

THE SECRETARY BIRD.

country ; not only on account of its size, **but because it always**
abounds in fat. The meat of it is not unlike that of the
turkey, but is certainly superior as possessing the flavour of
game.

Birds constantly attend the varieties of rhinoceros, and
are consequently called rhinoceros birds. Their object is to

THE CAPE TURTLE.

prey upon the parasitic insects that swarm on these animals. They are nearly as large as the common thrush, and are of a grayish colour. However soundly the rhinoceros may sleep, a bird of this kind will arouse him, when, springing to his feet, he looks round in every direction, prior to a flight; it is, therefore, an enemy to the hunter.

Mr. Gordon Cumming says: "I have often hunted a rhinoceros on horseback, which led me a chase of many miles, and required a number of shots before he fell, during which chase several of these birds remained with the rhinoceros to the last. They reminded me of mariners on the deck of some bark sailing on the ocean, for they perched along his back and sides; and as each of my bullets told on the shoulder of the rhinoceros, they ascended about six feet in the air, uttering their harsh cry of alarm, and then resumed their position. It sometimes happened that the lower branches of trees, under which the rhinoceros passed, swept them from their living deck, but they always recovered their former station. They also adhere to the rhinoceros during the night. I have often shot these animals at midnight, when drinking at the fountains; and the birds, imagining they were asleep, remained with them till morning, and on my approaching, before taking flight, they exerted themselves to the utmost to awaken 'Chukuroo' from his deep sleep."

A bird, common in some parts of Africa, is called "the little shepherd," from its familiarity in approaching the Hottentots while tending their sheep. In one part of his journey, Mr. Burchell remarks, "Here, in the dead of the night, I heard the soft warbling of some bird, whose wild notes afforded me the greater delight, and seemed the sweeter, from breaking forth so unexpectedly in the cheerless waste, and recalling to me, in the midst of a scene so different, the plaintive nightingale."

A beautiful hoopoe, entirely of a deep purple; a small long-tailed pigeon, seen only in pairs, generally running along the ground as it picks up its food; a very small bird, resembling the golden-crested wren, and of a yellowish green; a small blackish-brown bird, singing with very soft and sweet notes, and apparently not shy; the barbets; and a small

THE SACRED VULTURE

familiar bird, resembling the redstart, hopping under the bushes; are also among the feathered tribes described by travellers.

The species of vulture known as the sacred vulture of

Egypt, may sometimes be seen sailing in the air in great numbers—a constant attendant near the abodes of men, where it descends to feed on carrion and offal. The birds with brown plumage are males, while those with white are females.

An immense flock of the locust-bird may sometimes be seen alighting on the surrounding bushes. It is of the thrush species: the head, breast, and tail of a pale cinereous colour, the wings and tail black. These birds destroy multitudes of locusts, and hence their name.

A beautiful green sugar-bird frequents the thorn trees, attired in splendid plumage. One bird whose habit is to hollow out for itself a hole in the earth, instead of one in the trunk of a tree, is a singular anomaly in the woodpecker tribe. A handsome bird is called the eland-vogel, or eland-bird, from the Hottentots believing it to be an attendant on the eland, or, at least, that it indicates that animal being near. A small finch is a very common bird, and widely dispersed over the whole country. A partridge is observable of a uniform ash-brown colour, everywhere marked with fine white lines, excepting the quill-feathers and the head; the feathers of the breast, each with a white stripe down the middle; the beak and legs of a bright red; but the ridge of the upper mandible, the nails, and the eyes are black.

Klaas, the servant of Le Vaillant, in one of his journeys through a wood of mimosas, discovered and brought to his master a beautiful nest, bearing a strong resemblance to a small horn, suspended, with the point downward, between two branches. Its greatest diameter was two inches and a half, and it gradually diminished towards the base.

" It would be difficult," says this naturalist, " to explain the principle on which such a nest had been built, particularly as three-fourths of it appeared to be entirely useless; for the part which was to contain the eggs, and which was alone indispensable, was not more than three inches from the sur-

face. All the rest of this edifice, which was a tissue closely
and laboriously woven of slender threads taken from the

THE SOCIABLE GROSBEAK.

bark of certain shrubs, seemed to be of no service. The
interior of the nest was not furnished with any kind of soft

material, such as down, wool, or hair; but as the female had not laid her eggs when Klaas brought it to me, it is probable that the nest was not quite finished; a fact proved by the birds being still at work at the time."

Campbell observed two remarkable nests. One was about four yards in circumference, the other three, each being about a yard in depth. They were built of coarse grass, "by," he says, "a small bird which resembles our goldfinch." One of these nests had seventeen holes in the bottom, by which the bird entered; the other had seven. At one time he saw about a hundred birds come out of them.

"Instead of being the nest of a single pair of birds," he says, "they seem to be kraals, or towns of birds. Perhaps one may be the property of a single pair, in which they accommodate all their descendants. A horned owl had taken possession of the outside of the roof of the largest for a nest. She was sitting on it, and it appeared from the bones and hair strewed about that she lived upon the field-mouse. I had the curiosity to climb the tree on purpose to examine this phenomenon in nature. The roof was neatly thatched, and a hollow in the middle to contain the owl, but no passage leading to the inside. I had no way to examine the apartments within, without destroying a great part of the nest, which would have been a cruel operation; wherefore I left it in the state in which I found it, contented with making a drawing of the tree and the two nests."

Another nest was not suspended from the branch, but firmly attached to it. It was about the size of a hogshead, composed of strong, coarse straw, regularly thatched, the ends of the straw pointing downwards, so that no rain could possibly enter. It had eight holes in the bottom for admitting the birds, each leading to a separate apartment. All were lined with the soft, downy heads of a particular species of grass, well suited for the purpose. On dividing the nest across, the large mass above was found to be a solid body of straw.

A still more remarkable structure was observed by Le Vaillant. Having seen a tree with an enormous nest of birds, he sent a few men with a wagon for it, that he might open the hive, and minutely examine it. On its arrival he cut it to pieces with a hatchet, and saw that the chief portion of the structure consisted of a mass of Bushman's grass, without any mixture, but so compact and firmly basketted together as to be impenetrable to the rain. This was the commencement of the structure, each bird building its particular nest under this canopy, the upper surface remaining void, without, however, being useless, for as it had a projecting rim, and was a little inclined, it served to let the rain-water run off, and preserved each little dwelling from the rain.

Thus, then, there was a huge, irregular, sloping roof, all the eaves of which were completely covered with nests crowded against one another. Each one was three or four inches in diameter, which was sufficient for the bird; but as they were all in contact with one another round the eaves, they appeared to the eye to form but one building, and were only distinguishable from one another by a little aperture which served as an entrance to the nest; and even this was sometimes common to three different nests, one of which was situated at the bottom, and the other two at the sides. As the number of cells increased in proportion to the increase of the inhabitants, the old ones, it is said, became streets of communication formed by line and level. "No doubt," says Le Vaillant, "as the republic increases, the cells must be multiplied also; but it is easy to imagine that, as the augmentation can take place only at the surface, the new buildings will necessarily cover the old ones, which must therefore be abandoned. Should these, even, contrary to all probability, be able to subsist, it may be presumed that the depths of their situation, by preventing any circulation and renewal of the air, would render them so extremely hot as to be un-inhabitable. But while they would thus become useless, they would remain what they were before, real nests, and change neither into streets nor sleeping-rooms.

"The largest nest that I examined was one of the most considerable that I had anywhere seen in the course of my journey, and contained three hundred and twenty inhabited cells, which, supposing a male and female to each, would form a society of six hundred and forty individuals. Such a calculation, however, would not be exact." The structure thus described is that of the Sociable Grosbeak.

CHAPTER XXII.

"THE GREAT T'SOMTSEU."

The Curiosity of Colonel Napier excited—Who is this Person?—The Question answered—An Interview with "the Great T'Somtseu"—Story of his Sleeping in a Lion's Den.

LIEUTENANT-COLONEL NAPIER states that he had heard so much of the great T'Somtseu of the South, such marvellous relations of his skill, daring, and eccentricities, that he determined, if possible, to become acquainted with this remarkable character, who, it was stated, had just returned from one of his distant expeditions to Cape Town, where the colonel then was. The extraordinary person alluded to has since become extensively known as Mr. Gordon Cumming.

A few days after receiving much information respecting him from the colonel's host, "a privileged old Life Guardsman," "while sauntering," he says, "under the shade of the fine young oak trees, which line each side of the broad main street at Graham's Town, I beheld an athletic young man, whose extraordinary costume instantly attracted my attention. His dress consisted of a pair of rough 'Veldschoenen,' white trowsers, and shirt, without waistcoat or jacket; a leather girdle tightly encircled his waist, whilst on his head he wore a broad-brimmed hat adorned with jackals' tails, and surrounded by a magnificent plume of the finest ostrich feathers.

"That, thinks I to myself, must be the very man I want to see; I therefore stepped across the street, and asked him at once if his name were not Cumming; and, on his saying it was, after duly introducing myself, I told him I had heard so much of his exploits that I determined to form his acquaintance; and, moreover, having brought out from England a rifle of great calibre, as I found such an article was to me perfectly useless, he might perhaps like to take it off my hands, which reason would, I trusted, be accepted as an apology for so very abrupt a mode of introduction.

"The 'lion-slayer' I had pictured to myself as a swarthy, hairy, sunburnt Salvator Rosa brigand-looking fellow, with a voice of thunder, and with the manners of a savage—in short, in every respect a very Morok *—what was, therefore, my surprise on beholding quite the reverse of all I had imagined! Before me stood a noble-looking young man of about six-and-twenty years of age, standing at least six feet high in his stockings (had he worn such a superfluous article of dress), and, although built like a Hercules, his manly form was most elegantly moulded, surmounted by a finely-shaped head, luxuriantly adorned with silken locks of a flaxen hue, which negligently hung over a countenance of an almost feminine cast of beauty beaming with good nature, and the mildest light blue eyes; and, when he spoke, his silvery and gentle tones emulated the softness of a woman's voice.

"Such was the appearance of the 'great T'Somtseu,' who, after expressing himself flattered at what he pleased to call the undeserved compliments I had paid to his well-earned reputation : 'I dare say,' continued he, in the same soft and attractive tone of voice, 'you have heard that I have turned a regular smouch,† but I think I have a right, as long as I molest no one, to choose my own course of life; for, whilst indulging in the roving and adventurous existence I ever delighted in, I earn what I consider a gentlemanly livelihood, which enables me to follow to the utmost the bent of my inclinations. My wagons are now laden with ivory, carosses, ostrich feathers, and other articles, which I hope will realise

* The tamer of wild beasts, in the story of the " Wandering Jew."
† The colonial term for trader.

17

almost a thousand pounds. This is the produce of nearly a year's amusement; and, when turned into cash, I shall be able therewith to replace the many horses and oxen I have lost, and re-equip myself to start again in quest of fresh excitement, profit, and adventure. However,' added he, 'if you will come to my wagon just outside the town, I shall be very happy to show you its contents, and to give you any information you may require, or, first, if you prefer, we can go and look at your large "elephant roer."' *

"I remarked, as we walked along, I had heard so many marvellous stories put down to his account, that, unless confirmed by himself, they were certainly beyond my power of belief. For instance, said I, only last night, in a circle of friends assembled at Fort England, I heard it positively stated, that you recently not only 'bearded a lion' in his very den, but slew him there, and were afterwards found asleep with your head pillowed on his lifeless carcase.

"'These sort of things,' said he, 'are always exaggerated, and the only credit I deserve is, that of being a tolerable shot, and having pretty good nerves, the sole qualifications required on such occasions. As to the story of sleeping in the lion's den, I have never to my knowledge proved such a Daniel—though, on more than one occasion, I certainly have been asleep, whilst those gentlemen were prowling about so close to me, that I have been awakened by their angry growls.'

"Pray tell me how you ever came to be placed in such a very unpleasant situation."

"'From experience,' replied he, 'I found that the easiest and perhaps safest way of destroying lions was to do so from a hole deep enough to conceal a man's body; and, when I shot a large animal, such as a rhinoceros or buffalo, near a pool of water, or a brook—I often had recourse to the same device. The hole was dug very near the carcase, and, at

* The name for a large gun.

nightfall, I would ensconce myself therein, to wait till the animals that had come to drink should have thoroughly gorged themselves ; when they were, generally speaking, easily knocked over from my place of concealment. I have, however, been so thoroughly fagged on taking up my position, as to have fallen asleep, and been awakened by angry discussions occurring over the mangled remains of the slain. On one occasion, when thus disturbed from my slumbers, I found myself surrounded by five enormous lions, one of which took it into his head to look down over the ledge of the hole which concealed me—but a discharge right in his face caused him to pay with his life the penalty of such impertinent curiosity, and this perhaps may be the story about my nap in the lion's den.' "

CHAPTER XXIII.

THE body of the crocodile, in its figure, resembles that of a lizard; it is depressed, and the back is protected by solid buckles, of a bony texture, with longitudinal elevated ridges, or by large osseous plates, ridged above, and disposed in longitudinal rows. The sides are covered with small rounded or oval plates; and the under surface is sheathed with square, smooth, scaly plates, disposed in transverse rows. The tail is long and tapering, thick at the base, and compressed at the sides, so as to form a paddle. Along its upper surface ridged plates are continued from the back, at first in four rows, which at length emerge into a single row of ridges. The sides of the tail are covered with square scales.

The limbs are short; the fore feet have each five distinct toes, of which the two outermost are destitute of nails. The hind feet have four toes, of which the last has no nail; they are partially webbed. The head is flattened above, the bones, which are rugged, are closely covered with a tough and almost horny skin; this skin is furrowed into compartments, like scales, and it also dips into the winding intervals, between the rugosities of the bone, so as to render them visible.

The entire structure of the crocodile adapts it to its circumstances. In its stomach there are frequently found several stones of various sizes, which have been swallowed, some suppose, to serve as ballast, but this is an error. The fact is, that the stomach of the crocodile bears a strong resemblance, both in its form and structure, to the gizzard of birds; and they, as is well known, swallow stones to triturate the food and assist digestion.

The crocodiles are essentially carnivorous, the scourge of the lakes and rivers in which they dwell. As the eagle is among birds, as the lion is among beasts, so is the crocodile among reptiles. The principal food of these animals consists of fishes, aquatic birds, and such quadrupeds as they can seize on the borders of the water. They employ cunning as well as force in the supply of their wants. Like all carnivorous animals which have often to endure a long deprivation of food, their prey being scarce, these aquatic reptiles can fast for weeks, or even months, without inconvenience. But when opportunity serves, they glut themselves and become indolent and torpid.

When excited by hunger, the crocodile specially displays his force and activity. Where a river enters a lake, or where a lake discharges its superfluous waters, there does the reptile lurk, watching for fish; on which as they pass it darts with surprising velocity. It conceals itself near the spot where animals come to drink, and suddenly rushes from its ambuscade upon them; in the same way it seizes water-birds, and often, also, catches them by swimming quietly under them, and then pulling them down by their legs.

Although sometimes carried inland by floods, the crocodile seldom advances far on shore in pursuit of prey. On land it is by no means difficult to escape its attack; for the legs of the animal are ill-formed for running; and the vertebræ of the neck are so constructed and fitted together, as to render a lateral motion difficult, and the turning out of a straight line not to be accomplished without describing a considerable compass.

The number of eggs varies from twenty to sixty. To deposit them the female comes to a bank, or border of the water, and chooses a sandy place, exposed to the sun ; scraping a cavity for their reception, lining it with dry leaves, and carefully covering them with leaves and sand. The eggs are about as large as those of a swan, and are covered with a parchment-like membrane. In about forty days the young are hatched, and are then about five or six inches in length. The female, who watches the eggs, conducts the young to the water, and supplies them with half-digested food, attending to them till they are able to capture their own prey. The male takes no part in the care of the young. As a proof of their innate ferocity, it may be stated that crocodiles only a foot long have violently bitten the arrows with which they were wounded, and snapped at the archers with malignant fury. Crocodiles of different species are found in South Africa.

On the lower tiers of rivers, amidst flowering bushes and evergreens, alligators bask ; dexterous in the pursuit of fish, by driving a shoal of them into a creek, and then plunging into the terrified mass, and preying on its victims at pleasure. Woe be, too, to the other animals that roam in imaginary safety on the river's banks. Antelopes are eagerly seized, and rarely do they escape the grasp of their subtle and powerful foe. If the animal is too large to be swallowed entire, the alligator conceals it in some hole of the bank, until it begins to putrify, when it is dragged out and devoured under the concealment of the trees and shrubs fringing the river.

The most favourable season for catching the crocodile is the winter, when the animal sleeps, as he usually does, on sand-banks, enjoying the warmth of the sun ; or the spring, after the pairing time, when the female regularly watches the sand islands, where she has buried her eggs. The native discovers the place; and on the south side of it (that is to the leeward), he digs a hole in the sand, throwing up the earth to the side which he expects the crocodile to take.

There he conceals himself; should the crocodile fail to observe him, it comes to the accustomed spot, and soon falls asleep. The huntsman then darts his harpoon with all his force into the animal; for, in order that the stroke may be successful, the iron ought to penetrate to the depth of four inches. The crocodile, on being wounded, rushes into the water; and the native retreats to a canoe, with which a companion hastens to his assistance. A piece of wood attached to the harpoon, by a long cord, swims on the water; and shows the direction in which the crocodile is moving. The natives, pulling by this rope, drag the creature to the surface of the water, when it is pierced by a second spear.

The feat appears more easy in description than it proves in fact. Considerable skill is required in piercing through the crocodile's coat of mail. When, too, the animal is struck, it by no means remains inactive; on the contrary, it lashes violently with its tail, and tries to bite the rope asunder. To prevent this, the rope is made of about thirty separate thin lines, not twisted, but simply placed together, and bound at intervals of every two feet. The thin lines, however, get between the teeth, or become entangled round them. It frequently happens, however, that the harpoons, by the pulling of the men, break out of the crocodile's body, and it escapes.

"If," says Rüppell, " I had not seen the fact with my own eyes, I could hardly have believed that two men could draw out of the water a crocodile fourteen feet long: fasten his muzzle, tie his legs over his back, and finally despatch him by plunging a sharp instrument into his neck, so as to divide the spinal cord."

In some of the rivers of Africa the natives are bold enough, and indeed skilful enough, to combat with the crocodile in its own element; and, armed only with a sharp dagger, dive beneath him, and plunge the weapon into his belly. It often happens, however, that the combat is fatal to the man ; and frequently his only chance of escape is to force his dagger, or, if this be lost, his thumbs, into the animal's eyes with all his might, so as to produce great pain and blindness.

In America the method usually adopted of capturing the alligator is by baiting an extremely formidable four-pointed hook composed of well-constructed wooden spikes, and suffering it to float in the river ; on the creature swallowing it, he is hauled on shore by the rope attached to it, and then slaughtered. Waterton's account of catching a cayman, as it is sometimes called, is amusing. The reptile had swallowed the hook, and was being towed to the shore. The naturalist was waiting for him, armed with the mast of the boat, and determined to force it down the throat of the alligator should he prove restive.

" By this time," he says, " the cayman was within a few yards of me ; I saw he was in a state of fear and perturbation. I instantly dropped the mast, sprung up, and jumped on his back, turning half round as I vaulted, so that I gained my seat with my face in a right position. I immediately seized his fore-legs, and by main force twisted them on his back ; thus they served me for a bridle. He now seemed to have recovered from his surprise, and probably fancying himself in hostile company, he began to plunge furiously, and lashed the sand with his long and powerful tail. I was out of the reach of the strokes of it by being near his head. He continued to plunge and strike, and made my seat very uncomfortable."

In South Africa a similar feat was performed still more recently. A crocodile was shot at and wounded, but though it did not seem that he was much hurt, he immediately rose out of the pond, and attempted to reach a morass. At this juncture a native came up, and, before the crocodile could get away, he threw himself astride over the creature's back, snatched up his fore-paws in an instant, and grasped them doubled up. The crocodile was immediately thrown on his snout ; and though able to move freely his hind feet, and keep his tail in motion, he could not budge half a yard, though he put forth all his power to go forward. The native bravely kept his seat ; his place across the beast being at the shoulders, he only suffered the jerks that were made to throw him off. In this way a huge reptile eighteen feet long was firmly held until another shot pierced his brain.

CHAPTER XXIV.

THE FLY TSETSE.

Its Ravages among Horses and Horned Cattle—Adventure of Mr. Gordon Cumming—His dreadful loss of Oxen by the Tsetse—The Zimb of the Traveller Bruce.

" THERE is an extraordinary fly," says Mr. Gordon Cumming, "in the interior of South Africa, whose bite is certain death to horses and to horned cattle. This interesting, but most destructive fly is called by the natives 'tsetse.' Its bite is never-failing death to horses and horned cattle, though it has no permanent evil effect on man nor on any of the wild beasts.

" I found the buffalo and the zebra, closely allied as they are to the horse and the horned cattle, and a variety of other animals frequenting the districts of this insect, scathless from the poison. The tsetse is fortunately confined to a distance of about two or three miles from the base of the mountain ranges which intersect the forests of the far interior. Thus, a traveller having a correct knowledge of its locality, may penetrate beyond the countries it frequents without losing his cattle, by avoiding the vicinity of the mountains ; whereas, if he has the misfortune to pass through its districts, he will to a certainty lose every horse and ox which he possesses. In the fourth year in which I hunted in Africa I lost, by the bite of this insect, all my draught oxen, and most of my horses. It is no joke to find yourself and your wagons without a horse or an ox at command, a thousand miles from the habitation of your nearest countryman.

" It was in the mountains of Linguapa that I suffered most from the fly tsetse. I was homeward bound on my fourth hunting trip, with my two wagons heavily laden with ivory and other hunting spoils. I had halted under the mountains of Linguapa to hunt the rare and beautiful sable antelope, being assured by a party of hostile natives that the tsetse was not there. My live stock was already much reduced by the varied chances of a hunter's life ; I had suffered much loss by lions ; one night in particular my two especially favourite black shooting horses had been killed and eaten by a troop of five lions.

" After hunting the sable antelope in the romantic mountains of Linguapa for about a fortnight, I remarked, with sorrow and surprise, that my oxen, which were my mainstay, were rapidly falling off in their condition. I became alarmed, and hastily struck my camp, and left the fair, but fatal mountains of Linguapa. My oxen and horses now daily lost their strength, and soon death began to fell their ranks ; their heads were swollen with poison, and, day after day they dropped dead beneath their yokes, and then began a race between death and myself for the Colony.

" Troops and lions and hyænas followed in our tracks, serenading us with their deep and ominous voices by day and night. At length there remained only sufficient oxen to draw one wagon. I then struggled on for a few days longer, bringing on one wagon at a time a short distance, and then sending back the dying team to bring up the other wagon. One day when I had thus parted my two wagons, a long and heavy thunderstorm (such as you never see in England) descended upon our devoted heads. It was with the greatest difficulty that I managed to bring up the second wagon to the first; it was a severe and last struggle for my poor oxen, having accomplished which, most of them lay down and died. I now "hove to," as sailors would say, and having sharpened my axes, I fortified my camp with wait-a-bit thorn trees. and there for weary weeks and weeks, my two wagons lay, like the *Erebus* and *Terror* in the ice, far in the desert, a thousand miles from my nearest countrymen, whom I hardly hoped to see again.

" I remember feeling very desolate on that occasion, and could not help being in low spirits, and entertaining sad forbodings of still greater evils. I had left the colony with a gay cavalcade of sixteen fiery young saddle horses, upwards of forty powerful draught oxen, a herd of she-goats for milk, and a pack of about thirty serviceable dogs, all of which, marching along in their pride and strength, imparted to my caravan something of the appearance which we might fancy exhibited by the patriarchs of old. Such was my caravan when I left the colony nine short months before—to-day, how sad the contrast! The fell hand of the destroyer had swept them from me, like the leaves of the forest before the autumnal gale. *They were all gone!* the hyænas and the vulture had fought over their remains, and their skeletons bleaching on the glowing plain, strewed my line of march ; and, worse than all, poor Hendrick! my faithful follower, had been snatched from my fireside by a ruthless lion. I can never forget the feelings of gratitude with which I beheld the converted natives approach my forlorn position with the teams of draught oxen so generously sent to my relief by the worthy missionary Dr. Livingstone, by whose assistance I eventually regained the colony."

Bruce describes an insect which he calls the Zimb, and remarks : "All the inhabitants of the sea-coast of Melinda, down to Cape Sardefan, Saba, and the south coasts of the Red Sea, are obliged to put themselves in motion and change their habitation to the next sand in the beginning of the rainy season, to prevent all their stock of cattle from being destroyed.

" Of all those that have written upon these countries, the prophet Isaiah alone has given an account of this animal and the manner of its operation (Isa. vii. 18, 19): 'And it shall come to pass in that day, that the Lord shall hiss for the fly that is in the uttermost part of the rivers of Egypt. . . · and they shall come, and shall rest all of them in the desolate valleys, and in the holes of the rocks, and upon all thorns, and upon all bushes.' " It is now generally believed by eminent entomologists, that the tsetse is the Zimb of Bruce.

CHAPTER XXV.

VISIT TO KING MOSELEKATZE.

Moselekatze, the King of the Matebele—Approach to his Capital—Salutes
to Royalty—Um' Nombate, a Peer of the Realm—His Majesty approaches
the Wagons—The Despot described—Offering of Presents—The King's
Return to his Kraal—Adventures with some of the Matebele.

CAPTAIN HARRIS describes a visit which was paid him by
Moselekatze, the king of the Matebele. It was a soft golden
morning, and five miles' travelling over a fertile plain, broken
only occasionally by isolated hills of inconsiderable altitude,
and covered with large herds of oxen, brought him and his
attendants within a short distance of three conical mountains,
disposed in a triangular form, within the area inclosed by
which they were told that the royal kraal would be found.
As their approach was discovered, the tops of the hills became lined with natives, some of whom ran down at intervals
to report their progress; but it was not until they had actually
reached the gorge that a miserable hamlet was perceived, which
was pointed out as the imperial residence.

Two persons guided the wagons, one Hottentot drove the
cattle in the rear, and six others proceeded to advance with
solemn step, saluting the king with repeated discharges of
musketry, as a complimentary mode of announcing their
arrival. Several of the subordinate chieftains, who were
standing near the gateway of the kraal, then advanced, and,
as the wagons ascended the acclivity, took the hand of each
of the party in succession, repeating the word *Fellow! fellow!*
fellow! several times.

"The principal of these men," says Captain Harris, "was

Um' Nombate, a peer of the realm. He was an elderly man, of slight figure, benevolent aspect, and mild but dignified demeanour. He wore the usual tails, consisting of a few strips of wild cat and monkey skin, dangling in front, and some larger, and more widely apart, behind. The elliptical ring was surmounted by the inflated gall-bladder of a sheep. Andries, Piet, and April were old acquaintances, and he appeared glad to see them.

"In reply to our inquiries respecting the health of the king, and whether it was the royal pleasure that we should visit him, he observed that his majesty was very glad we had arrived, and would come to the wagons anon, at the same time directing them to be drawn up outside the gate. The next in rank was a chief of mean and contemptible exterior, whose repulsive manners were but too exactly indicated by his scowling profile. He was deeply scarred with small-pox, and, excepting a necklace of lions' claws, three inflated gall-bladders on his pate, and a goodly coat of grease on his hide, was perfectly naked. I saw nothing remarkable about many of the others. They all carried snuff-boxes stuck in their ears, a collection of skin streamers, like the tails of a lady's boa, attached to a thin waist-cord, being the nearest approach to an habiliment amongst them. All their heads were shaven, sufficeint hair only being left to attach the elliptical ring, which is composed of sinews sewn to the hair, and blackened with grease.

Shortly after the oxen were unyoked, and the tent erected, Mohanycan, the king's page, came forth from the kraal, bearing the congratulations of his majesty. Still he did not come; and Captain Harris, persuaded that he "was dying of impatience" for the presents he had brought, dispatched a messenger, saying that they were extremely anxious to pay their respects, and that everything was prepared for his reception. He soon appeared, attended by his chiefs and some of his warriors. As he advanced, others rushed up with a shout, brandishing their sticks. A number of women followed with calabashes of beer on their heads; and two pursuivants cleared the way by roaring, charging, prancing, and caricoling, flourishing their short sticks in a most furious manner, and proclaiming the royal titles in a string of unbroken sentences. As they advanced to meet him, several of the crowd exclaimed "*Haiyah! haiyah!*" a shout of congratulation and triumph. Having shaken hands they led him into the tent, and seated him in a chair, the courtiers and great men squatting themselves on their hams on the ground, in semicircular order, on either side.

"The expression of the despot's features, though singularly cunning, wild, and suspicious, is not altogether disagreeable. His figure is rather tall, well turned, and active; but through neglect of exercise, leaning to corpulency. Of dignified and reserved manners, the searching quickness of his eye, the point of his questions, and the extreme caution of his replies, stamp him at once as a man capable of ruling the wild and sanguinary spirits by which he is surrounded. He appeared about forty years of age, but being totally beardless, it was difficult to form a correct estimate of the years he had numbered. The elliptical ring on his closely-shorn scalp was decorated with three green feathers from the tail of the paroquet, placed horizontally, two behind and one in front. A single string of small blue beads encircled his neck; a bunch of twisted sinews encompassed his left ankle, and the usual girdle, dangling before and behind with leopards' tails, completed his costume."

Conversation now ensued, and Captain Harris's gifts were presented; but though the king considered it for some time beneath his dignity to evince any symptom of astonishment, at length the sight of so many fine things threw his decorum off the balance. Putting his thumb between his teeth, and opening his eyes to their utmost limits, he grinned like a schoolboy at the sight of gingerbread, patting his breast, and exclaiming repeatedly, "*Monanti, monanti, monanti; tanta, tanta, tanta;*—good, good, good; bravo, bravo, bravo." Ordering an attendant, who was crouching at his feet, to take everything to his kraal, and resuming his solemnity and his seat, tea was then brought in.

Various questions were now put, and answers given on both sides, when the king sent for his dress of state, to show how well he had arranged some materials that had been pre-sented to him by Sir Benjamin D'Urban, Governor of the Cape. It was an apron composed of black goat-skin streamers, loaded with beads of every size and colour, and with a pro-fusion of brass chains and ornaments, disposed in an endless variety of patterns. The production of this article led the king to inquire after the health of the sovereign of England, of whom he said he had heard, and whom he declared to be, next to himself, the greatest monarch of the universe, adding, that the white king's nation was undoubtedly second to his own in power. The dialogue proceeded now very slowly in consequence of the necessity of its being conducted through the tiresome medium of four different languages. At length it flagged altogether. Directing a sheep and sundry calabashes of beer to be placed before his visitors, the king arose, and abruptly, without the slightest compliment, made his exit amid the congratulations of his loyal subjects. The heralds, preceding him as before, rent the air with shouts and exclamations, until "the great black one" had returned to his kraal.

Captain Harris fell in subsequently with several parties of Matabele warriors escorting large droves of oxen towards Kapain. The Africans appeared shy, but the adventurers, unable to hold any communication with them, felt con-vinced that they formed a part of Kalipi's commando—a plundering party. Skirting the deep sedgy channel of the Similakate several miles, they arrived at a point where the river bends suddenly to the eastward, and falls, with no

18

little violence, over a stratum of granite, forming a rough, but complete pavement. It was a considerable task to cross this stony drift, threatening to dislocate the joints of the wagons, requiring the guns and all brittle wares to be removed, and producing some concussions of unusual violence.

A beautiful spot was chosen in which to unyoke for breakfast; it was in the midst of a large grove of mimosas, where the airy parasol-shaped foliage was intertwined above their heads so as to be a perfect defence from the sun's rays, and where the constant and delicious shade allowed the growth of a rich carpet of grass, amidst which arose innumerable gaudy flowers. While the oxen were revelling in this abundance, Captain Harris strolled down the river with his gun in search of some riet-bucks, some of which had before been seen. Here the scenery was beautiful. Three cascades fell brawling over descents of several feet, within a quarter of a mile of each other, flanked by stately timber trees of splendid growth and graceful foliage, which, bending over the limpid stream, were beautifully reflected in its bosom. Huge isolated masses of rocks reared at intervals their stupendous heads. On the top of these were cormorants, those voracious birds devouring an almost incredible amount of fish, and so skilful in diving and chasing the finny tribes under the water that they seldom, if ever, return without having secured their prey; and below were alligators.

On resuming their journey about noon, the route towards an opening in the mountains led Captain Harris's party nearly due south, through an exceedingly rich and fertile part of the country, abounding in verdant savannahs and hamlets, around which large droves of cattle were enjoying a most luxuriant pasture. They were tended by armed herdsmen, and it was surprising to see the oxen leave their grazing and flock around the wagons as they proceeded, snorting and exhibiting signs of pleasure, as though recognising objects with which they were familiar. The appearance, shortly afterwards, of several hundred Matabele warriors in their war costume explained the riddle, and showed that they must be some of the cattle taken from the unfortunate emigrants.

Shortly after this Mohanycan, the guide, left the wagons, and proceeded to a kraal at some distance, for the purpose of communicating to Lingap, the subordinate captain who resided there, the king's orders that he should attach himself to the suite of the travellers. The consequence of this ill-judged proceeding was, that they were deprived of his services at the very moment when they were most required. The warriors, not perceiving any of their own tribe with the party, and having had their hands but lately imbrued in the blood of the white men, could think of nothing but war and plunder. Suspecting, or rather hoping that they had found means to enter the country without the king's knowledge, they closed round the wagons with every demonstration of hostility, instantly and peremptorily requiring the drivers to halt; several, at the same time, placing themselves in front to obstruct the passage. The Hottentots looked aghast, and one of them, in a state of extreme agitation, fainted when he saw a number of wounded warriors borne past on the shoulders of their comrades, whilst others groaned under the weight of accoutrements that had been stripped from the bodies of the slain.

The situation of the party was now critical; one of them, Andries, whether from terror or disgust at having been superseded, showed no disposition to extricate them by explaining the true state of affairs. No one else understood a word of the language. The crowd was now fast encroaching upon them, and their pacific intentions were becoming every moment more questionable. Some even clambered into the the wagons, overhauling their contents, whilst others cast a longing eye at the oxen and sheep. Andries was at length seized by a brawny savage, an event which proved highly

favourable, for, in his agony of distress at the supposed approach of death, he found his tongue, and stuttered out a
brief intimation that they had been the honoured guests of
the king. The name of Moselekatze acted like magic on
his followers. The barbarians were instantly appeased, and,
in a few seconds, were petitioning in an abject tone for snuff,
beads, and tobacco, which being given, allowed them all to
proceed joyfully on their way.

CHAPTER XXVI.

Young Monkey captured by Le Vaillant—Immense Troops of Dog-faced
Baboons—Sagacity and Frolics of one named Kees—The Coranna and
the tame Baboon.

In one of Le Vaillant's excursions he killed a female monkey,
which had been carrying a young one on her back. The
young one continued to cling to her dead parent till the evening quarters of the naturalist were gained, and the assistance
of a Hottentot was even then required to separate the living
and the dead.

No sooner, however, did the young one find itself alone,
than it darted towards a wooden block, on which was placed
the wig of Le Vaillant's father. To this it clung by its
fore-paws most tenaciously; and such was the force of this
deceptive instinct, that it remained in the same posidion
for about three weeks, apparently mistaking the wig for
its mother. It was fed from time to time with goat's milk ;
and at length voluntarily relinquished the refuge of the
peruke. The confidence it ere long assumed, and the amusing
familiarity of its manners rendered it a favourite with the
naturalist's family.

But alas! one morning on entering his private room, the
door of which had imprudently been left open, a strange sight
met his view; for there was the little monkey actually making a hearty breakfast on a noble collection of curious insects.
In the first ebullition of anger, he resolved to strangle the
creature in his arms ; but his wrath soon subsided into pity;
for the crime had carried with it its own punishment—

13

several of the pins by which the beetles were transfixed having been swallowed with them by the monkey. Its agony
became consequently great; and all efforts were unavailing
to preserve its life.

FEMALE MONKEY AND HER YOUNG.

Immense troops of dog-faced baboons inhabit the mountains in the neighbourhood of the Cape, from whence they
descend to the plains to ravage the gardens and orchards. So
cunning are they, that they always place sentinels, to prevent

the main body of depredators from being surprised. They break the fruit to pieces, cram it in their pouches, and keep it till they are hungry. Whenever the sentinel discovers any one approaching, he sets up a loud yell, when all retreat with the utmost precipitation.

Lade describes his going with a party to a mountain, and their amusement in hunting large apes. The arts they practised, and the nimbleness and impudence with which they returned after being pursued, were alike indescribable Sometimes they allowed him to approach so near that he was almost certain of seizing them; yet when he made the attempt, they sprang, at a single leap, two paces from him, and mounted trees with equal agility, from whence they looked at their assailants with great indifference, and seemed to derive pleasure from the astonishment they excited. Some of them were so large, that if the interpreter had not assured them the baboons were neither ferocious nor dangerous, their number would not have appeared a sufficient protection from attack. As it could answer no purpose to kill them, they did not use their guns. One of the party levelled his piece at a very large baboon, that had rested on the top of a tree, after being long and vainly pursued; this so terrified the creature, that he fell down motionless at their feet: they had therefore no difficulty in seizing him, but, when he recovered from his stupor, it required all their dexterity and efforts to make him a captive.

Le Vaillant had a dog-faced baboon with him on his expedition, to which he gave the name of Kees.* This animal was of great service to his master: for he was a better sentinel than any of his dogs; warning him of the approach of beasts of prey, when they seemed to know nothing of the danger. Even they, at length, seemed to rely on him with entire confidence, for they continued to sleep in perfect tranquillity.

* This name is generally given by the farmers in Africa to tame baboons.

Another service was equally singular. "I made him," says the naturalist, "my taster. Whenever we found fruit or roots with which my Hottentots were unacquainted, we did not touch them till Kees had tasted them. If he threw them away, we concluded that they were either of a disagreeable flavour, or of a pernicious quality, and left them untasted. The ape possesses a peculiar property, wherein he differs greatly from other animals, and resembles man—namely, that he is by nature equally gluttonous and inquisitive. Without necessity, and without appetite, he tastes everything that is given him, or that falls in his way."

Kees was often taken by his master when he went hunting; and no sooner did he detect any preparation for the sport, than he evinced the greatness of his joy. On the way he would climb into the trees to seek for gum, of which he was very fond. Sometimes he pointed out to his master the honey he found in hollow trees, or the clefts of rocks. But if he could not meet with either honey or gum, and his appetite was sharpened by running about, he went eagerly in pursuit of roots.

To draw them out of the ground, he laid hold of the herbage with his teeth, stemmed his fore-feet against the ground, then drew back his head, and so gradually pulled out the root. But if this expedient (on which he tasked his whole strength) failed, he laid hold of the leaves as before, as close to the ground as possible, and then threw himself heels over head, which gave the root such a concussion, that it never failed to come out.

Such roots he ate with great greediness, especially one, which, to his cost, his master found very refreshing, and therefore insisted on having his share. Here the cunning of Kees was specially apparent. As soon as he found this root and his master was not near enough to seize upon his share, Kees devoured it in the greatest haste, keeping his eyes all the while riveted on his master. "He accurately measured," says Le Vaillant, "the distance I had to pass before I could get to him; and I was sure of coming too late. Sometimes, however, when he had made a mistake in his calculation, and I came upon him sooner than he expected, he endeavoured to hide the root, in which case I compelled him, by a box on the ear, to give me up my share. But this treatment caused no malice between us; we remained as good friends as ever."

When Kees happened to tire on the road, he mounted on the back of one of the dogs, who was so obliging as to carry him hour after hour. One of them, larger and stronger than the rest, hit on an ingenious artifice to avoid being pressed into this singular piece of service. As soon as Kees leaped on his back he stood still, and let Le Vaillant's train pass without moving from the spot. Till they were almost out of sight the baboon persisted in his purpose, when, finding it was literally "no go," he dismounted; and the two joined the party at their utmost speed. The dog, however, gave the baboon the start, and kept a good look out that he might not be served the same trick again. Still Kees had a certain authority with all the dogs. He could not endure a competitor; if any one came too near him when he was eating, he gave him such a box on the ear as immediately compelled him to retire to a respectful distance.

With the exception of serpents, there were no animals of whom he stood in so much dread as of his own species. Sometimes he heard the cry of other apes among the mountains, and, terrified as he was, he yet answered them. But, if they approached nearer, and he saw any of them, he fled, with a hideous cry, crept between the legs of any persons that were near, and trembled over his whole body. It was very difficult to compose him at all, and it required some time entirely to recover him from his fright.

Kees was addicted to stealing. He well understood how

to loose the strings of a basket, in order to take victuals out, especially milk, of which he was very fond. Chastisement for his thefts produced no amendment. Le Vaillant sometimes whipped him; but then he ran away, and did not return again to the tent until it grew dark. Once, as the naturalist was about to dine, and had put the beans which he had boiled for himself on a plate, he heard the voice of a bird with which he was unacquainted. He left his dinner standing, seized his gun, and ran out of the tent. After about a quarter of an hour he returned with the bird in his hand; but, to his astonishment, found not a single bean on the plate. Kees had stolen them all, and taken himself out of the way.

When he had committed any trespass of this kind he used always, about the time his master took tea, to return quietly, and seat himself in his usual place, looking as innocent as if nothing had happened; but this evening he did not allow himself to be seen. On the following day, too, he was not observed by any of the party, and in consequence some apprehension arose of his being entirely lost. But, on the third day, one of the people who had been to fetch water said he had seen Kees in the neighbourhood; but that as 'soon as the baboon espied him, he was off. Le Vaillant went immediately out, and beat the whole neighbourhood with his dogs. All at once he heard a cry, like that which Kees used to make when his master returned from shooting, and had not taken the baboon with him. He looked about, and at length espied the creature endeavouring to hide himself behind the large branches of a tree. He now called to him with a friendly voice, and made motions to him to come down. But the baboon's trust was gone, and his master was obliged to climb up the tree to fetch him. " He did not attempt to fly," said Le Vaillant, " and we returned together to my quarters; here he expected to receive his punishment; but I did nothing, as it would have been of no use.

"When exhausted with the heat of the sun and the fatigues of the day, with my throat and mouth covered with dust, and my body with perspiration, I was ready to sink gasping to the ground, in tracts destitude of shade, and longed even for the dirtiest ditch-water; but, after seeking long in vain, lost all hopes of finding any in the parched soil. In such distracting moments Kees never moved from my side. We sometimes got out of our carriage, and then his sure instinct led him to a plant. Frequently the stalk was broken off, and then all his endeavours to pull it out were in vain. In such cases he began to scratch in the earth with his paws; but as that would also have proved ineffectual, I came to his assistance with my dagger or my knife, and we hastily divided the refreshing root between us."

An officer, wishing one day to test the fidelity of this baboon, pretended to strike Le Vaillant. Instantly Kees flew into a violent rage, and from that time could never endure the sight of the officer. If he only saw him at a distance, he began to cry, and made all sorts of grimaces, evidently showing that he wished to avenge the insult that had been done his master; he ground his teeth; and tried, with all his might, to fly at his face; but that was out of his power, as he was chained down. The offender several times endeavoured to conciliate him by offering him dainties, but Kees was long implacable.

When any eatables had been pilfered, the fault was always laid first on Kees; and rarely was the accusation unfounded. For a time the eggs laid by a hen were regularly taken away, and Le Vaillant wished to know if the baboon were the offender. For this purpose he went out one morning to watch, and waited till the hen announced by her cackling that she had laid an egg. Kees was sitting on one of the vehicles, but the moment he heard the hen's voice he leaped down, and was running to fetch the egg. When he saw his master he suddenly stopped, and affected a careless position, swaying himself backwards on his hind legs, and assuming a very innocent look. Hypocritical movements, however, only confirmed suspicion, and therefore Le Vaillant pretended not to see him, and turned his back to the bush where the hen was cackling, upon which Kees immediately sprang to the place. His master ran up to him at the instant when, having broken the egg, he was swallowing it. Catching the thief in the fact, a good beating followed, but the severe chastisement did not prevent Kees from stealing new-laid eggs again.

As Le Vaillant was convinced that he should never be able to break Kees of his vices, and that unless he chained him up every evening, he should never be able to get a fresh egg, he endeavoured to accomplish his purpose in another manner. He trained one of his dogs, as soon as the hen cackled, to run to the nest and bring him the egg without breaking it. In a few days the dog had learned his lesson ; but Kees, as soon as he heard the usual sound, ran also to the nest. A contest now took place between them who should have the egg ; and often was the dog foiled, though the stronger of the two ; but if he gained the victory, he ran joyfully with the egg and put it in his master's hand. Kees, nevertheless, followed him, and did not cease to grumble and make threatening grimaces at the dog until he saw the egg was taken, as if he were comforted for the loss of his booty in its not being enjoyed by his adversary. If Kees had got hold of the egg, he endeavoured to run with it to a tree, when, having devoured it, he threw down the shell on his adversary, as if to make game of him. In that case the dog returned with his tail between his hind legs, and that he had met with an unlucky adventure was at once apparent.

Mr. Moffat told Mr. Methuen of a Coranna who had a tame baboon, which, in common with all the monkey race, entertained an intense dread of snakes. Its master from mere wantonness, forcibly entwined a dead snake round the baboon's neck, when the animal sat motionless for upwards of an hour, stupefied with fear, and, on the snake being removed, stole timidly into the hut of the Coranna.

After a short time the baboon, according to custom, was called on by its master to scratch its head, but, though angrily required to do so again and again, it refused to move. The Coranna rose and struck it with a stick, and immediately the aggrieved and enraged creature sprang upon him, and there was a tremendous struggle, the noise of which brought in some of the neighbours.

On entering, however, they could see nothing through the dust raised in the interior of the hut except cinders, which were kicked about in all directions from a fireplace in the centre. The screams of the man and the baboon continued intermingled, till at length the creature dashed out through the by-standers, and escaped to the mountains.

In this encounter the Coranna had been severely bitten, and some weeks elapsed before his recovery. On regaining strength, he determined on revenge, and scoured the mountains in search of the baboon. At last he descried his foe peering over a crag, and instantly levelled his gun. But the baboon was equally prompt in withdrawing his head, and held up, as he chattered loudly in defiance, a monkey companion for the fire of the Coranna. Utterly foiled, he returned to his hut, leaving the baboon in the mountains.

13*

CHAPTER XXVII.

HUNTING THE HIPPOPOTAMUS.

Adventures of Captain Harris—A Hippopotamus Steak—Exploits of Mr. Gordon Cumming—Two of the best Hippopatami in a Herd captured.

CAPTAIN HARRIS and his party arrived at the Gariep of Moselekatze's dominions. Fed by many streams from the Cashan range, this enchanting river springs into existence as if by magic, and rolling its deep and tranquil waters between tiers of weeping willows, through a passage in the mountain barrier, takes its course to the northward.

"Here," he says, "we enjoyed the novel diversion of hippopotamus shooting—that animal abounding in the Limpopo, and dividing the empire with its amphibious neighbour, the crocodile. Throughout the night, the unwieldy monsters might be heard snorting and blowing during their aquatic gambols, and we not unfrequently detected them in the act of sallying from their reed-grown coverts to graze by the serene light of the moon ; never, however, venturing to any distance from the river, the stronghold to which they betake themselves on the smallest alarm.

"Occasionally during the day they were to be seen basking on the shore amid ooze and mud ; but shots were more constantly to be had at their uncouth heads, when protruded from the water to draw breath, and if killed the body rose to the surface. Vulnerable only behind the ear, however, or in the eye, which is placed in a prominence, so as to resemble the garret-window of a Dutch house, they require the perfection of rifle practice, and after a few shots become exceedirgly shy, exhibiting the snout only, and as instantly withdrawing it.   The flesh is delicious, resembling pork in flavour, and abounding in fat, which, in the colony, is deservedly esteemed the greatest of delicacies.   The hide is upwards of an inch and a half in thickness, and being scarcely flexible, may be dragged from the ribs in strips, like the planks from a ship's side.   Of these are manufactured a superior description of *sjambok*, the elastic whip, indispensable to every boor proceeding on a journey.   Our followers encumbered the wagons with a large investment of them, and of the canine teeth, the ivory of which is extremely profitable."

On killing a hippopotamus, Mr. Burchell remarks : " The landscape resembled a flesh-market, where bushes were converted into shambles, and their branches were bending to the ground overloaded with meat.   Whatever way I turned my head, I beheld men, or women, or dogs eating; several large fires were crowded with cooks; all around was carving, broiling, gnawing, and chewing.   Nor did I myself feel the least inclined to reprobate the practice, for, after a long, fatiguing walk, and eight hours' fasting, I confess that a *hippopotamus steak* was not a thing to be rejected; and, even at this moment, I still remain convinced that, if our English lovers of good eating could but once taste such a steak, they would not rest till they had caused ' fine lively hippopotami' to be an article of regular importation."

Mr. Gordon Cumming, while riding along the bank of a river, heard a loud plunge, which was immediately followed by the welcome blowing of sea-cows.   He instantly divested himself of his leather trowsers, and went into the reeds, when he came suddenly on a crocodile of average size, lying in a shallow back stream, and, on the creature attempting to gain the main river, he shot him dead on the spot.   This was the first crocodile he had managed to lay his hands on, though he had killed many.   Soon after breakfast, the chief Seleka, and some of his aristocracy, paid him a visit.

Two days after he sent men down the river, before it was clear, to look for sea-cows, and they soon came running after him to say they had found some. The adventures that ensued are thus given :—

"I followed accordingly, and in a long, broad, and deep bend, came upon four hippopotami, two full-grown cows, a small one, and a calf. At the tail of this pool was a strong and rapid stream, which thundered along in Highland fashion over large masses of dark rock, and on coming to the shady bank, I could at first see only one old cow and a calf. When they dived, I ran into the reeds, and, as the cow rose, shot her in the head; she, however, got away down the river, and I lost her. The other three took up the river, and became very shy, remaining under the water for five minutes at a time, and then popping their heads up only for a few seconds ; I accordingly kept behind the reeds in the hope of their dismissing their alarms. Presently the two smaller ones, apparently no. longer frightened, showed their entire heads, remaining above water for a minute ; but the third, which was by far the largest, and which I thought must be a bull, continued extremely shy, diving under the water for ten minutes and more, letting us see her face but for a second, and, making a blowing like a whale, returning to the bottom. I stood there with a rifle on my shoulder, and my eye on the sight, till I was quite tired. I thought I should never get a chance at her, and had just resolved to let fly at one of the smaller ones, when she shoved up her head and looked about her ; I fired, the ball cracked loudly below her ear, and the huge body of the sea-cow came floundering to the top.

"Though not dead, she had lost her senses, and continued swimming round and round, sometimes beneath, and some-times at the surface of the water, creating a fearful commo-tion, when I finished her with a shot in the neck, upon which she instantly sank to the bottom, and disappeared in the strong and rapid torrent at the tail of the sea-cow hole. Here she remained a long time, and I thought I had lost her, but the natives said she would soon reappear, and while taking my breakfast there was a loud hue and cry that the hippopotamus had floated and was sailing down the river. It was so, and my Hottentots swam in and brought her to the bank; her flesh proved most excellent. In the afternoon I shot a splendid old water-buck, with a princely head, which I kept.

"The next day I rode down the river's bank, with two after riders, to seek for hippopotami, which the natives reported would be found in a pool in advance, where another river joined the Limpopo. After riding a short distance, I found the banks unusually green and shady, and in a broad, deep, and long still bend of the stream the game I sought.

"They were lying in their sandy beds among the rank reeds at the river side, and on hearing me galloping over the gravelly shingle, the deposit of some great flood, they plunged into their native stronghold in dire alarm, and commenced blowing, snorting, and uttering a sound very similar to that made by the musical instrument called a serpent. It was a fairish place for an attack, so, divesting myself of my leather trowsers, I ordered my after riders to remain silent, and then crept cautiously forward, determined not to fire a shot until I had thoroughly examined the herd, to see if there was not a bull, and at all events, to secure, if possible, the very finest head amongst them.

"The troop consisted of about fourteen hippopotami, ten of them being a little further down the stream than the other four. Having carefully examined these ten, I made out two decidedly larger than the others. I then crept a little distance up the river behind the reeds, to obtain a view of the four, and saw that they were two enormous old cows, with two large calves beside them. The two old ones had

19

exactly the same size of head as the two best cows below. I accordingly chose what I thought the best of these two, and, making a fine shot at the side of her head, at once disabled her. She disappeared for a few seconds, and then came floundering to the surface, swimming round and round, diving and reappearing with a loud splash and a blowing noise, and getting slowly down the river, until I reattacked and finished her, about an hour after, a quarter of a mile further down. The other sea-cows were now greatly alarmed, showing, and that only occasionally, but a small part of their heads. I managed, however, to select one of the three remaining ones, and, making a perfect shot, sent a bullet cracking into her brain; this caused instantaneous death, and she sank to the bottom. I then wounded two more sea-cows in the head, both of which I lost; the others were so alarmed and cunning, that it was impossible to do anything with them.

"The one I had first shot was now resting with half her body above water, on a sand-bank in the Limpopo, at the mouth of the river Lepalala, which was broad, clear, and rapid, and from this position I started her, with one bullet in the shoulder, and another in the side of the head. This last shot set her in motion, when she commenced struggling in the water in the most extraordinary manner, disappearing for a few seconds, and then coming up like a great whale, setting the whole river in a vortex. Presently she took away down the stream, but returning I killed her with a shot in the middle of the forehead. This proved a most magnificent specimen of the female hippopotamus. She far surpassed the brightest expectations I had formed of her, being a larger, a more lively, and in every way a more wonderful and interesting animal than certain writers had led me to expect. On securing this fine sea-cow, I immediately cut off her head and placed it high and dry, and this was a work of considerable difficulty for four men. We left the body in the water, being, of course, unable to do anything with it there, and it was well I secured the head when I did, for next morning the crocodiles had dragged away the carcase.

"The body of the other huge sea-cow which I had shot, now floated and became stationary within about twenty yards of the opposite bank of the river. I accordingly held down the river to the tail of the pool, where the stream was broad and rapid, and less likely to hold crocodiles, and although cold and worn out with fatigue, swam across to secure my game. Two of my Hottentots swam over to my assistance; but just as we were going to lay hold of the animal, she became disengaged from the invisible fetters that had held her, a gigantic old tree that some flood had lodged in the bottom of the pool, and floated down the middle of the river; when she neared the tail of the pool we swam in, and, inclining her course to shore, stranded her on a fine gravel bank.

"This truly magnificent specimen was about the same size as the first, and apparently older, but her teeth were not quite so thick. Ordering the natives at once to cut off her huge head, and having seen it safely deposited on the bank, along with that of her comrade, I held for my wagons, having to cross the Lepalala to reach them. I was very much knocked up, but most highly gratified at my good fortune in first killing, and then securing, two out of the four best cows in a herd of fourteen."

CHAPTER XXVIII.

ENON—REV. R. MOFFAT AND KURUMAN.

Explorations of Travellers—A King's Punishment of a Criminal—A Hide asked for as Food—Story of a Damara Doctor—Strange Credulity—The Batlapis—Eloquence of the Basuto King—Disinterested Tribute to Missionaries—Moravian Settlement of Enon—New Lithako or Kuruman, the Station of Rev. R. Moffat, visited by Mr. Methuen—The Balala—Mr. Moffat's account of Moselekatze and Chaka, the Zoolah Tyrant—Station of Dr. Livingstone—His story of the Lion's Attack—Singular Ledge of Rock.

In 1820 the Rev. John Campbell returned to Lithako, and proceeded thence as far east as to the hitherto unvisited city of Mashow, from which he directed his course northward till he reached Kureechanee, about latitude 25° S. South-west from this last town he found himself on the borders of a desert which he was informed extended an immense distance to the westward. In 1823 Lithako was once more visited by Mr. George Thompson, whose accounts of many parts of the country lying between this point of the colony, as well as of some of the Kaffir tribes to the east, were more complete than any previously published.

Mr. Gordon Cumming was the first to penetrate into the interior of the Bamanguato country; his axe and spade pioneering the way which others have since followed. He would have pushed still further onwards, but the great losses he experienced in cattle and horses prevented him from so doing.

One traveller mentions that the king of the Mashows sent for some people to assist him in punishing a criminal. The offender a few minutes before had stolen a goat, and on him summary judgment had been passed. He was laid flat on the ground, and four men held his arms and legs. The chief stood at his head and a servant at his feet, each one provided with a large whip of rhinoceros' skin, and with these they scourged his back with great force. On his receiving a severe beating, the chief was requested to be satisfied; he immediately desisted and ordered his servant to cease beating also. The young man, on rising from the ground, began to say something doubtless in his own behalf, but he was instantly and severely struck by one of those who assisted to punish him. On attempting to speak a second time, he received the same treatment as before, on which he went quietly and put on his cloak. The colour of the man's skin was nearly dark blue, and every stroke left a white mark, so that almost the whole of his back appeared as if it had been rubbed over with a chalk stone.

Sir J. E. Alexander, when passing through Namaqua Land, was asked by some natives for the hide of an ox, for the purpose of eating. The condition of his party at the time, he thus describes: "We had not got any game for some days; a sheep was made to go a long way; and none of us had even sufficient to appease our hunger. The Namaquas asked for a hide that we had kept to make shoes of, and, roasting it at the fire, they pounded it between two stones, and ate it up. I partook of it also, and found it very tough, but not disagreeable to the taste. To be sure at the time I could have eaten my saddle for hunger; and certainly thought that our leather trowsers must soon furnish us with a meal."

The Damaras, in their physical appearance and black colour, approximate to the negroes and natives of Congo, on the west coast. On the state of these people much light has been thrown by Mr. Frank Dalton, a recent traveller.

A young Damara doctor showed Sir J. E. Alexander the way in which he treated his patients—a way not a little singular. He provided himself with a clean wooden milk vessel, and applying it, covered with a piece of skin, to the breast of a man who was lying on his side, and groaning as if sick. The doctor then left him, and sitting down opposite a stone, began to strike it with the stick of his fox-tail handkerchief, and to sing at the same time, "To, to, to, tehei; to, to, to, tehei."

After this he got up and danced round, and looked as if for something on the ground; at last he stopped suddenly, and appearing to find what he sought, he called out sharply, "tet, tet, tet." He then went to the patient, took from his chest the vessel, blew upon it, and pretended to find in it some blood, grease, or a bone, which had been introduced by sleight of hand. Carefully covering the vessel, the doctor ran off with it a little way, buried in the sand what he pretended to have conjured from the patient, and then stamping over it, pronounced the sick to be well!

Instances are given of greater imposture on the one hand, and credulity on the other. Campbell says that numbers of the Corannas had a joint taken from the little finger, which was done with a sharp stone. This operation was performed merely for the purpose of bleeding, in order to remove some pain. "The inconvenience through life," he adds, "arising from such a dismemberment, perhaps never occurred to this ignorant people."

Burchell, who resided for some time among the Batlapis, remarked : "The foulest blot on their character is the indifference with which murder is viewed among them. It excites little sensation, excepting in the family of the person who has been murdered ; and brings, it is said, no disgrace upon him who has committed it ; nor uneasiness, excepting the fear of revenge. Shall we not hesitate to assert that human nature is superior to the brute creation, when we find among this people instances of the fact, that the shedding of human blood, without the pretext of provocation or of offence, and even by the basest treachery, has fixed no infamy on the perpetrator of so awful a crime ; and rarely drawn upon him any punishment from the chief authority ; an authority which the

Giver of Power intrusts to mortal heads, only for the weak, and for the common good ? Such, at least, are the sentiments which they express, and such were their replies to my questions on this subject."

Instances are recorded in which the language used by the natives of Africa, and more especially by the chiefs, has been highly eloquent and impressive. As an example, we may take that of Mosheste, the famous Basuto king, when congratulating his people on the arrival among them of three missionaries :

"Rejoice, you Makare and Mokatchani !—you rulers of cities, rejoice ! We have all reason to rejoice on account of the news we have heard. There are a great many sayings among men. Among them some are true, and some are false; but the false have remained with us, and multiplied—therefore, we ought to pick up carefully the truths we hear, lest they should be lost in the rubbish of lies. We have been told that we have all been created by one Being, and that we all spring from one man. Sin entered man's heart when he ate the forbidden fruit, and we have got sin from him. These men say that they have sinned ; and what is sin in them is sin in us, because we came from one stock, and their hearts and ours are one thing. Ye Makare have heard these words, and you say they are lies. If these words do not conquer, the fault will lie with you. You say you will not believe what you do not understand. Look at an egg ! If a man break it, there comes only a watery and yellow substance out of it; but if it be placed under the wing of a fowl, a living thing comes from it. Who can understand this ? Who ever knew how the heat of the hen produced the chicken in the egg ? This is incomprehensible to us, yet we do not deny the fact. Let us do like the hen. Let us place these truths in our hearts, as the hen does the eggs under her wings ; let us sit upon them, and take the same pains, and something now will come of them."

Alluding to different tribes, such as Bushmen and Corannas, Mr. Thompson remarks : " Persons who have visited them, and are best qualified to appreciate the difficulties to be surmounted in instructing and civilising them, will, if they are not led away by prejudice, be far more disposed to admire the exemplary fortitude, patience, and perseverance of the missionaries, than to speak of them with contempt and contumely. These devoted men are found in the remotest deserts, accompanying the wild and wandering savages from place to place, destitute of almost every comfort, and at times without even the necessaries of life.

" Some of them have, without murmuring, spent their whole lives in such service. Let those who consider missions as idle, or unavailing, visit Gnadenthal, Bethelsdorp, Theopolis, the Kaffir stations, Griqua Town, Kamiesberg, &c. &c. ; let them view what *has* been effected at these institutions for tribes of the natives, oppressed, neglected, or despised by every other class of men of Christian name ; and if they do not find all accomplished which the world had perhaps too sanguinely anticipated, let them fairly weigh the obstacles which have been encountered, before they venture to pronounce an unfavourable decision. For my own part, utterly unconnected as I am with missionaries or missionary societies of any description, I cannot in candour and justice withhold from them my humble mead of applause for their labours in Southern Africa. They have, without question, been in this country not only the devoted teachers of our holy religion to the heathen tribes, but also the indefatigable pioneers of discovery and civilisation.

" Nor is their character unappreciated by the natives. Averse as they still are in many places to receive a religion the doctrines of which are too pure and benevolent to be congenial to hearts depraved by selfish and vindictive passions; they are yet everywhere friendly to the missionaries, eagerly invite them to reside in their territories, and consult them in all their emergencies. Such is the impression which the disinterestedness, patience, and kindness of the missionaries have, after long years of labour and difficulty, decidedly made even upon the wildest and fiercest of the South African tribes with whom they have come in contact ; and this favourable *impression*, where more has not yet been achieved, is in itself a most important step towards full and ultimate success."

The Moravian settlement oi Enon, situate near the centre of the Valley of the White River, and in the midst of the rich and picturesque scenery already described, was visited by a traveller. It stands upon a level spot of alluvial soil, near the margin of one of the largest lagoons formed by the river, and which has been named the Leguan's Tank, from its being frequented by numbers of the large amphibious lizard called the leguan or guana. It was also once stocked with a species of carp common to many of the South African rivers.

The village was laid out in the form of a long street, at the upper end of which were the church and school-room, work-shops, and dwelling-houses of the missionaries. The building of these was interrupted for a time by the Moravians being driven out by the Kaffirs, as has been related. At that period nearly the whole of their cattle had been carried off, and several of the herdsmen slain ; and on their retreat, the missionary village, which was then situate somewhat lower down the valley, had been totally burned down and laid waste by the remorseless enemy. In the brief space, however, of less than six months after their return, and with only a few efficient workmen, these industrious people erected buildings sufficient for their immediate necessities, and for prosecuting the several handicrafts they practise. Extensive gardens and orchards were laid out, and full arrangements made for the completion of their settlement.

The dwellings of the Hottentots at this time were, with a few exceptions, small cabins of a very simple construction. The walls were formed by fixing stakes in the ground, wattling these with sapplings from the thicket, and plastering the whole, both in and outside, with a mixture of cow-dung and sand. This sort of plaster, where lime is scarce and expensive, is used even in the best houses of the colony, as it is in New South Wales, South America, and other countries where the aridity of the atmosphere renders it suitable. If preserved from damp, it is in such climates almost equal in durability to lime, and when well smoothed and white-washed, is in no respect inferior in appearance. The roofs of these huts were generally thatched with reeds or long grass; but, for the superior buildings, a species of very hard rush was used, which will last, it is said, without repair for twenty or thirty years.

The most substantial buildings next to those erected by the missionaries, were two or three small houses built by Kaffir women, who by some accident had been left in the colony, had become Christians, and had joined the institution. In their own country, the Kaffir females have generally the task allotted to them of building the huts, as well as tilling the gardens; they are thus inured to labour, and are consequently more generally industrious and neat-handed than the Hottentot women.

Most of the cottages had little gardens behind, stretching on the one side to the foot of a woody hill, on the other to the bank of a river. In these plots were cultivated maize, Kaffir millet, pumpkins, musk and water-melons, onions, parsnips, potatoes, and some other vegetables. A few young fruit-trees were scattered among them. The extent of cultivation here was certainly much inferior to that at the elder settlement of Gnadenthal, where the whole village was enveloped in a forest of fruit-trees; but, considering the short period that had elapsed since the inhabitants had returned to Enon, as much had been accomplished as could reasonably have been expected. The appearance of the whole place was neat, orderly, and demure. There was no hurried bustle, no noisy activity, even in the missionary workshops, though industry plied there its regular and cheerful task; but a sort of pleasing pastoral quiet seemed to reign throughout the settlement, and brood over the secluded valley.

At the time of the visit now described, there were four missionaries, all natives of Germany. The eldest of these, who was also the superintendent of the institution, was the venerable Mr. Schmitt, well known throughout the colony for his mild urbanity, and his affection for the Hottentot race. After having spent his earlier years as a labourer in the missions of the United Brethren on the desolate coast of Labrador, he was sent to South Africa, where he previously founded another missionary settlement about fifty miles from Cape Town, named Groenekloof (Greencleugh); and having established that on a prosperous footing, he was appointed to his present service. His wife was an English woman; at this period the only white woman in the settlement, and in truth like a mother to every family in it.

The younger brethren were plain German mechanics, but well informed and intelligent in matters relating to the improvement and education of uncivilised people. One was a carpenter, another a blacksmith and cutler. Three businesses they carried on by the aid of Hottentot apprentices, to the great advantage of the institution and the people under their charge.

The missionaries of the United Brethren are usually, if not uniformly, regularly-instructed artisans, educated with this view at Herrnhutt, or some other of the European establishments. The trades selected are of course such as are most likely to be useful amongst a rude and simple people, those of smith and carpenter being the most common. Besides his peculiar trade, each missionary is acquainted more or less with practical husbandry and gardening. Thus, Mr. Schmitt, as well as his younger brethren, had been bred a mechanic, and had assiduously practised his trade as wagon maker when the more important duties of his charge admitted of it.

They are generally excellent workmen; not quite so neat perhaps in matters of taste and finish as first-rate English mechanics; but scarcely to be surpassed in regard to the substantial qualities of the articles they manufacture. In South Africa the wagons made by them, and their knives, and other articles of cutlery, are in high request, and have a very considerable sale, although the cutlery is greatly higher in price than similar goods from Birmingham imported into this colony.

Besides the important advantage of being gradually enabled to instruct a number of the natives in these useful trades, and thus train them to habits of regular industry (one of the most difficult of all tasks with a nomadic and semi-barbarous race), the profits derived from this source are so considerable as to defray a large portion of the expenses of the respective institutions where they are carried on. Being conducted also wholly for the advantage of the missions, and the profits thrown into one general fund, no opportunity is afforded for the growth of unbecoming rivalry, the clashing of private interests, or the development of sordid or selfish passions among the brethren themselves, while, at the same time, without any apparent exertion, a sufficient excitement to steady industry is kept up by the sacred sense of duty, by habits of strict regularity, and the observance of exact hours for every occupation.

There is unquestionably something very touching, as well as tasteful and picturesque, in the appearance of a Moravian burial-ground in South Africa. Situate at some little distance from the village, yet not far from the house of worship, cut out of the centre of a grove of evergreens, and kept as neat as a pleasure-garden, the burial-ground of Enon formed a pleasing contrast to the solitary graves heaped with a few loose stones, or the neglected and dilapidated churchyards usually met with in the colony.

The missionaries here, all without exception Germans,

have, like their countrymen in general, a fine taste for music. The voices of the Hottentots, too, are peculiarly sweet and plaintive ; so that there was nothing vulgar or discordant in their singing, but, on the contrary, a sweet, solemn, and pathetic harmony. Nothing, indeed, can well be conceived more exquisitely affecting than the rich, though simple melody of one of these missionary hymns, when sung by a Hottentot congregation in the bosom of their wild native woods, where, only a few years before, no voice was heard save the howling of wild beasts, or the discordant yell of heathen hordes scarcely less savage.

Another station of great interest is found not far short of a thousand miles from Cape Town ; it was originally called New Lithako, but subsequently it received the name of Kuruman. It has been visited by many travellers, among whom is Mr. Methuen, who, in his "Life in the Wilderness," describes Kuruman as "a sort of metropolis of missionary stations." " Here," he continues, " we found Messrs. Hamilton and Moffat, both in good health, and active as ever in their sphere of usefulness and benevolence. Enduring, at the commencement of their ministerial labours, hunger, thirst, heat, and cold, privations of all kinds, and living in constant danger of death both from men and beasts, they persevered with a resolution and faith reminding us of the apostolic times, and their efforts have been blessed with success.

" They now have few difficulties to contend with. Possessing comfortable cottages, built after the Dutch model, with no upper story, walled and well-stocked gardens, and all necessary furniture, they live independent of, and cut off from the civilised world, beloved by the Bechuanas, who are visibly improving under their teaching. There is a chapel here, built of stone and thatched, capable of containing three hundred persons : the body of it is provided with movable benches and a pulpit. This building and the cottages are all the results of missionary labour.

14

" The appearance of the Kuruman (Anglicé, the Tortoise)
is very pretty; a broad grass walk dividing the cottages

A BECHUANA.

which occupy the one side from the garden or rivulet, and a
rank of drooping Babylonian willows on the other. The

native huts have nothing picturesque about them, and at a distance resemble a collection of hay-ricks ; they are superior to the bee-hive pattern dwellings of the Kaffirs and Corannas, being formed of an outer wall of stakes about three feet high, driven into the ground in a circle, and surrounded by a conical roof thatched with grass. Each hut has a low doorway, with an equally low verandah before it, and round it is a circular court inclosed either with rush mats or a wattle-hedge ; in this court they commonly make their fires, and cook their food in fire-proof clay-pots of their own manufacture.

" Mr. Moffat and his lady were unbounded in their hospitality towards us; they begged us to treat their house as our own, and during the rest of our sojourn in the village we took all our meals there."

In his minute on " Sunday," Mr. Methuen says : " The sound of a bell strangely resounded in these remote regions, calling the Bechuanas to devotion. The service in the chapel was performed in the native tongue; and the congregation was numerous, orderly, and less disturbed by some circumstances which occurred at the time than many English ones would have been. The men wore, mostly, fustian jackets and leather trowsers, the women petticoats of divers patterns, or carosses, with either fur caps on their heads or turbans made of handkerchiefs ; some sat on the mud floor, some on the benches."

The Bechuanas were full of amazement on first seeing good portraits of Mr. and Mrs. Moffat, whose presence they said they were glad of, for otherwise they should have concluded that these were their ghosts, or their skins stuffed. The same idea arose in the minds of some natives to whom Dr. Smith showed some of his drawings of animals; nor could they be convinced that they were not looking merely at their skins until he sketched their own likenesses. No wonder that a galvanic battery filled some of them, as they grasped the brass rods, with superstitious dread, or that one was sure it was an evil spirit, "for," said he, "I saw the blue flame!"

Among the Bechuana tribes are great numbers of people called "Balala"—poor ones—"who stand," says Mr. Moffat, "in the same relation to the Bechuanas in which the Bushmen formerly stood to the Hottentots, and whose origin, doubtless, was of the same nature.

"These Balala were once inhabitants of the towns, and have been permitted or appointed to live in country places for the purpose of procuring skins of wild animals, wild honey, and roots for their respective chiefs. The numbers of these country residents are increased by the innate love of liberty, and the scarcity of food in towns, or within the boundaries to which they are confined by water and pasture. These again formed themselves into small communities, though of the most temporary character, their calling requiring migration, and having no cattle of any description. Accustomed from infancy to the sweets of comparative liberty, which they vastly preferred to a kind of vassalage in the towns or kraals, they would make any sacrifice to please their often distant superiors, rather than be confined to the irksomeness of a town life. Such is their aversion that I have known chiefs take armed men, and travel a hundred miles into desert places, in order to bring back Balala, whom they wished to assist them in watching and harvesting the gardens of their wives; and in such seasons they will frequently wander about, and fix their domiciles in the most desert and unfrequented spots, to escape this easy, but to them galling, duty, which is only required in a year of plenty." Mr. Campbell called them, very correctly, the "Bechuana Bushmen."

Mr. Methuen subsequently remarks: "Many were the interesting anecdotes which Mr. Moffat, with his happy mode of telling a tale, related to us of his former life, and his interviews with Moselekatze. This chief was in the habit of calling Mr. Moffat his father Matchuabi, and used often to say to him, after receiving reproof for his cruelty, 'You can say to me what nobody else dares; were you not my father I should kill you.' Mr. Moffat often prophesied to him his fall (which has since occurred), as well as that of all such bloody oppressors. He would say in reply, 'I cannot make you out ; you do not come here to trade ; you do not seem to fear death, and yet you so much dread others being put to death.'

" By this missionary's account, Moselekatze was short and stout; he was son to Matchuabi, and revolted, in the following way, from Chaka, the Zoolah tyrant. Chaka continually sent commandos, or marauding parties, against the surrounding tribes for the purpose of stealing their cattle. Moselekatze, then one of his captains, was always successful in his attacks, and cunningly reserved portions of the stolen property for himself. He was at last dispatched against a very powerful tribe, on which all former attempts had failed : he gained the victory, and at the same time attended to his own interests.

"Chaka discovered his artifices, and, vowing vengeance, came upon him so suddenly, that Moselekatze and a handful of men, after fighting desperately, only escaped under cover of darkness, he himself hiding in a tree. At daybreak he rallied his men, and defeating in detail three divisions sent against him, fled to the sources of the Likeva River, and established an independent nation there, now called Matabile. His subjects are marked by a slit through their ears like sheep, by which they may be always known, and for desertion the punishment is death. His formation of regiments, regulation of arms and discipline, and his victories, prove him to be a man of great energy and talent."

Not far from the station at Kuruman, is one where Mr., since Dr., Livingstone was zealously labouring as a mission-

20

ary; and he had married a daughter of Mr. Moffat. Just before the visit of Mr. Methuen, he had passed through that struggle with a lion, which he has lately so graphically described.

"We found the lions," he says, "on a small hill, about a quarter of a mile in length, and covered with trees. A circle of men was formed round it, and they gradually closed up, ascending pretty near to each other. Being down below on the plain with a native schoolmaster, named Mebaleve, a most excellent man, I saw one of the lions sitting on a piece of rock within the now closed circle of men. Mebaleve fired at him before I could, and the ball struck the rock on which the animal was sitting. He bit at the spot struck, as a dog does at a stick or a stone thrown at him ; then leaping away, broke through the opening circle, and escaped unhurt. The men were afraid to attack him, perhaps on account of their belief in witchcraft.

"When the circle was reformed, we saw two other lions in it ; but we were afraid to fire, lest we should strike the men, and they allowed the beasts to burst through also. If the Bakatla had acted according to the custom of the country, they would have speared the lions in their attempts to get out. Seeing we could not get them to kill one of the lions, we bent our footsteps towards the villages. In going round the end of the hill, however, I saw one of the beasts sitting on a piece of rock as before, but this time he had a little bush in front. Being about forty yards off, I took a good aim at his body through the bush, and fired both barrels into it. The men then called out, 'He is shot! he is shot!' Others cried, 'He has been shot by another man too; let us go to him !' I did not see any one else shoot at him, but I saw the lion's tail erected in anger behind the bush, and turning to the people, said, 'Stop a little till I load again.'

"When in the act of ramming down the bullets, I heard

a shout. Starting, and looking half round, I saw the lion just in the act of springing upon me. I was upon a little height; he caught my shoulder as he sprang, and we both came to the ground below together. Growling close to my ear, he shook me as a terrier dog does a rat. The shock produced a stupor similar to that which seems to be felt by a mouse after the first shake of the cat. It caused a sort of dreaminess, in which there was no sense of pain nor feeling of terror, though quite conscious of all that was happening. It was like what patients partially under the influence of chloroform describe, who see all the operation, but feel not the knife.

"This singular condition was not the result of any mental process. The shake annihilated fear, and allowed no sense of horror in looking round at the beast. This peculiar state is probably produced in all animals killed by the carnivora ; and if so, is a merciful provision by our benevolent Creator for lessening the pain of death. Turning round to relieve myself of the weight, as he had one paw on the back of my head, I saw his eyes directed to Mebaleve, who was trying to shoot him at a distance of ten or fifteen yards. His gun, a flint one, missed fire, in both barrels ; the lion immediately left me, and, attacking Mebaleve, bit his thigh. Another man, whose life I had saved before, after he had been tossed by a buffalo, attempted to spear the lion while he was biting Mebaleve. He left Mebaleve, and caught this man by the shoulder ; but at that moment the bullets he had received took effect, and he fell down dead."

Mr. Methuen describes his going with a party to inspect a singular overhanging ledge of rock, about ten miles to the west of Kuruman, and says —" We found Mr. Livingstone from the Mabotsa station awaiting our return ; his arm had been broken and much lacer d by a lion he had assisted in destroying. The foolish natives, the Bakatlas, believed that Sobiqua, chief of a neighbouring tribe, was practising witchcraft on them by sending lions, because they had suffered some losses by the attacks of these brutes. They would not permit Livingstone to keep the skin of the lion which had injured him, but buried it carefully, their sages performing some ridiculous ceremonies, which they said would in future deter all lions from visiting Mabotsa."

CHAPTER XXIX.

DISCOVERIES OF LIVINGSTONE.

Knowledge of a Lake in the Interior—Livingstone's first Journey—The Kalahari Desert—The Zouga—The Bayeye—The Lake Ngami—Livingstone's second Journey—His third Journey—Visit to Sebitoané—River of the Barotse—The River Casai—Adventures and Sufferings—The Victoria Falls—Mr. Moffat's Visit to Sechele—His Visit to Moselekatze—Theory of Sir Roderick Murchison—Its establishment by Livingstone—His subsequent Course.

In the years 1835 and 1836 Dr. Andrew Smith made an interesting journey, ascending the mountain heights of Kaffirland, and advancing as far as the southern tropics in the tracks of the traders. The chief object, however, of this expedition was the discovery of a large lake, long reported to be in the interior, but in this he was unsuccessful. This lake had been indicated on maps dated so far back as 1508, relying on the native accounts received by the early Portuguese settlers in South Africa. Campbell, Harris, and other travellers heard of it, and more than twenty years ago, a place was assigned it on the map, which, under the circumstances now to be narrated, it has been found to possess.

On the 1st of June, 1849, Dr. Livingstone, accompanied by Messrs. Oswell and Murray, left the missionary station at Kolobeng, which lies 200 miles north of Kuruman, the station of his father-in-law, the Rev. Robert Moffat.

His object was to gain the lake Ngami, which lies to the north-west of his starting point, and is separated from it by the Kalahari desert, which had hitherto presented an insurmountable barrier to European enterprise. This desert is inhabited by numerous Bushmen and Kalahari, the tract of land probably deriving its name from the latter. They are

14*

a black people, speaking the Bechuana language, and though they possess no large cattle, they rear goats in abundance; they also cultivate beans, pease, calabashes, pumpkins, and water-melons.   The latter appears to be their chief support, and a failure of the annual crop is frequently followed by famine.

In the rainy season water is as abundant in the Kalahari as in any other ·part of the neighbouring countries; and though, from the nature of the country, it is scarce in the dry season, it is by no means entirely wanting. It is well wooded in many parts, and as regards pasturage, may be said to rival the finest prairies of South America.   Of wild animals, such as the giraffe, the zebra, the gnu, the spring-buck, and even the ponderous elephant, which migrates to these regions in the rainy season, there is no want.   It is in search of the latter animal that the enterprising Griqua often risks his life. The Bechuanas make regular excursions into the Kalahari, for the sake of the skins of animals, particularly those of the leopard, the panther, and the jackal.

Many attempts had been made to cross this desert, but all of them had failed.   Determined to explore it by a new path of his own, Dr. Livingstone carefully gathered information from the natives, and, availing himself of this, he advanced by a circuitous route which skirted the desert, and thus diminished the perils of his journey.

Pursuing this route in a northerly direction, for a distance of 300 miles, he and his party suffered much, particularly for want of water ; but at the end of a month, they emerged from the dreary regions they had traversed, and were surprised and delighted by the change.   They now found themselves on the banks of the Zouga, a noble river, flowing in a south-easterly direction, and richly bordered with trees, many of which bore fruit, and were of a gigantic height, and were, moreover, new to the traveller.

The natives of the soil gave Dr. Livingstone and his party

a friendly welcome. The travellers learned from them that the river Zouga flowed out of the lake Ngami, and that it was situated at a distance of about 300 miles. Dr. Livingstone therefore left his travelling-wagon slowly to follow the windings of the stream, and embarked in a native canoe, which had been hollowed out of the trunk of a tree. In this small craft, paddled by fresh-water sailors, he sailed up the Zouga, visiting on his voyage many of the villages, which were surrounded by the broad reeds which grow on its margin, or were built on the limestone rocks through which the waters had found their way.

Captain Messum states that he had heard the inhabitants of the lake regions represented as monsters with only one eye in the centre of the forehead, and feeding on human flesh, as the giants of old used to take their breakfasts. " A baby was nothing ; they swallowed it whole." The researches of our travellers have shown, however, that the people who dwell on the shores of Lake Ngami are called Batoana, and under the rule of Lecholètébè. They are, in fact, a small tribe of the Bechuanas. The Batoana, according to Mr. Andersson, have not long been dwellers in the lake regions ; they arrived as conquerors under the father of Lecholètébè. Having dispossessed the aborigines, they reduced them to a state of slavery, giving them a name corresponding to their condition, namely, *Bakoba* or *Macoba*, that is " serfs." These people, however, style themselves Bayeye, or " Men."

The Bayeye have apparently been established at the lake for a considerable period, if not from time immemorial. They are tall, of a robust form, and of a sooty complexion. Their dress consists simply of a piece of skin, broad in front, tied round the waist, with a tassel attached to it on each side falling down over the hips ; and in addition to this they wear a skin, or light caross, which they accommodate to the body according to the state of the weather. The women wear a short skin shirt.

The only weapon in use among the Bayeye is a light javelin, having sometimes two or three barbs. The older ones have a shield, made of a single fold of ox-hide ; but they have only become acquainted with this defence since they were subdued by the Bechuanas, as to the want of a shield they entirely attribute their own defeat.

They are much given to habits of pilfering and lying, are suspicious and deceitful, and, like most black natives, addicted to intoxicating liquors, and fond of the dance. This is commonly a mimic representation of the playful sports and the courting of different wild animals. They understand the art of making beer from malt, on which they frequently get intoxicated. The men are inveterate snuff-takers, and the women " dakka "—smokers. They live in large round huts, covered with matting made of rushes. Polygamy prevails among them to almost any extent.

In earlier times the Bayeye possessed numerous herds of cattle, but these passed into the hands of the Bechuanas on their assuming the mastery of the country. They are permitted, however, to rear a few goats, which they do less for the milk and flesh than for the skins, which they convert into carosses and other articles.

The country inhabited by the Bayeye before their subjection must have been of great extent, and is still of considerable size, consisting, it is believed by Mr. Andersson, to whom we are indebted for these particulars, of one continued plain, intersected by rivers, with extensive marshes. The banks of the river are in general very low, but wherever they rise a few feet above the level of the water, they are shaded by a rank and wild vegetation ; the trees, of a gigantic size, having their stems and branches entwined and interwoven with beautiful parasitical plants and creepers.

The soil is fertile, and yields the necessaries of life in abundance with but little labour. A month or two before the rainy season, the ground for cultivation is selected, cleared, and slightly worked by a small short hoe. After the first heavy rains they begin to sow the corn, of which there are two kinds indigenous to the country, namely, the common "Kaffir," and another sort very small grained, not unlike canary-seed, which is much more nutritious. Tobacco, calabashes, water-melons, pumpkins, beans, small peas, are also grown, as well as different kinds of edible earth-fruits.

Moreover, the country produces a variety of wild fruit-trees, which serve no less to beautify the scenery than to afford good and wholesome sustenance to the inhabitants. Among the most handsome and useful trees the *moshoma* stands perhaps pre-eminent, on account of its great height, the straightness of the trunk, and the distance at which it begins to branch out. The fruit is gathered on the ground, exposed to the sun for some time, and when sufficiently dried, is put into a hollow piece of wood, a sort of mortar, and pulverised, and is fit to use at any time by simply mixing it with water. It is then not unlike honey in appearance, and has a sweet agreeable flavour, but must be cautiously used by strangers at first, for if eaten in any quantity, it is apt to derange the stomach. The *moshoma* invariably grows on the banks of rivers, or in their immediate neighbourhood, and may be easily conveyed down the Tiogé to the lake. The Bayeye use the timber extensively for canoe building, and in the manufacture of utensils.

Already Dr. Livingstone had expressed the feelings by which he was actuated :—" I do not wish to convey hopes of speedily effecting any great work through my own instrumentality ; but I hope to be permitted to labour, as long as I live, beyond other men's line of things, and plant the seed of the Gospel where others have not planted." These emotions were strong in his bosom as he was passing up this remarkable river. His hope of the benefit of others was increased by the tidings of the natives. He heard that other rivers flowed from the north into the Zouga, and into the lake which was the object of his visit. He was also animated and gladdened by the report that a friendly and powerful chief, named Sebitoané, whom he proposed to visit, lived at the distance of only ten days' journey from his present position.

The object of his search was now speedily gained, and standing on the banks of the lake Ngami, he looked across its broad expanse, and beheld the dim outline of its opposite shore. He found that the lake was 2,825 feet above the level of the sea, and that its length was about sixty miles. Through the unwillingness of the natives, the Bayeye, among whom he now sojourned, to assist the party in visiting the people who dwelt farther north, and from their own want of proper means for crossing the river, he was reluctantly compelled to postpone his visit to Sebitoané. He learned, however, that the Ngami is merely a reservoir for the surplus waters of a much larger lake or marsh, containing numerous islands, about 150 or 200 miles beyond, on one of which was the residence of this chief. The river which falls into the Ngami at its north-west extremity, called the Teoge, has a very strong current, and frequently brings down large trees and carcases of animals. Other rivers were reported as being beyond Sebitoané's district, and a large population was said to live on the banks.

In the year 1850, accompanied by Mrs. Livingstone, his family, and Sechele, the chief of the Bakwains, Dr. Livingstone paid his second visit to the newly-discovered region ; but his hope of reaching the country of Sebitoané was frustrated by the unexpected prevalence of marsh-fever, and of the venomous fly called "tsetse," already described. As, however, the acquaintance obtained with the district on which the lake is situated, and with that through which the Zouga flows, satisfied Dr. Livingstone that neither would afford a salubrious centre for a new mission, and as sickness began to prevail among his party, he was reluctantly compelled to return to his station.

In the spring of 1851 Dr. Livingstone, now rejoined by Mr. Oswell, and accompanied by his own family, left Kolobeng again for the north. Early in June they entered a tract of country excessively dry and difficult for travellers until they reached a small stream called Mambali, emptying itself into a dismal swamp, ten miles broad, through which they had wearily to work their way. Having emerged from this they crossed the Souta, and reached the banks of the Chobe, a large and deep river falling into the Zambese, upon which Linyanti, the residence of Sebitoané, the chief of the Makololo, is situated.

Sebitoané received the party with great kindness, and related the adventures and disasters of his eventful history. For nearly thirty years he had been engaged in warfare, principally with the Matabele, the people of Moselekatze. Several times had he lost his all, and now he owed his security to the noble rivers Chobe and Lecambye, whose broad, deep streams prevented the incursions of his powerful enemies. Amidst a region of swamp and river, dreadfully fatal as it was, he was the ruler of a larger number of people, composed of Basuto, Bakwains, Bamanguato, and the black races, and was also richer in cattle than any other chief in South Africa with whom Dr. Livingstone was acquainted. He had long wished for intercourse with Europeans, and had sent large presents to chiefs who were at a distance to aid in accomplishing this purpose.

.The missionary conducted two religious services amongst these people the day after his arrival. But these were the only ones attended by Sebitoané. The desire he had so long felt seemed now likely to be realised, but he was seized with mortal disease, and in a fortnight he was numbered with the dead. Sorrow was therefore blended with pleasure in the heart of the missionary; pleasure at having seen this chief, sorrow that he had so unexpectedly expired. He was in the midst of the most savage people he had yet beheld; and yet, strange to say, they now gathered around him, en-

treated that he would remain with them, and asked that the
children of Sebitoané might be treated as he would have been
had he lived.

The country is a dead level for hundreds of miles, but
intersected by rivers in all directions, having tributaries absolutely countless, and hence has received the name "Linot-
kanska"—rivers on rivers. It is therefore a contrast to the
region it was long supposed to be. Dr. Livingstone remained
there for two months, but his hope of bringing his own
people here, that they might no longer be troubled and impeded in their progress by the Dutch boors, became entirely
extinct. The land was indeed of extraordinary fertility, but
the tsetse was dreadfully prevalent, and, had this not been
the case, there was a fatal objection in the periodical rise of
the rivers of the country.

It was now that he visited the magnificent stream whose
course to the Mozambique Channel he afterwards traced.
At the point first reached it is called the Sechcke, but, in
different parts of its course, it bears the name of Lecambye
and Zambese ; these various designations meaning simply
"the river." "It is," says Dr. Livingstone, "from 300 to
500 yards broad, and at the end of a remarkably dry season
had a very large volume of water in it. The waves lifted
the canoes, and made them roll beautifully, and brought back
old scenes to my remembrance ; and though the banks are from
sixteen to twenty feet in height, we saw evidence of its annual
overflow fifteen miles beyond. When the wind blows waves
of considerable size rise on its surface, and accidents frequently
occur in crossing. It was quite calm when I went over on
the next morning to hold a service in the town, but as the
time for taking an altitude of the sun approached, the waves
were running so high that it was only by great persuasion I
could induce the people to paddle me back again."

Such was his first glance at the Zambese, which has since
proved to be the key of southern and central Africa. On

the people, however, his interest was specially concentrated; he longed to labour among them as a missionary, and felt that it was only by efforts of this character that they would become truly prosperous. With these emotions he retraced his course partly over the land he had traversed, and partly on the Tamanakle and the Zouga.

The vegetation all along the course of the Zouga is varied and luxuriant, and in some places the scenery is quite charming; the banks of the river being often, to the very water's edge, covered with majestic trees of beautiful and dense foliage. The baobob is particularly conspicuous, attaining not unfrequently round its stem a girth from sixty to seventy-five feet.

Dr. Livingstone says, in a letter to a friend : " The higher we ascended the river the broader it became, until we often saw more than one hundred yards of clear deep water between the broad belt of reed which grows in the shallow parts. . . . . . One remarkable feature in this river is its periodical rise and fall. It has risen nearly three feet since our arrival, and this is the dry season. That the rise is not caused by rains is evident from the water being so pure. Its purity and softness increased as we ascended towards its junction with the Tamanakle, from which, although connected with the lake, it derives its present increased supply. The people could give no reason for the rise of the water, further than that a chief who lives in a part of the country to the north, called Mazzekiva, kills a man annually, and throws his body into the stream, after which the water begins to flow."

Having subsequently accompanied his family to Cape Town, and from thence sent them to England, Dr. Livingstone entered on his fourth and greatest exploratory enterprise. Proceeding towards Kuruman, his course was impeded by trying circumstances; but he proved, to his joy and gratitude, that they were overruled by Providence for good : for during the delay that thus arose, the Trans-Vaal Boors, who had become, unhappily, under the sanction of the British Government, a free republic, cruelly attacked the Bakwains, only because Sechele, their chief, would not obtain for them a monopoly in ivory, by forbidding English traders to pass through his country on their way to the north.

As the boors attributed his refusal to gratify their desire to the influence of Dr. Livingstone, they determined to take on him a murderous revenge. Desolating the station at Kolobeng, and killing sixty of the Bakwains, they hastened to the mission-house, the commandant declaring that he would have Livingstone's head. Frustrated in his purpose by the missionary's absence, the boors proceeded to steal or destroy his property to an amount exceeding in value £300.

After staying some little time at Kuruman, Dr. Livingstone proceeded N.N.W. ; but, anxious to avoid the fly tsetse, by a different route to that he had taken on former occasions. It lay through a densely wooded country, where vines grew luxuriantly, adorned by rich clusters of purple grapes. The grass, however, was from eight to ten feet high, and rendered it necessary for him to have his axe or his whip in hand throughout the day—a toilsome journey, therefore, to man and beast.

On approaching the Chobe, where he had previously found a net-work of rivers, he met with other difficulties, as they now flooded the country. His attendants, with the exception of one lad, were, to add to his anxieties, suddenly attacked by disease ; and, compelled to leave the invalids and the wagon behind, he, almost unaided, worked his way onwards. Crossing the smallest of the streams, not without considerable effort, he and his youthful companion reached one half a mile broad, and abounding with hippopotami. Employing a pontoon which he had brought with him from Cape Town, they now traversed the flooded country in pursuit of the Chobe.

After doing so for about twenty miles, Dr. Livingstone climbed a high tree, and saw to his delight the object of his search ; but a broad *chevaux-de-frise*, formed of various aquatic plants, among which was the papyrus, interlaced with a creeper resembling the convolvulus, almost forbade an approach. Breaking them down so as to secure a foothold above the water, often deep, he and his native attendant urged their way towards the Chobe, taking the pontoon with them. But now appeared another barrier. He says : " A horrid sort of grass, about six feet high, and having serrated edges which cut the hands most cruelly, wore my strong moleskin unmentionables quite through at the knees, and my shoes, nearly new, at the toes." Amidst this, however, he struggled for three days, wading along and wet up to the middle, and at length reached the Chobe, down which they paddled for twenty miles, when they landed at a village of the Makololo. Their astonishment was indescribable ; " we had fallen on them," they said, " as from a cloud, yet came riding on a hippopotamus."

No sooner did the intelligence of their arrival reach Linyanti, than a number of the people were sent from that town in canoes to bring Dr. Livingstone, his companions, and the wagon thither ; there their welcome was most cordial. Sekeletu, the successor of Sebitoané, was filled with delight, and the people were disposed to exult in the anticipation of no ordinary benefits at the hands of their visitor.

In the neighbourhood of the Zambese Dr. Livingstone had the pleasure of observing an immense mass of waters, since called the "Victoria Falls." At a distance of six miles he came in sight of the columns of vapour rising like smoke, and looking like it—for below they were white, and became dark higher up. When about half a mile from the Falls, he left the heavy canoe by which he had come from Secheke, and embarked in a lighter one, with men well acquainted with the rapids, who, by passing down the centre of the stream in the eddies and still places caused by the jutting rocks, brought him to an island situated in the middle of the river, and on the edge of the lip over which the water rolls. Although now within a few yards of this lip, he found it impossible to perceive where the vast body of water went; it seemed to lose itself in the earth, the opposite lip of the fissure into which it disappeared being only eighty feet distant. Creeping with awe to the verge, he saw the solution of the problem.

"I passed down," he says, "into a large rent which had been made from bank to bank of the broad Zambese, and saw that a stream of a thousand yards broad leaped down a hundred feet and then became suddenly compressed into a space of fifteen or twenty yards. The entire falls are simply a crack made in a hard basaltic rock from the right to the left bank of the Zambese, and then prolonged from the left bank away through thirty or forty miles of hills.

"If one imagines the Thames filled with low tree-covered hills immediately beyond the tunnel, extending as far as Gravesend, the bed of black basaltic rock instead of London mud, and a fissure made therein from one end of the tunnel to the other down through the keystones of the arch, and prolonged from the left end of the tunnel through thirty miles of hills, the pathway being one hundred feet down from the bed of the river instead of what it is, with the lips of the fissures from eighty to one hundred feet apart, then fancy the Thames leaping bodily into the gulf, and forced there to change its direction and flow from the right to the left bank, and then rush boiling and roaring through the hills,—he may have some idea of what takes place at this the most wonderful sight I had witnessed in Africa.

"In looking down into the fissure on the right of the island, one sees nothing but a dense white cloud, which at the time when we visited the spot had two bright rainbows on it. The sun was in the meridian, and the declination about equal to the latitude of the place. From this cloud rushed up a great jet of vapour exactly like steam, and it mounted two or three hundred feet high; then condensing, it changed its hue to that of dark smoke, and came back in a constant shower, which soon wetted us to the skin. This shower falls chiefly on the opposite side of the fissure; and a few yards back from the lip, there stands a straight edge of evergreen trees, whose leaves are always wet. From their roots a number of little rills run back into the gulf, but as they flow down the steep wall there, the column of vapour, in its ascent, licks them up clean off the rock, and away they mount again. They are constantly running down, but never reach the bottom."

Dr. Livingstone's stay at Linyanti was not without its important results. It appeared, for example, that Sebitoané had intended a daughter to be his successor, but that she had heartily and gracefully surrendered her title to Sekeletu, who reluctantly accepted it, as there was a claimant of his authority. As Sekeletu had forbidden the sale of children, the pretender to the chieftainship brought into his dominions a slave-trading party, who gave him a small cannon as a reward. Confident now of wresting the authority from the grasp of Sekeletu, he came to the spot where the chief was conferring with Dr. Livingstone, having arranged with his followers that on a signal being given, they should hamstring Sekeletu with a battle-axe. The presence of the missionary, however, saved the life of the chief. The plot was disclosed the same evening by some of the conspirators; and their leader was immediately executed.

Dr. Livingstone overthrew the plans of others who came from the west to purchase slaves; and some of them, hearing that he had crossed the Chobe, fled with great precipitation to their country. He also restrained the Makololo from attacking a stockade in the valley of the Barotse, within which some slave-traders had entrenched themselves, and the

21

consequences of which attack must have proved fatal to many. In various ways he attracted the regard of the people ; and their chief, Sekeletu, indeed, did all in his power to retain his visitor. It was only after considerable delay he was prepared to proceed farther to the north.

Meanwhile Dr. Livingstone's father-in-law, Mr. Moffat, was anxious to send him some supplies, and his own journey for this purpose was one of great interest. After a visit to Sechele and his people, he left his village, in company with Messrs. Chapman and Edwards, whose objects were hunting and trading. They travelled in a northerly direction through a country rather thickly wooded. All this country, and far to the south, was not long since swarming with elephants, giraffes, rhinoceroses, buffaloes, elks, and many species of antelopes, and it might have been thought, from the immense extent of comparatively uninhabited country, that they would have continued to abound for generations to come, but the musket, the rifle, and the swift steed have made them scarce, and the poor natives have to suffer from this cause.

Lopepe is always talked of as a den of lions. It is a valley, at the upper end of which there is a deep hollow covered with reeds, along the outsides of which are deep pits. Lions were heard roaring at a distance.

After visiting Sekhomi, Mr. Moffat and his party journeyed onwards for some days, and on one night halted for a short time at a river, which they afterwards learned was the Serule, literally "do not sit or remain." It appeared to deserve the name, for not only was the water very brackish, but the shores showed that they were the abodes of lions and rhinoceroses. Mr. Edwards obtained here a supply of game.

They subsequently entered amidst a number of high hills, and saw under one a small village of poor people. Some of the men on observing the wagons came, and, as the travellers thought, kindly put them in the right direction, but which afterwards proved too far east. They stated that Sekhomi had sent word that no one should direct them to where Mose-lekatze lived. "Poor fellows," says Mr. Moffat, "as they appeared willing to serve us, they got over the difficulty by stating that if we went in that direction we should reach the Shashe River, which was the same thing. Mr. Edwards very kindly shot a giraffe and a quagga for these hungry children of the desert. They looked very thin, and miserably clad."

About fifteen of the inhabitants of a neighbouring village came with their children to see the wagons, all miserably poor, but very willing to serve the travellers for a few beads. They therefore left with their guides the following morning, and before proceeding far, they passed one of the gigantic moana trees, which may be called "the forest king," and, when in foliage, much resembles an enormous cabbage on a very thick stalk. The height from the ground to the first branches was about twenty feet, with a circumference of thirty-six. Some, it is said, are double this size. It is so soft that a knife may be pushed into the trunk with little difficulty. They halted in time to cut down thorn trees to make a fold. This, though hard, being the work of every day, the Sabbath excepted, they thought nothing of it, having good axes.

They now traversed the eastern verge of the great Kala-hari. When the wagons stood, they had to walk almost to the ankles in fine white sand, which extends in all directions. This part of the country wears a dreary aspect; not a living creature was to be seen except a few cows; and, towards evening, flocks of doves and wild pigeons coming to drink. At a distance an adjutant crane was observed—a place appa-rently not in keeping with its rapacious habits.

On passing through the first range of the Bamanguato hills the scenery became fine. They then passed over a level plain covered with bushes, a few trees, and thick grass. To this succeeded extensive fields of native grain. The town extends for miles along the base of a range of mountains appearing black and sterile, and scantily covered with trees and grass.

Here they met with three traders, and also Sehunéloe, one of the native converts at Kuruman, who had, previously to his settling among the Baharutse at Mosega, as an assistant missionary, come here on a visit. They soon had a swarm of natives around them, as they had heard of the approach of the party, and had seen the missionary's fellow-travellers before. He was set down for the veritable Moffat, of whom they had long heard. They stared at him inquisitively; some asking "Is it he?" while others answered, "It is himself—salute him." Among other curious salutations, they heard some in broken Dutch call out "Good evening—morning." On observing his helper fastening the dogs to the wagons as soon as the oxen were unyoked, he inquired the cause, and found that the Bamanguato were shameless thieves, of dogs not excepted, from the chief to the beggar.

" I sent," says Mr. Moffat, "to convey my respects to his most uninviting majesty, Sekhomi, with a message that my heart was grieved to find that all Livingstone's letters and papers were still here, though Sekhomi had promised to forward them half-way to Livingstone, where was a person waiting to convey them to Livingstone. From all that I have heard of Sekhomi, he has not only a forbidding appearance, but is the very personification of greediness, selfishness, impudence, tyranny, and deceit. Of course I shall treat him with all due respect."

On the following day, having arrived at Shoshong, Sekhomi's town, Mr. Moffat says : " This morning, at an early hour, Sekhomi, who had been often heard to say that he would not give up the letters and papers until Livingstone himself should come with a large reward, sent down the parcels, the very sight of which grieved me. Most of them ought to have been sent a twelvemonth ago.

"Soon after, a number of men presented themselves before

my wagon, and a rather insignificant-looking person saluted me, to which I answered by remarking that I was going to see the chief. He laughed, and added, '*I* am Sekhomi!' I remarked that he was beforehand with me, as it was my duty to wait on him as my superior, according to custom. He admitted this with something like a smile, but appeared quite at a loss to know what to say. He felt he had got into a difficulty and lost my esteem (if ever I had any for him) by not forwarding Livingstone's parcels, for which he knew well he would be rewarded. He tried to get out a sentence or two in palliation of his ungrateful conduct to Livingstone, who I knew had been kind to him, but made such a bungling excuse, that I recommended him to confess at once that he had behaved badly, and I should then hope he would improve some day. I tried to convince him how sorry I was, but he only laughed, and tried to divert my thoughts from the subject, by telling me how glad he was to see me. The subject of Christian instruction was introduced, and its importance enlarged upon, but it proved most unwelcome."

He now proceeded to visit Moselekatze, one object of his doing so being to convey various communications and supplies for Dr. Livingstone, to some point in his proposed journey eastward. That object was finally accomplished by Moselekatze, who appointed twenty of his men, with an officer, to carry on foot seventeen boxes and other packages to the south bank of the Zambese. When the party arrived there with their treasure, they hailed the Makololo on the opposite shore, informed them of the purpose of their visit, and invited them to take charge of what they had brought for "the Doctor"—the name by which the traveller was best known in Africa. Suspecting treachery, the Makololo at first declined. In consequence, the Matabele left the supplies on the banks of the river, and devolved on their suspicious neighbours the responsibility of keeping them safely. After the Matabele had left, the Makololo crossed the Zambese, conveyed the packages to an island, protected them from the weather, and, in that state, Dr. Livingstone found them, more than a year afterwards, in perfect safety.

It was a splendid morning, when thirty-three canoes, manned by 160 rowers, were waiting his signal at Linyanti; and he entered one in which were six athletic and experienced men, who, though the Zambese rolled down in ample volume against them, swept through it at a surprising rate. It is often more than a mile broad, and adorned with numerous islands of from three to five miles in length. These, and the banks, too, are covered with forest, and most of the trees on the brink of the water send down roots from their branches like the banian. The islands at a little distance seem rounded masses of sylvan vegetation of various hues, reclining on the bosom of the glorious stream. The beauty of the scene is greatly increased by the date palm, and lofty palmyra towering above the rest, and casting their feathery foliage against a cloudless sky. The banks are rocky and undulating, and many villages of the people are situated upon them. They are expert hunters of hippopotami and other animals, and cultivate grain extensively. North of this point the river, here called the Lecambye, passes through the country of the Barotse.

The previously unknown region through which Dr. Livingstone had proceeded, like a large portion of the country, watered by the same noble river, abounds with game. Beyond Barotse, the herds of large animals surpassed all that he had ever seen. Among these were elands ; while eighty-one buffaloes defiled slowly before his fire one evening, and sometimes roared at him. Various kinds of antelopes were in great abundance. Multitudes of birds were on the river, and the sand-martins never leave it. And many new trees were observed with interest. The temperature in the shade was about 100 deg. Fahr. during the day, and often 90 deg. at nine at night. At Naride he parted company with the

Makololo, and proceeded with some Barotse to the confluence of the Leeba with the Lecambye.

Pursuing his course with his party first up the Lecambye, and then up the Leeba, he was at length compelled to exchange his pleasant canoe for the back of an ox. On arriving at the latitude of Loando, they pursued a westerly course. Never did he endure such drenchings; and all the streams being swollen, many had to be forded, the water flowing on the rustic bridges waist deep. Others were crossed by sticking to the oxen, and some were swum over. "The Barotse," he says, "did not know I could swim ; and the first broad stream we came to excited their fears on my account. ' Now, hold on fast by the tail. Don't let go.' I intended to follow the injunction, but tail and all went so deep I thought it better to strike out alone for the bank, and just as I reached it I was greatly gratified to see a universal rush had been made for my rescue. Their clothes were all floating down the stream, and two of them reached me breathless with the exertion they had made. If we could march, I got on very well : I don't care much for fatigue ; but when compelled to stand still by pouring rain, then fever laid hold with his strong fangs on the inner man, and lying in a little gipsy tent with everything damp or wet, was sore against the grain."

Dr. Livingstone describes the Casai as a most beautiful river, greatly resembling the Clyde. A finely wooded valley has a slope towards the stream of about five hundred yards. The river itself, about a hundred yards broad, winds slowly from side to side in a glen of great beauty, and then goes to the north and north-east. The traveller was told that he might sail along it for months, and return without reaching its termination.

As he wished now to cross it, and proceeded to do so, serious difficulties arose to his progress. A boy belonging to his party picked up a knife, little thinking that it was dropped as a snare by one of the tribe holding the eastern bank of the river. No sooner had one half of the traveller's attendants crossed the stream, than a charge of theft was made. As Dr. Livingstone was satisfied with their integrity, he desired the complainant to search the luggage for the missing article ; whereupon the lad came forward, and told how he had picked up the knife. Compensation was now demanded by its owner, and it was granted, by the boy giving up a shell which he had worn round his neck.

On another occasion, the missionary, with his attendants, were spending their Sabbath in peace, when they were surrounded by a whole tribe armed with guns, arrows, spears, and short swords, shouting vociferously, and at the same time brandishing their weapons. Dr. Livingstone now asked the chief to sit down as he did, and requiring silence, inquired what was the matter. The reply was one which the reader could not have imagined.

A crime, it was stated, had been committed in one of the Barotse allowing a small drop of his saliva, when spitting, to fall on one of the Chiboque ! Dr. Livingstone replied, that if the chief could seriously declare that this accident was a crime, he was willing to pay a fine ; which was, unhappily, only adding to the long string of exactions which had previously been made. The chief accepted a fine, but it was refused by his warriors, who demanded one thing after another until they required one of the attendants to be sold as a slave. It was now clear that their only object was plunder, and Dr Livingstone and his twenty-seven companions prepared for the worst. Though as a company they were not actually ready for a mortal struggle, a repulse of their antagonists would have been dreadful. They resolved, therefore, to wait for their foes shedding the first drop of blood, and looked calmly on them, shouting as before. This courageous bearing produced the desired effect ; the Chiboque accepted an ox as a fine, and even returned a few pounds of flesh.

So frequently, however, were oxen demanded by the

tribes through whom the party had successively to pass, that they were at length nearly all gone. The traveller's wits came to his relief in this extremity. Having noticed the rejection of an ox which had lost part of his tail, he conjectured that the natives supposed this part had been removed that witchcraft medicine might be inserted, and he cut short the tails of the remaining oxen. His expedient succeeded; henceforth, happily for the state of the supply, the demand ceased.

After a wearisome passage, amidst heavy rains and through a country covered with thick forests, Dr. Livingstone beheld the spectacle which he has thus described:—
" Below us lay the valley of the Quango. If you sit on the spot where Mary Queen of Scots viewed the battle of Langside, and look down on the vale of the Clyde, you may see in miniature the glorious sight which a much greater and richer valley presented to our view. It is about a hundred miles broad, clothed with dark forest, except where the light green grass covers meadow-lands in the Quango, which here and there glances out in the sun as it winds its way to the north. The opposite side of this great valley appears like a range of lofty mountains, and the descent into it of about a mile, which, measured perpendicularly, may be from a thousand to twelve hundred feet. Emerging from the gloomy forests of Londa, this magnificent prospect made us all feel as if a weight had been lifted off our eyelids.

" A cloud was passing across the middle of the valley, from which rolling thunder pealed, while above all was glorious sunlight; and when we went down to the part where we saw it passing, we found that a very heavy thunder-shower had fallen under the path of the cloud: and the bottom of the valley, which from above seemed quite smooth, we discovered to be intersected and furrowed by great numbers of deep-cut streams. Looking back from behind, the descent appears as the edge of a tableland, with numerous indented dells and spurs jutting out all along, giving it a serrated appearance. Both the top and sides of the sierra are covered with trees, but large patches of the more perpendicular parts are bare, and exhibit the red soil, which is general over the region we have now entered."

After the Quango, or, as it is sometimes called, the Congo, was crossed, Dr. Livingstone found himself on Portuguese ground, where he and his party were most kindly received by the half-castes occupying the first settlement on the borders of the river. It bears the name of Cassange, and has in it thirty or forty traders' houses, built of wattle and daub, and scattered irregularly about. The traders are all officers in the Portuguese militia, and are forbidden by the government to cross the Quango, as constant skirmishes with the natives would otherwise take place.

Great as are the resources of the country, they are almost entirely wasted by the Portuguese. Though corn might be grown and cattle fed to an incalculable extent in the splendid valley of the Quango, it yields under their management scarcely anything to the support of man. Moral and physical stagnation and decay press as an incubus on the whole settlement. Still they are remarkably kind and hospitable; and the government is anxious to suppress slavery, and to foster enterprise and trade. Half-castes are nowhere so well treated. Dr. Livingstone remarks : " It was particularly gratifying to me to view the liberality with which people of colour were treated by the Portuguese. Instances, so common in the south, in which half-caste children are abandoned, are rare here."

Most opportune were the attentions received by the traveller until he reached Loando. Already had he suffered from repeated attacks of fever, and from dysentery, so that he could not sit upon his ox for more than ten minutes at a time; and when he entered the city, for which he had long been looking, he was little more than a skeleton. But now among many considerate and generous friends—the most so was her Majesty's Commissioner at Loando, and the only Englishman in the place, Edmund Gabriel, Esq. "I shall never forget the delicious pleasure," Dr. Livingstone says, "of lying down on his bed, after sleeping six months on the ground; nor the unwearied attention and kindness through a long sickness, which Mr. Gabriel invariably showed. May God reward him."

His inquiries and personal observations made during his stay at Laondo, led him to form a high estimate of the beauty and fertility of the province of Angola; and he felt assured that, with proper culture, few regions of the African continent would prove more productive. He found, for instance, that from some seeds many years ago introduced by the Jesuit missionaries, the Mocha coffee had so propagated itself as to spread to the distance of three hundred miles from the coast, where he met with it growing in a wild state. Here its culture is so simple, and its productiveness so great, that a settler, by merely clearing the ground, might, with ordinary application and skill, soon raise large crops, and amass a fortune.

Refreshed by rest, and by the great kindness with which he had been received, Dr. Livingstone set out, under the protection of the Portuguese government. He started intent on fresh discoveries. Emerging from the province of Angola into the country occupied by the Chiboque, the Bushingo, and the Bangala tribes, his progress was retarded by their cupidity and violence. After a time, however, he discovered a great change in the character of the natives, and travelled among friendly tribes. But he found them all deeply imbued with the spirit of trade, and felt great difficulty in getting past many villages, every artifice being employed to detain him and his companions, so that they might purchase their supplies from the natives.

Dr. Livingstone now reached the country of the Barotse,

at a place 800 miles from Loando, where he substituted the
light canoe and the rapid river for the tedious and troublesome mode he had been compelled to adopt.   Having constructed such vessels as were sufficient for his purpose, he
thus wrote to his friends : " You will be pleased to hear that
my men are all in high spirits, and quite prepared for another
trip ; although, as we have had to sell almost everything for
food, they have but little to show after their long absence
from home."

The· current of the river being in their favour, they proceeded rapidly down the Lecambye, and on reaching Linyanti, were heartily welcomed by the chief and his people.
Here Dr. Livingstone thoroughly prepared for his travels to
the east coast.   During the first part of the journey, which
was among the Makololo, he and his companions had nothing
to fear.   Of these there are several races.   The tribe among
which he had resided was only a remnant of those who had
migrated some years before, from the Kalahari desert to
their present locality.   Composed originally of tribes of
Bechuanas, they have introduced the Sichuana language
among the mixed race.   By the persevering labours of Mr.
Moffat, the sacred Scriptures have been translated and printed
in this language.   During his descent of the Zambese, Dr.
Livingstone chiefly came in contact with a tribe of the natives
called the Balonda, a numerous, athletic, and skilful race,
living principally by agriculture, and under the sway of the
Makololo.

Among these people, the relative position of man and
woman is reversed; and although polygamy is practised, the
husband is the worst off.   The women sit in the councils of
the nation.   A young man on marrying is compelled to
move from his own village to that of his wife; he binds himself to provide her mother with fire-wood, as long as she
lives; the wife alone can divorce the husband; and, in the
event of their separation, the children become the property

of the mother. The husband cannot enter into even the simplest contract without the sanction of his wife.

In return, however, for his deference, his wives are expected to supply him with food. The women never want a husband, and an old maid—sometimes, by the way, a very valuable person—is not to be seen from the Cape to the equator. Dr. Livingstone found no instance of rebellion on the part of a husband, but he discovered that a conspiracy among the wives was not uncommon. When the husband happens to offend them, they inflict that cruel punishment of—withholding his dinner; the first sending him to the second, and so on through the series, only to increase his hunger. All he can do—poor mortal—is to climb a tree, and to pour forth such lamentations as these : " Listen, oh listen! I thought I had married women, but they are only witches! I am a bachelor! I have no wife! Is that right for a gentleman like me?"

It may be a few cuffs and blows are added to hunger; but now the authorities of the village interfere, and the tyrannical wife is punished by being compelled to carry her spouse on her back from the place of judgment to his own house. Taunted as she goes by the jeers and gibes of the men, she is cheered by the sympathy and words of the women, such as " serves him right—give it him again." " The first time," says Dr. Livingstone, " I ever had such a sight, was in the case of a great masculine creature, and a withered scraggy old man; and as I was graceless enough to laugh, she could not help joining in it, to the great scandal of young Africa."

Gross ignorance and idolatry are frightfully prevalent among the people. As he passed along the highways, he saw footpaths leading to consecrated spots in the dark recesses of their forests, dedicated to the worship of departed spirits. He saw also idols among them, such as a block of wood with a rough human head carved upon it, or a lion made of clay, with two shells for eyes. They are otherwise

15*

very superstitious; they would neither eat with the traveller, nor in his sight; they took meat from him, but they
ate it at home.

Their treatment of himself and his companions was,
however, uniformly kind. On approaching a village, a messenger generally met them with a polite invitation to enter,
and to choose a tree under which they would like to rest.
They then brought and arranged beneath the shadow of the
tree as many of the roofs of their own dwellings as were
sufficient for shelter from the mid-day sun and the nightly
dews.. They added to these favours a supply of food; but,
as to this, the travellers were soon independent, from the
abundance of the large game with which the country swarmed.
The most dainty meat of the Makololo—his roast beef—is
the flesh of the zebra; the giraffe supplies him with his
veal, the hippopotamus with his pork, and the various antelopes with venison. These delicacies were commonly enjoyed
by the travellers; while geese, ducks, and smaller birds
crowded along their path; and fish were scarcely less plentiful.

On leaving Linyanti, Dr. Livingstone kept, for a considerable time, within sight of the Zambese, and carefully tracked
its course. So constantly did he use the sextant and artificial
horizon, that it was rumoured that "a white man was coming,
who brought down the sun and moon, and carried them
under his arm." And the Astronomer Royal of Cape Town
declared that, "beyond the Cape district of the colony, there
is no river laid down so accurately as the Zambese, in the
centre of Africa, by his observations."

Kalai was now visited, an island on the Zambese, and
renowned as the mausoleum of a once powerful chief, named
Sekote. No fewer than seventy large elephants' tusks were
observed around his grave, and thirty more over the graves
of his relations. The people of this chief were among the
most degraded barbarians of South Africa. Between fifty

and sixty human skulls, mounted on poles, were counted in a single village; and so eagerly were they coveted, that strangers were often murdered solely to add to their number.

Leaving the Zambese at Kalai, Dr. Livingstone, taking a north-east direction for about 140 miles, rejoined it at its confluence with the Kafiré. At this point he came on a fine range of rivers, stretching far away to the north. The elevation he now attained was 4,000 feet above the level of the sea. Connecting this discovery with his previous observations of another ridge on the continent of about the same height, he came to the conclusion that the centre of Africa is an extended hollow, flanked by those two ridges, and that into the basin thus formed, numberless streams flowed from the water-sheds, which empty themselves into the Zambese, the great trunk river of South Africa. The most important fact, however, is, that this is the commencement of a healthy district, stretching eastward to Tete. Here, then, the great object was gained, for which through nearly six years' of toil and suffering, he had been in quest.

This ridge, unlike the low grounds, has neither forest nor marsh. The country is open and undulated, carpeted with short grass, somewhat resembling an extended lawn or park. It is peculiarly adapted both for pastoral and agricultural pursuits, for it grows wheat of superior quality and abundant yield, with other cereals, and a great variety of excellent roots.

With fresh spirit our traveller now pursued his way to the point at which the Loangua pours its ample volume into the Zambese, and to the deserted Portuguese town, called Zumbo, or Jumbo. After leaving this, his way lay among savage tribes, strange to him as he was to them. Still further, they were then at war with the Portuguese, a small colony of whom they had for two years besieged in Tete. The traveller, moreover, had no canoes, and even if he had possessed them, the rapids would have forbade their use for any

great distance in this part of the Zambese. Lions were all
but deified by the natives, who, though they slept for safety
in trees, clapped their hands when any of these animals were
in sight, in token of their veneration. And, to complete
the sum of Dr. Livingstone's discomfort, he was without
an ox.

"It was not likely," he writes, "that we should know our
course well, for the country there is covered with shingle and
gravel, bushes, trees, and groves, and we were often without
path, skulking out of the way of villages where we were
expected to pay after the purse was empty. It was excessively hot and steamy; the eyes had always to be fixed on
the ground to avoid being tripped. After that I say, let
those who delight in pedestrianism, enjoy themselves. It is
good for obesity; but for me, who had become as lean as a
lath, the only good I saw in it was to enable an honest sort
of fellow to realise completely the idea of a treadmill."

When the traveller first came into contact with the
people, they took him for a Portuguese, and would have
attacked the party had they not been undeceived. But when
they learned he was an Englishman, they regarded him as one
of "the nation that loves a black man." On arriving within
eight miles of Tete, where he knew he would be heartily welcomed, he was so exhausted that he could proceed no further.
The Portuguese governor of that place hearing of his condition, sent him what he calls "the materials of a civilised
breakfast," and with this he was so greatly refreshed that he
was enabled to continue his journey. The governor received
him with the greatest cordiality, and for a time he took up
his abode at Tete.

As he surveyed the region around, he found that Tete
stood in the centre of an extensive coal-field, two seams of
which he discovered on the banks of a river, besides two
others at a place called Chicova. A large gold-producing
district, which partly surrounded the coal-field, was now com-

paratively unproductive, because it was inefficiently worked. Iron, equal to the finest produced in Sweden, is abundant here. So tough and fibrous is it, that Dr. Livingstone says he has repeatedly seen the spear-heads of the natives, when hurled against the skulls of the hippopotami, coiled round like the proboscis of a butterfly, and then beat out again with stones, into their previous state. There are also numerous fibrous plants, and a species of cotton which grows wild in great abundance. Sugar and indigo are indigenous to the country. Bee's-wax, too, may be obtained in large quantities.

Sir Roderick Murchison, in his address to the Royal Geographical Society in 1852, observed : "The old rocks which form the outer fringe of South Africa unquestionably circled round an interior marshy or lacustrine country. The present aspect and meridian zone of waters, whether lakes or marshes, extending from Lake Ngami to Lake Tchad, are therefore but the great modern residual geographical phenomena of those of a mesozoic age." This was a very remarkable anticipation of the results of actual investigation made by Dr. Livingstone, who was the first to discover the true configuration of the southern portion of the African continent.

After a visit to this country, in which his fame and popularity have spread far beyond the limits of any particular circle, he has gone forth again with all the encouragements and aids that science can bestow upon him, with an unparalleled amount of public sympathy, and with even the recognition and authority of government to give dignity to his further labours in behalf of South Africa.

22

Richardson, Barth, and Overweg—Objects of the North and Central African Expedition — Tripoli — Ghat — Taradshit — Deaths of Richardson and Overweg—Tin-Tellust—Kanó—Bórnu—Zinder—The Mart of Say—Timbuktu—Great Perils.

WHILE the circumstances just narrated were transpiring, another expedition was engaged in northern Africa. It originated with Mr. Richardson, who, after having returned from his travels in the northern portion of the Sahara, in 1845 and 1846, induced the English Government to send him out for the purpose of concluding commercial treaties with the chiefs of the desert regions between Tripoli and Lake Tchad, or Tsad. On the proposal of Mr. A. Petermann, and through the lively interest taken in it by various distinguished persons, it was arranged that Dr. Barth and Dr. Overweg, two Germans, should accompany Mr. Richardson for the purpose of making scientific observations. Lord Palmerston sanctioned this proposal, and most liberally afforded the two travellers pecuniary assistance, in addition to their own private means and to the grants from the Geographical Society in Berlin and the King of Prussia.

To Dr. Barth we are indebted for a record of what was accomplished by this most interesting and promising expedition. "His qualifications," says the *Athenæum*, "place him in the first rank of scientific explorers. He is a man of large and exact information, trained in all the intricacies of African or Arabian race, or language, and religion,—prepared by a three years' previous travel under the shadow of palm trees or in the societies of camels, by colloquies with Arabs

and Tunisian slaves, to undertake long solitary wanderings,—
is singularly free from prejudice, a circumstance which
enabled him to carry a Koran along with him, and by a
quick understanding of Moslem laws and doctrines, at times
to silence native disputants, and in the main to disarm native
antipathy for a Christian,—and, moreover, a man of such
patience as to foil the intrigues of his treacherous Arab
servants, bearing for the sake of mankind with the thousand
ills which African travellers are ever heir to,—and of a
kindliness of heart that made him treat his camel as himself,
and by recollections of dates and orange-peel made the
animal, when his servant had forgotten to tether it, like a
Christian beast return to the tent. Something, too, of a
more painful interest the reader cannot divest himself from
as he watches the pair of Africanised travellers measuring
the slow miles with a lengthening chain at each remove from
civilisation,—floating on yoked calabashes over the rivers,—
occasionally buttering their legs on account of inflammation
caused by the damp,—then exposed to flies and heat and
very uncertain odours, — kept in irksome duress in the
fanatical towns,—languishing in close huts under fever or
the fear of instant death,—suffering from a barbarous rate of
exchange, or the perpetual exorbitance of African duns,—
then separating at last under an arrangement which death
prevented the one from keeping, and left the survivor only
the duty of visiting the lonely burial-place under a fig-tree,
and taking care that a sufficient fence of thorns protected
the European's grave."

The travels extend over a tract of country of twenty
degrees from north to south, and embrace a period of six
years, in the first part of   iich is surveyed the country
southward from Tripoli, th   gh the dreary Hammada, the
Berber land of Fezzan ; thr   the salt district of Asbeu to
Agades, a corn-trading town   7,000 inhabitants; and thence
to Kanó, the Manchester of   ntral Africa.

One object of the expedition being to open communications with the African chiefs, Dr. Barth relates the result of
the negotiation with the leader of the Tawarek, a powerful
tribe, which levies tolls on the caravans passing by the south-
eastern and western routes. The failure of the envoys he
traces to the deficiency of means, as well as to a want of tact
in producing a letter, written by the government, in which an
express stipulation is made for the abolition of the slave
trade, at the time when the chiefs were ready to sign the
treaty. It is evident from the latter part of the work that a
combination of firmness and confidence is required to cope
with native cunning ; though it may be doubtful whether
much of the annoyance that Dr. Barth and his companions
experienced did not arise solely from the supposition of their
wealth ; and an increase of means, unless accompanied by a
proportionate company, would probably enhance a thousand-
fold the difficulties of an African expedition.

Previously to starting from Tripoli, the mountainous region to the south was thoroughly explored and surveyed by
the two Germans. An unexpected degree of cold was experienced in these excursions ; as one day before sunrise the
thermometer stood so low as 26 deg. Fahr. ; and on the
2nd and 3rd of February, 1850, the snow obliged the travellers to remain in their tents. After their return to Tripoli several weeks were required for their preparations ; and
the transport of the boat for navigating Lake Tchad caused
considerable difficulty. For this purpose a beautiful wherry
had been constructed, by the direction of the admiral, at
Malta, broad in the beam, and as light as a cork on the water ;
but it was necessary to take it to pieces ; and several camels
were requisite to carry it across the burning sands of the
Sahara.

The travellers started on the 23rd of March, the great
caravan having departed before them ; but the party formed
a small caravan of itself, having about forty camels laden

with their effects and merchandise. Every possible assistance was rendered by her Majesty's consuls at Tripoli and Murzuk to the undertaking, so that the expedition started under the most favourable circumstances.

The direction of the route to Murzuk was almost due south from Tripoli, beyond the Gharian defile, the country consisting of a continuous tableland of an average elevation of 2,000 feet. As far as the well of Taboniyah many deep wadis intersect this tableland, and the ruins of several Roman monuments and columns were discovered by the travellers. Southward of that place is a tableland, or hamadah, an immense desert of considerably greater elevation, and extending for about 110 geographical miles in the same direction. As far as the eye can reach, neither trees nor indications of wells are visible, and the scanty vegetation which occurs is only found scattered in the trifling irregularities of the surface. The ground is covered with small stones, pyramids of art erected with great labour serve as road-marks to the intrepid camel-drivers by day, while the polar-star and Antares are their guides by night. Wadi Shiati is another plateau of equally dismal aspect. It is composed of a black sandstone, the disintegration of which forms a dark yellow sand, covering the inequalities of the stony surface, from which stands out prominently the black rock in high cones of the most fantastic forms, strikingly resembling basaltic rocks. Murzuk is very unhealthy and dangerous for Europeans; but happily none of the party suffered during their stay.

An interesting result of their journey towards Ghat was the discovery of several curious sculptures on the rocks of the Wadi Felisjareh. One of them consists of two human figures with the heads of birds, and a bull, armed with spears, shields, and arrows, and fighting for a child; the other is a fine herd of oxen going to a watering-place, most skilfully grouped and executed. In the opinion of the travellers the two rocks bear a striking and unmistakable resemblance to the sculptures of Egypt. They are evidently of much higher antiquity than many other sculptured tablets found by the travellers, on which camels were generally the principal objects.

From Ghat the general surface of the country continues to rise, and at Selufiel the travellers saw around them the highest mountain-masses met with during the journey. After the middle of August they experienced the influence of the Soodan rains; the atmosphere then beginning to be humid, and the evenings or mornings being accompanied by fogs.   Frequent thunder-storms and heavy rains also occurred. Under the influence of these rains the appearance of the road is become completely changed, luxuriant plantations of palms being everywhere met with to the south of Taradshit.   According to the natives the rainy season lasts till the end of September.

At Taradshit, near the frontiers of Soodan, the travellers, having accomplished the exceedingly difficult and dangerous journey across the Great Desert, believed themselves in perfect safety from the attacks of considerable numbers of furious Tuaricks, who had for some time followed their caravan, with the intent to murder and plunder them ; but on the 25th of August they were attacked, the first time by forty, and the second time by a hundred armed men, mounted on camels. By their own courage, however, and the bravery of the Kelowis, their companions, their lives were saved at the expense of a high ransom, and they reached Tin-Tellust, the residence of the Prince Annoor, to whom they were strongly recommended, and by whom they were kindly received.

The inhabitants of Tin-Tellust and the country around lived entirely on the productions of Soodan, in exchange for which they supply Soodan with salt.   Every year the Prince Annoor takes to the south from 2,000 to 3,000 camels laden with salt, and returns with slaves and provisions.   At

Damergu the travellers separated, Mr. Richardson going by the most direct route to Kuka, but he died before he reached this city, the capital of Bórnu. Dr. Overweg proceeded to Lake Tchad, where he put together and launched the boat with which he was provided ; he then explored the lake, visiting the Biddumas, who inhabit the islands, of which there are about a hundred large ones scattered over the lake. He was the first European who had visited this independent nation.

Dr. Barth, who had proceeded Southward to Karro, subsequently reached Kuka, and presented himself at the Sheik's palace as one of the surviving Christians who had come from England to bring presents from her British Majesty. Dr. Overweg also arrived. The two travellers were kindly received by the Sultan, and were assisted by him in all their objects and wishes. Again the travellers separated, and engaged in other tours.

As they pursued their course, the effects of the slave-trade became increasingly evident. While the proofs had already been abundant of the manufacturing industry of the natives of Karró, in weaving and dyeing cotton, in smelting iron, in making salt, in irrigation and agriculture, the human and material desolation caused by the slave-hunts was deeply affecting. It appears that an African chief usually clears off his debts by making a foray upon a hostile or sometimes a friendly tribe. Whole districts, which on his first visit Dr. Barth found flourishing and populous, pasture-fields of herds of cattle and *entrepôts* of trade and industry, when he passed by only two years later, were mournful wastes, without the least vestige of human or animal life, tall reed grass covering the fields which had been formerly cultivated. The chief argument which the Vizier of Bórnu alleged in favour of the slave-trade was, that it enabled the people to furnish themselves with muskets ; and on its being represented that Bórnu contained other products that might be exchanged for fire-arms, the Governor declared, "in the most distinct manner, that if the British Government were able to furnish them with a thousand muskets and four cannons, they would be willing to subscribe any obligatory article for abolishing the slave-trade in their country." This proposal Dr. Barth sagaciously parried by hinting that a road ought to be made first from Bórnu to the Benuwé, so as to open a through communication.

The death of Dr. Overweg left Dr. Barth to pursue his researches alone. In November, 1852, with a train of seven servants and a broker, he set out from Kúkawa on his expedition to Timbúktu, from which place at first he represented to the Government that his principal object was to reach the Niger at the town of Say. The cold at that time of the year was great, and Dr. Barth had not recovered from sore legs, the effects of the damp in crossing the rivers.

Well-tilled fields, then flocks of guinea-fowl, enlivened the landscape, until the site of the ancient capital of Bórnu was reached. It is six miles in circumference. The aisles of the mosque, the area of the palace built of baked bricks, and the six or seven gates, are still traceable; but the only living things in the ruins were a pair of ostriches, that hurried through the rank grass. After encountering thieves, who stole a blanket from under one of his servants—after exchanging the region of the monkey bread tree for that of the date trees—he arrived at a little market-town, called "the sweetness of the world," and thence entered Búndi.

"I entered the town," he says, "from the north-east quarter, and here found a large open space laid out in fields of wheat, kitchen-gardens, with onions, and cotton-grounds, all in different stages of cultivation. Most of the beds where wheat was grown were just being laid out, the clods of dry earth being broken and the ground irrigated, while in other places the green stalks of the crop were already shooting forth. The onions were very closely packed together. Everywhere the fertilising element was close at hand, and palm-trees were shooting up in several detached clusters; but large mounds of rubbish prevented my taking a comprehensive view over the whole, and the more so as the village is separated into four detached portions lying at a considerable distance from each other, and forming altogether a circumference of about three miles, with a population of from 8,000 to 9,000 inhabitants. But the whole is merely surrounded by a light fence.

"The principal cluster, or hamlet, surrounds a small eminence, on the top of which stands the house of the head man or mayor, built of clay, and having quite a commanding position, while at the north-eastern foot of the hill a very picturesque date grove spreads out in a hollow. The ground being uneven, the dwellings, like those in Gúre, are mostly situated in hollows, and the courtyards present a new and characteristic feature—for although the cottages themselves are built of reed and stalks of Negro corn, the corn-stacks, far from presenting that light and perishable appearance which they exhibit all over Háusa, approach closely that solid style of building which we have observed in the Músgu country, being built of clay, and rising to the height of ten feet. Wúshek is the principal place for the cultivation of wheat in the whole western part of Bórnu; and if there had been a market that day, it would have been most profitable for me to have provided myself here with this article, wheat being very essential for me, as I had only free servants at my disposal, who would by no means undertake the pounding and preparing of the native corn, while a preparation of wheat, such as mohamsa, can be always kept ready; but the market of Wúshek is only held every Wednesday.

" In the whole of this country, one hundred shells, or kúngona, which are estimated equal to one gábagá, form the standard currency in the market; and it is remarkable that this sum is not designated by the Kanúri word 'miye or 'yéro,' nor by the common Háusa word 'darí,' but by the name 'zango,' which is used only in the western parts of Háusa and in Sókoto. I had pitched my tent near the south-eastern hamlet, which is the smallest of the four, close to the spot where I had entered the place, not being aware of its extent; and from here I made, in the afternoon, a sketch of the mountain range towards the south, and the dry shelving level bordered by the strip of green verdure, with the palm trees in the foreground. In the evening I was hospitably regaled by each of the two bíllama who govern the town, and I had the satisfaction of making a 'tailor to his majesty Múniyóma,' who was residing here, very happy by the present of a few large darning-needles for sewing the líbbedi or wadded dress for the soldiers."

Agricultural industry was everywhere apparent until the traveller reached two remarkable lakes. One was of natron, having the dark green colour of sea-water; the other was smooth and of a dark blue. After leaving Zinder, the capital of Western Bórnu, and making purchases of cotton and silk, and prescribing for a number of patients, he passed into the Sókoto country, the prince of which expressed regret for the fate of Clapperton, the traveller, whose vigorous constitution gave way under the effects of climate and privation, and who died of dysentery on the 13th of April, 1827, at Chemgarrey, a village four miles from Sókoto, a spot which Dr. Barth visited with melancholy interest. A pair of richly orna- mented pistols won the chieftain's heart, and he readily allowed the traveller to pass through his land to Timbúktu.

Dr. Barth thus describes the great mart of Say, on the Niger:—

"While passing along the streets, I was delighted to ob- serve a certain degree of industry displayed in small handi- crafts, and in the character of the interior of the households. Everything was very dear, but particularly butter, which was scarcely to be procured at all. All the currency of the market consists of shells; but I found the most profitable merchandise to be the black cloth for female apparel from Gando, which realised a profit of eighty per cent., while the Kanó manufactures did not find a ready sale. The black Núpe tobe, of common manufacture, bought in Gando for 3,300 shells, here fetched 5,000; while the black zenne, manufactured in Gando itself, and bought there for 1,050, sold here for 2,000. Of course all depends, in this respect, upon the momentary state of the intercourse of this quarter with Háusa; and at the present time almost all communication with that manufacturing province being interrupted, it is easy to explain how an article produced in Gando could realise such a per-centage in a town at so short a distance from that place—a state of things which cannot form the general rule. At any rate, for the English or Europeans in general, Say is the most important place in all this tract of the river, if they ever succeed in crossing the rapids which obstruct the river above Rabba, and especially between Búsa and Yaúri, and reaching this fine open sheet of water, the great highroad of Western Central Africa. The traffic of the natives along the river is not inconsiderable, although even this branch of industry has naturally suffered greatly from the rebellious state of the adjacent provinces, more especially those of Zabérma and Déndina; so that at present boats did not go farther down the river than Kirotáshi, an important place situated about fifteen miles lower down on the western bank; while, in the opposite direction, up the river, there was constant intercourse as far as Kindáji, with which place I made myself sufficiently acquainted on my return journey.'

On entering the Songha territory, Dr. Barth met an Arab, under whose protection he put himself in order to reach Timbúktu. Adopting the advice of his companion, he represented himself as a scheriff, carrying books from the east to the Sheikh, a *ruse* which turned downwards the points of 150

spears raised against him, and obliged him to lay his hands
and bestow his blessing on the unclean spear-bearers.   As
he advances he is able to propitiate the industrious natives
by presents of darning-needles, and makes progress in the
Songha language.   His Arab companion now proves treacherous, his race is suspected, and to avoid suspicion he repeats
the opening prayer of the Koran.   Dr. Barth attributes the
subsequent difficulties he experienced on his entrance into
Timbúktu to the want of a sufficient firman from the Sultan.

The day after his arrival he heard that Hammadi, the
rival of the Sheikh, had informed the Fúlbe, or native people
of the town, that he was a Christian, and they had come to
the determination of killing him.   He thus describes his
circumstances :—

"I was not allowed to stir about, but was confined within
the walls of my house.   In order to obviate the effect of this
want of exercise as much as possible, to enjoy fresh air, and
at the same time to become familiar with the principal
features of the town, through which I was not allowed to
move about at pleasure, I ascended as often as possible the
terrace of my house.   This afforded an excellent view over
the northern quarters of the town.   On the north was the
massive mosque of Sánkoré, which had just been restored to
all its former grandeur through the influence of the Sheikh
el Bakáy, and gave the whole place an imposing character.
Neither the mosque Sídi Yáhia, nor the 'great mosque,' or
Jíngeré-bér, was seen from this point ; but towards the east
the view extended over a wide expanse of the desert, and
towards the south the elevated mansions of the Ghadámsíye
merchants were simple.   The style of the buildings was
various.   I could see clay houses of different characters, some
low and unseemly, others rising with a second story in front
to greater elevation, and making even an attempt at archi-
tectural ornament, the whole being interrupted by a few
round huts of matting.   The sight of this spectacle afforded

me sufficient matter of interest, although, the streets being very narrow, only little was to be seen of the intercourse carried on in them, with the exception of the small market in the northern quarter, which was exposed to view on account of its situation on the slope of the sand-hills, which, in course of time, have accumulated round the mosque. But while the terrace of my house served to make me well acquainted with the character of the town, it had also the disadvantage of exposing me fully to the gaze of the passers-by, so that I could only slowly, and with many interruptions, succeed in making a sketch of the scene thus offered to my view. At the same time I became aware of the great inaccuracy which characterises the view of the town as given by M. Caillié; still, on the whole, the character of the single dwellings was well represented by that traveller, the only error being, that in his representation the whole town seems to consist of scattered and quite isolated houses, while, in reality, the streets are entirely shut in, as the dwellings form continuous and uninterrupted rows. But it must be taken into account that Timbúktu, at the time of Caillié's visit, was not so well off as it is at present, having been overrun by the Fúlbe the preceding year, and he had no opportunity of making a drawing on the spot."

Of the town, which has a population of 10,000, he says,—

"Situated only a few feet above the average level of the river, and at a distance of about six miles from the principal branch, it at present forms a sort of triangle, the base of which points towards the river, whilst the projecting angle is directed towards the north, having for its centre the mosque of Sánkoré. But, during the zenith of its power, the town extended a thousand yards further north, and included the tomb of the fáki Mahmúd, which, according to some of my informants, was then situated in the midst of the town. The circumference of the city at the present time I reckon at little more than two miles and a half; but it may

16

approach closely to three miles, taking into account some of
the projecting angles. Although of only small size, Timbúktu may well be called a city—medína—in comparison
with the frail dwelling-places all over Negroland. At
present it is not walled. Its former wall, which seems
never to have been of great magnitude, and was rather more
of the nature of a rampart, was destroyed by the Fúlbe on
their first entering the place in the beginning of the year
1826. The town is laid out partly in rectangular, partly in
winding, streets, or as they are called here, 'tijeráten,' which
are not paved, but for the greater part consist of hard sand
and gravel, and some of them have a sort of gutter in the
middle. Besides the large and the small market there are
few open areas, except a small square in front of the mosque
of Yáhia, called Túmbutu-bóttema. Small as it is, the city
is tolerably well inhabited, and almost all the houses are in
good repair. There are about 980 clay houses, and a couple
of hundred conical huts of matting, the latter, with a few
exceptions, constituting the outskirts of the town on the
north and north-east sides, where a great deal of rubbish,
which has been accumulating in the course of several centu-
ries, is formed into conspicuous mounds. The clay houses
are all of them built on the same principle as my own residence, which I have described, with the exception that the
houses of the poorer people have only one courtyard, and
have no upper room on the terrace."

On the arrival in the town of the Sheikh El Bakáy, the
traveller's confidence increased, though the rival chieftain
was incessantly intriguing for his death. Some years ago
Major Laing succeeded in making his way across the desert
from Tripoli to Timbúktu, and had transmitted home some
notices of that famous city, where he spent some weeks; but
he was murdered in the desert on his return. In an interview with El Bakáy, Dr. Barth found that Major Laing had,
after being plundered by the Tawárek, been the guest of the

Sheikh's father. None of that unfortunate traveller's papers were, as far as he could ascertain, in existence. Several attempts were made to convert the traveller to Islamism; and in December news arrived that the Bérabish, who had murdered Major Laing, had resolved on his death.

The festival of the birthday of Mohammed brought an influx of strangers into the town, and one of no little interest. Dr. Barth says:—

"The chief A'wáb, who paid me a long visit, in company with his màllem, and gave me the first account of the proceedings of that Christian traveller Mungo Park (to use his own words), who, about fifty years ago, came down the river in a large boat; describing the manner in which he had been first attacked in the Tawárek below Kábara, where he lost some time in endeavouring to open a communication with the natives, while the Tin-ger-égedesh forwarded the news of his arrival, without delay, to the Igwádaren, who, having collected their canoes, attacked him, first near Bamba, and then again at the narrow passage of Tósaye, though all in vain; till at length, the boat of that intrepid traveller having stuck fast at Ensýmmo (probably identical with Ansóngo), the Tawárek of that neighbourhood made another fierce and more successful attack, causing him an immense deal of trouble, and killing, as A'wáb asserted, two of his Christian companions. He also gave me a full account of the iron hook with which the boat was provided against hippopotami and hostile canoes; and his statement altogether proved what an immense excitement the mysterious appearance of this European traveller, in his solitary boat, had caused among all the surrounding tribes."

The sudden death of the Bérabish chieftain who had been intriguing for Dr. Barth's death, produced an impression on the people, who generally believed him to be the son of Major Laing. But after a sojourn of seven months he was compelled to leave it, and he thus describes a disagreeable incident :—

" The Zoghorán officer, the companion of Férreji, had come out on some errand, while I was staying with the three brothers in the large tent, which had been erected for Sídi Mohammed. I wanted to leave, but Bakáy begged me to stay. I therefore remained a short time, but became so disgusted with the insulting language of the Zoghorán, that I soon left abruptly, although his remarks had more direct reference to the French, or, rather, the French and half-caste traders on the Senegal, than to the English or any other European nation. He spoke of the Christians in the most contemptuous manner, describing them as sitting like women in the bottom of their steam boats, and doing nothing but eating raw eggs : concluding with the paradoxical statement, which is not very flattering to Europeans, that the idolatrous Bámbara people were far better people, and much farther advanced in civilisation than the Christians. It is singular how the idea that the Europeans are fond of raw eggs (a most disgusting article to a Mohammedan), as already proved by the experience of Mungo Park, has spread over the whole of Negroland, and it can only be partially explained by the great predilection which the French have for boiled eggs."

After an excursion to Gógó, parting with his steady friend El Bakáy, Dr. Barth finally quitted the Songhay territory, and the return journey to Tripoli concludes his narrative, which occupies five octavo volumes.

CHAPTER XXXI.

MR. MOFFAT'S LAST JOURNEY.

Journey to the Residence of Moselekatze—His Reception by the Chief—He promises to receive Missionaries—Liberation of Macheng, the Captive —A Native Parliament.

MR. MOFFAT determined, in the summer of 1857, to visit once more the great chief of the Matabele, to secure his concurrence in the establishment of the proposed missions on the Zambese River. In one part of his eventful journey, he says:—

"Having gone far to the east of my course, I turned to the direction of nearly north-west, in order to fall in with the most southern outpost of the Matabele. No one knowing a yard of the way, and buried in trees, I had recourse to my compass, as on my former journey, to thread my way through a rather dense forest, over fallen trees, rocky ravines, and hills, none of which were sufficiently high to enable us to look around for portions where the trees were more sparse. Very frequently the wagon had to stop till a road was cut through the trees. This excessively laborious mode of travelling continued till the sun set, when we found ourselves among high hills, with hopes of finding water. The day had been extremely hot, while a death-like silence pervaded the country, for we fell in with no kind of game nor saw a single bird, but occasionally crossed the narrow paths where lions had lately left their footprints. The wearied oxen were loosed from their yokes and fastened to trees, we being well aware that, if left to roam, they would wander in search of water. When this was done, every one laid them down on

23

the warm earth, indifferent to everything in the world but
'tired nature's sweet restorer,' although no one had tasted
anything since sunrise, except occasionally a drink of water.
A cup of tea or coffee, which is always valued by African
travellers, soon revived us, when the day's toils were re-
hearsed, and plans laid how we might the best get out of an
unenviable situation. We read and prayed, and with thank-
ful hearts retired to rest."

Next morning at dawn every one was on his feet in
search of water, but after in vain ascending hills, and
traversing ravines, the party returned by ones and twos
to the wagon. The prospect, as they proceeded, seemed
at times almost hopeless, but they were urged onwards by
stern necessity. It was evident that rain had not fallen in
that part of the country for a long time, as not a blade of
grass was to be seen, while in the open portions of it, through
which they had passed, the fire had swept off every vestige
of dry pasture. Ere long they descended the rugged steep
to the bank of the Shashe River. As soon as the gum trees
which line its bank were seen, every one with the greatest
eagerness got on the highest spot or rock within reach, to
assure himself of soon being able to quench his thirst. The
instant they halted, away went oxen, sheep, dogs, and men,
some heels over head, down the bank, to the sandy bed of
the river, whose refreshing water was in abundance. Now
a washing was enjoyed, a cup of coffee proved truly refreshing, and sitting down on the grass, under the shadow of a
spreading tree, an hour was passed in reading, singing, and
prayer. Gratitude was deep for the deliverance experienced
from many evils. Had any part of the wagon broken down,
or the oxen taken fright at the scent of the lion, and
dashed it against trees or rocks, their condition, without
water, would have been perilous indeed.

But an alarming incident occurred in the course of the
evening, when the oxen were being collected in order to

fasten them to trees close to the wagon. The sun had just set, Mr. Moffat had been writing down some observations, and had stepped out of his wagon to assist, as was his custom on such occasions. He had not proceeded many steps in front of the oxen, when they, having smelt the lion, rushed forward, and before he had time to be aware of the danger, galloped over him, knocking him down to the ground with great violence. As his head struck the hard soil, he was so stunned as to be unable to rise. While three of the people were in pursuit to turn the terrified oxen, one came to his assistance, and enabled him to stagger to the wagon, where he reclined with the feeling of a man who was scarcely sensible. As soon as he could use his legs he descended to the water, and was refreshed by bathing his head. At length the cattle were secured, and rest was obtained.

The compass was the only guide through an untrodden country, for human footsteps there were none. Gladly would Mr. Moffat have reclined on his couch, but necessity compelled him to shoulder the axe and cut out a road for the wagon. The Ramakhoabane River was next reached, where a small footprint of a human being was seen in the sand, and abundance of the rhinoceros, lion, hyæna, tiger, gnu, quagga, red-buck, and other animals. They cut down thorn trees, and made a cattle-fold strong enough to secure a night's repose. For if oxen are frightened so as to break through the thorny fence, they set off with the speed of race-horses, in some instances never to return.

Passing through ravines and tortuous turnings of the reedy river, they came at length in sight of the wished-for hills. There was no small stir among the people as Mr. Moffat and his companions passed through the villages, stuck up in corners and defiles of a multitude of hills, many of which had a fantastic appearance. All ages rushed to the wagon, and all exhibited unusual signs of joy. The fact was soon apparent that not only the chief but his people were earnestly desiring another visit. They affirmed that Mr. Moffat's teaching had made Mosclekatze more lenient and forgiving, and that he had raised many of his subjects to become *Mantato* (men); that is, allowing them to marry and wear a ring on their heads. They cherished, too, the hope that other improvements would arise from the missionary's influence.

On reaching the royal residence, the chief stretched out his hand and gave Mr. Moffat a hearty welcome, accompanied by many expressions of great joy at seeing him again. His ankles and knees had recently become weak, though he looked well, and was obliged to be moved by some of his wives, who are always in attendance. He was not able to attend the public service on the next day, which was the Sabbath, but a number of the Matabele, who understood the Sichuana language, were present. Mr. Moffat, however, saw Moselekatze in private.

"I told him," he says, "that I was come to tell him that the great teachers in England having heard of his kindness to me, and willingness to be instructed, had resolved to send him two teachers. He promptly remarked, 'You must come too. How shall I get on with people I do not know, if you are not with me?' and, snapping his fingers, added, 'By all means, by all means bring teachers; you are wise, you are able to judge what is good for me and my people better than I do. The land is yours, you must do for it what you think is good,' &c. I resumed by adding, that all I would ask was a place where there was a command of water, where the missionaries could live, make gardens, &c., and have many people to teach; that they would not look to him for food, but would plant, sow, and purchase what they might require. The subject was repeatedly referred to during my stay, and in no case did he deviate from what he assented to. I had now obtained the object of my desire—not that I ever doubted that the proposal would be acceptable, but I felt impressed with the importance of having from him a public sanction, so that, whatever might happen either to him or myself, missionaries might proceed to their destination with the greater confidence."

Macheng, the paramount chief of the Bamanguato tribe, is a young man, about twenty-six years of age, good looking, apparently of a mild disposition, and having a countenance not deficient in intelligence. He is the son of Khari, the king of his tribe, who was killed in an engagement with the Bashona, while he was yet a child. During the irruption of the tribes to the north, occasioned by the overwhelming prowess and power of the bloody Chaka, the despot of the Zoolus, the Bamanguato and other Bechuana tribes were scattered to the winds. Macheng, during his minority, with his eldest sister, afterwards one of Sechele's wives, were under the care of Sechele, who was at that time the head of but a small portion of the Bakuena. While Sechele was on one occasion absent from his town in a foray against the Banguaketse, a handful of the Matabele fell, on his undefended town, killed many, destroyed property, and carried away captive youths and women, among whom were Macheng and his eldest sister.

The latter escaped by finding her way back through the intricacies of forests, but Macheng was destined to be a captive for sixteen years. Though it was contrary to the rule of the Matabele to return a royal prisoner to his people, he was, from Mr. Moffat's influence with the chief, placed at his disposal.

The story of Macheng would not be complete apart from the detail of the following incidents :

" Some time before arriving at Sechele's town," says Mr. Moffat, " our approach was announced. He, the chiefs of the Bangwakeke and Barolong, with other chiefs of tribes congregated on his mountain, met me, some on horseback, to welcome Macheng. He appeared in no way elated, whatever might have been the emotions of his mind ; but nothing

16*

could induce him to leave me and ascend the mountain on which the town stood. On the Lord's day which followed, he accompanied me, and witnessed for the first time divine service performed in a house built and appropriated to the purpose of worshipping God. He was most surprised to witness the multitudes that had come to hear me preach. The next day had been appointed to hold a national assembly, to give a public expression of welcome to the returning captive. Sechele, after getting Macheng rigged out in a rather handsome costume, marched before us to the centre of a kind of natural amphitheatre, which had for an hour before been crowded with at least 10,000 people, in all their habiliments of war. After Sechele had stood up and commanded silence, he introduced the business of the meeting. One speaker followed another, expressing in enthusiastic language the pleasure they felt on the occasion of seeing the chief of the Bamanguato return from captivity. Of course, though very unwilling to be found a speaker in a native parliament, I had to take my share, though the detail of circumstances included also something like a sermon, to which, among so many thousands of heathen, the most profound attention was paid. Some of the speeches were very striking and figurative. The following are a few sentences from the brother of Sechele : 'Ye tribes, ye children of the ancients, to me this day is a day of wonder. That which awakes my heart to wonder is to see the Spirit's work. My thoughts within me begin to move. Verily, the things I have seen, and the words I have heard, assume stability. When I first heard the word of God, I began to ask, " Are these things true ? " Now, the confusion of my thoughts, and of my soul, is unravelled. Now I begin to perceive that those who preach are verily true. If Moffat was not of God, he would not have espoused the cause of Sechele in receiving his words, and delivering Macheng from the dwelling-place of the beasts of prey to which we Bechuanas dared not to approach.

There are, who contend that there is nothing in religion. Let such to-day throw away their unbelief. If he were not such a man, he would not have done what he has done, in bringing him who was lost, him who was dead, from the strong bondage of the mighty. I, Khosilintsi, say so, because Moselekatze is a lion; he conquered nations, he robbed the strong ones, he bereaved mothers. He took away the son of Khari. We talk of love. What is love? We hear of the love of God. Is it not through the love of God that Macheng is among us to-day? A stranger, one of a nation, who of you knows its distance from us? He makes himself one of us, enters the lion's abode, and brings out to us our own blood.' "

Besides two Matabele who accompanied Mr. Moffat, two others were sent by the chief to attest that it was his wish, as well as the missionary's, that Macheng should be placed in the first instance before Sechele, and to assure him that Macheng was a free man at Mr. Moffat's desire. One of them was the very individual who had charge of the captive from the first, and though a servant till he was enrolled among the warriors, appeared to look upon Macheng with paternal affection, but from the moment of his freedom honoured him as a chief of the Bamanguato.

"He arose," says Mr. Moffat, "and, facing the arena several times, moving about a staff he held in his hand (for the Matabele do not use weapons at a national assembly, as the Bechuanas do), and according to the usual form, called the tribes to give ear. Standing opposite to where Macheng and I sat, and laying his arms on his bosom, he walked round, and, raising a wailing voice, exclaimed, ' Pity me, O ye nations. Here I stand a lonely one. I am bereaved of my child. Whither shall I go? Will he forget his mother? Can I forget my son? I pressed him to this bosom. I carried him on these shoulders' (suiting the action to his words); 'then raising his voice in tones still more plaintive, he said, 'How happy

was I once with my boy ! Why was I made to bear him !
I have no more.' Looking round on the silent multitude,
he asked, rather sternly, ' Ye tribes, why did ye covet my
child ?' and, turning to me with softened tone, 'Why did
you, Moffat, prevail with the son of Machobane to make me
childless ? I shall return to the desert and weep. He is
gone from me, but I shall never forget that I am the father
of the son of Khari, who is now the son of Moffat,' &c. He
concluded his pathetic address with some remarks on the
light in which the tribes ought now to view Moselekatze.
The whole scene produced a thrilling effect, and the minds of
the assembly, which had been taken by surprise by the presence of the dreaded Matabele among them, were now in
raptures to hear such fraternising language from those who,
though distant, were. till now, a terror by night and day.
After this, I remained a few days, and saw every arrangement made. Macheng and his fifty attendants returned to
their own people, and 100 chosen men of the Bakuena, at
whose head was Khasilintsi, escorted them to the Bamanguato. Such a demonstration has rarely been made in the
country, and I should think will not soon be forgotten.
Previous to his departure a liberal subscription was made by
the nobles, of cattle, carosses, &c., so that he was not sent
away empty."

THE END.